Learning Microsoft® Excel 2010 Teacher's Manual

Betsy Newberry

PEARSON

Prentice Hall

Boston • Columbus • Indianapolis • New York • San Francisco • Upper Saddle River
Amsterdam • Cape Town • Dubai • London • Madrid • Milan • Munich • Paris • Montreal • Toronto
Delhi • Mexico City • Sao Paulo • Sydney • Hong Kong • Seoul • Singapore • Taipei • Tokyo

Editor in Chief: Michael Payne
Product Development Manager:
  Eileen Bien Calabro
Editorial Assistant: Nicole Sam
Director of Marketing: Kate Valentine
Marketing Manager: Tori Olson Alves
Marketing Coordinator: Susan Osterlitz
Marketing Assistant: Darshika Vyas
Senior Managing Editor: Cynthia Zonneveld
Associate Managing Editor: Camille Trentacoste
Production Project Manager: Lynne Breitfeller
Operations Director: Nick Sklitsis

Senior Operations Specialist: Natacha Moore
Text and Cover Designer: Vanessa Moore
Media Development Manager: Cathi Profitko
VP, Director of Digital Development: Zara Wanlass
Media Project Manager, Editorial: Alana Coles
Media Project Manager, Production: John Cassar
Editorial and Product Development: Emergent Learning, LLC
Composition: Linda Zerella
Printer/Binder: OPM Digital Print Services
Cover Printer: OPM Digital Print Services
Text: 10/12 Helvetica

Microsoft® and Windows® are registered trademarks of the Microsoft Corporation in the U.S.A. and other countries. Screen shots and icons reprinted with permission from the Microsoft Corporation. This book is not sponsored or endorsed by or affiliated with the Microsoft Corporation.

Copyright © 2012 Pearson Education, Inc., publishing as Prentice Hall, One L ake Street, Upper Saddle River, New Jersey, 07458. All rights reserved. Manufactured in the United States of America. This publication is protected by Copyright, and permission should be obtained from the publisher prior to any prohibited reproduction, storage in a retrieval system, or transmission in any form or by any means, electronic, mechanical, photocopying, recording, or likewise. To obtain permission(s) to use material from this work, please submit a written request to Pearson Education, Inc., Permissions Department, One Lake Street, Upper Saddle River, New Jersey, 07458.

Many of the designations by manufacturers and seller to distinguish their products are claimed as trademarks. Where those designations appear in this book, and the publisher was aware of a trademark claim, the designations have been printed in initial caps or all caps.

10 9 8 7 6 5 4 3 2 1

Prentice Hall
is an imprint of

PEARSON

www.pearsonhighered.com

ISBN 10: 0-13-511212-5
ISBN 13: 978-0-13-511212-0

TABLE OF CONTENTS

Introduction vi

Microsoft Excel 2010

Chapter 1
Getting Started with Microsoft Excel 2010 1
Lesson 1 – Touring Excel........................1
Lesson 2 – Worksheet and Workbook Basics 4
Lesson 3 – Adding Worksheet Contents 7
Lesson 4 – Worksheet Formatting 10
Lesson 5 – More on Cell Entries and Formatting......13
Lesson 6 – Working with Ranges.................16
Lesson 7 – Creating Formulas...................18
Lesson 8 – Copying and Pasting 20
Lesson 9 – Techniques for Moving Data............22
Lesson 10 – Charts, Sheet, Display, and Print Operations 24

End-of-Chapter Assessments 26

Chapter 2
Working with Formulas, Functions, and Worksheet Tools 29
Lesson 11 – Getting Started with Functions 29
Lesson 12 – Using Excel Tables..................31
Lesson 13 – The NOW Function and Named Ranges..................33
Lesson 14 – Working with IF Functions 35
Lesson 15 – Using Frozen Labels and Panes 38
Lesson 16 – Using Conditional Formatting and Find Replace 40

Lesson 17 – Rotating Entries and Resolving Errors 42
Lesson 18 – Adding Print Titles and Scaling a Printout....................44
Lesson 19 – Managing Worksheets and Performing Multi-worksheet Operations...........46
Lesson 20 – Summary Worksheets and Advanced Printing..................48

End-of-Chapter Assessments 50

Chapter 3
Charting Data 53
Lesson 21 – Building Basic Charts................53
Lesson 22 – Showing Percentages with a Pie Chart 56
Lesson 23 – Enhancing a Pie Chart................58
Lesson 24 – Adding Special Elements to a Chart or Sheet....................60
Lesson 25 – Completing Chart Formatting 62
Lesson 26 – Comparing and Analyzing Data.........64
Lesson 27 – Chart Printing and Publishing..........66
Lesson 28 – Using Charts in Other Files............68
Lesson 29 – Making Special Purpose Charts 70

End-of-Chapter Assessments 72

Chapter 4
Advanced Functions, PivotCharts, and PivotTables 75
Lesson 30 – Using Advanced Functions to Predict Trends.....................75
Lesson 31 – Using Advanced Functions for Data Analysis 78

Lesson 32 – Using LOOKUP Functions............81

Lesson 33 – Understanding PivotTables and PivotCharts......................83

End-of-Chapter Assessments 86

Chapter 5
Advanced Printing, Formatting, and Editing 89

Lesson 34 – Working with Graphics and Saving a Worksheet as a Web Page...........89

Lesson 35 – Working with Web Data 92

Lesson 36 – Linking and Embedding Data 94

Lesson 37 – Working with Workbooks 96

Lesson 38 – Working with Comments and Modifying Page Setup..............98

Lesson 39 – Modifying the Print Options 101

Lesson 40 – Using Copy and Paste Special 104

Lesson 41 – Moving and Linking Data Between Workbooks...............106

Lesson 42 – Working with 3-D Formulas 108

End-of-Chapter Assessments 110

Chapter 6
Managing Large Workbooks and Using Advanced Sorting and Filtering... 113

Lesson 43 – Customizing the Excel Interface and Converting Text...............113

Lesson 44 – Formatting Cells 115

Lesson 45 – Hiding and Formatting Workbook Elements......................117

Lesson 46 – Customizing Styles and Themes........................119

Lesson 47 – Using Advanced Sort 121

Lesson 48 – Using Advanced Filtering 123

Lesson 49 – Customizing Data Entry 125

Lesson 50 – Using Find and Replace 127

Lesson 51 – Working with Hyperlinks............128

Lesson 52 – Saving Excel Data in a Different File Format 130

Lesson 53 – Working with Subtotals 132

End-of-Chapter Assessments 134

Chapter 7
Creating Charts, Shapes, and Templates 137

Lesson 54 – Formatting Chart Elements...........137

Lesson 55 – Formatting the Value Axis 139

Lesson 56 – Creating Stacked Area Charts 141

Lesson 57 – Working with Sparklines.............143

Lesson 58 – Drawing and Positioning Shapes 145

Lesson 59 – Formatting Shapes 147

Lesson 60 – Enhancing Shapes with Text and Effects...................149

Lesson 61 – Working with Templates.............151

Lesson 62 – Protecting Data....................153

End-of-Chapter Assessments 155

Chapter 8
Using the Data Analysis, Scenario, and Worksheet Auditing Functions.... 157

Lesson 63 – Inserting Function and Using Logical Functions 157

Lesson 64 – Working with Absolute References and Using Financial Functions 160

Lesson 65 – Creating and Interpreting Financial Statements...............162

Lesson 66 – Creating Scenarios and
Naming Ranges 164

Lesson 67 – Finding and Fixing Errors in Formulas . . . 166

Lesson 68 – Ensuring Data Integrity. 168

End-of-Chapter Assessments 170

Chapter 9
Importing and Analyzing Database Data 173

Lesson 69 – Recording a Macro 173

Lesson 70 – Importing Data into Excel 176

Lesson 71 – Working with Excel Tables 178

Lesson 72 – Using Advanced Filters and
Database Functions. 180

Lesson 73 – Using Data Consolidation 182

End-of-Chapter Assessments 183

Chapter 10
Collaborating with Others and Preparing a Final Workbook for Distribution 185

Lesson 74 – Tracking Changes 185

Lesson 75 – Securing Workbooks 187

Lesson 76 – Finalizing a Workbook 189

Lesson 77 – Sending and Sharing a Workbook. 191

End-of-Chapter Assessments 193

The *Learning Microsoft® Excel 2010 Teacher's Manual* is a comprehensive guide to the student edition text. In addition to providing instructors with essential information about how to use the student edition in the classroom, it includes exclusive material such as additional activities, discussion topics, and suggestions for ways to customize lessons for tiered learning.

The Teacher's Manual includes:

- **Discussion Topics:** These discussion topics relate directly and indirectly to the content in the student edition.
- **Review and Reinforcement:** Topics covered in the previous section, or in previous chapters, that instructors may want to review before continuing are provided.
- **Teaching Tips:** These items help explain the content and provide additional information for instructors to use in the classroom.
- **Customized Instruction:** These include accommodations and additional activities for More Advanced, Less Advanced, ESOL, and Special Needs Students.
- **Skills Extensions:** These original activities expand on the student text.
- **Curriculum Connections:** Include cross-curricular activities tied into the computer skills that students are learning.
- **Quick Quizzes:** Provide questions to ask students. Sample answers are provided for the teacher.
- **Troubleshooting:** Offers additional instructions for areas where students may encounter difficulty.
- **Design Forums:** Include tips and suggestions on designing documents, spreadsheets, presentations, and database reports.
- **Workplace Skills:** These further define the types of files students are currently working on and how they are used within the workplace.
- **Job Focus:** Include information on which software skills and expertise are important for various jobs.
- **Data/Solution Files:** A listing of all of the student data files and solution files needed to complete the activities is provided for reference.
- **Try It! and Assessment Tips:** Include detailed notes and suggestions correlated to the steps in the activities.

Chapter 1: Getting Started with Microsoft Excel 2010

Lesson 1 Touring Excel

What You Will Learn

- ✓ Starting Excel
- ✓ Naming and Saving a Workbook
- ✓ Exploring the Excel Window
- ✓ Exploring the Excel Interface
- ✓ Navigating the Worksheet
- ✓ Changing Between Worksheets
- ✓ Changing Worksheet Views
- ✓ Exiting Excel

Words to Know

Active cell
Cell
Cell address or cell reference
Formula bar
Scroll
Sheet tabs
Tab scrolling buttons
Workbook
Worksheet

Tips, Hints, and Pointers

- Discuss each of the skills listed in the What You Will Learn section, and ask students if they have used any of these skills before.
- Discuss the scenario covered in the Application Skills section, and preview the tasks students will perform for Bike Tours and Adventures.
- Key skills covered in this lesson include learning about Excel 2010 features, navigating the worksheet, switching between worksheets, understanding worksheet views, and exiting Excel.

Starting Excel

- Excel is the spreadsheet application in the Microsoft Office suite of software programs. Spreadsheets enable you to organize data in columns and rows, calculate numerical data, display data in various formats, and speed the process of changing and updating data.
- Ask whether students have used spreadsheet software. If so, discuss the software programs they have used and the types of spreadsheets they prepared.

- **CUSTOMIZED INSTRUCTION: ESOL Students:** Have students make flash cards of the Words to Know. They should print the word in English and their primary language on one side, and the definition in English only on the other side.
- If students have already completed the Word section, point out the similarities in the Excel and Word interface, such as the location and general organization of the Ribbon, File tab, Quick Access Toolbar, status bar, program and workbook control buttons, Help button, etc.
- Explore keyboard and mouse procedures for moving in a worksheet. Make sure students understand that a cell must be active to accept entries and the active cell is identified by the heavy cell border. Demonstrate how to switch among the three default worksheets in a workbook.
- For students new to using spreadsheets, demonstrate how to use the mouse to change the active cell in a worksheet.
- Show students different methods for starting Excel. These are:

- Select the program from the Microsoft Office folder accessed from the All Programs menu on the Start menu.
- If the program has been used recently, or pinned to the Windows Start menu, you can select it directly from the Windows Start menu.
- If the program shortcut icon displays on your Windows desktop, you can double-click it.
- If the program icon has been added to the Taskbar, you can click it.

■ Remind students that all Office applications appear in windows that can be resized if desired.

■ Have students start Excel and locate the window elements.

■ Differentiate between a workbook and a worksheet. Have students identify rows, columns, and cells in their blank worksheets.

Naming and Saving a Workbook

■ Make sure students understand the difference between the Save and Save As commands. When you save a file for the first time, you can use either command. The Save As dialog box opens, prompting you to name the file and select the location where you want to save it. You use the Save command to periodically save changes you make to the file as you work on it. This reduces the risk of losing your work due to a power or computer failure.

■ Emphasize the importance of saving files with names that clearly identify their contents. If necessary, refer students to Lesson 2 in Basics Chapter 1 for more information on saving files.

■ **QUICK QUIZ:** What is the difference between the Save command and the Save As command?

You use the Save As command to assign a new name to a file and select the location where you want to store it. You use the Save command to periodically save your work. This helps eliminate the risk of losing your work due to a power failure or computer problems.

Exploring the Excel Window

■ Have students click in any cell to make it active. Point out the heavy black border of the active cell.

■ Explain that cell references are identified by the column letter and the row number of the current cell. Have students locate the cell reference of their active cell in the Name box and observe the shading of the cell's column and row labels.

■ **Try It! Exploring the Excel Window, step 5:** Remind students how a cell reference is formed from the column letter and the row number of the active cell. Check the reference of the active cell by looking in the Name box.

■ **Step 7:** Explain that the keyboard shortcut, Ctrl + Home, makes cell A1 the active cell.

■ **TROUBLESHOOTING:** If students' worksheets have numbers for both rows and columns, turn off the R1C1 reference style as follows: Click the File tab and then click Options. In the Excel Options dialog box, click Formulas in the left pane and under Working with formulas, remove the check mark from the R1C1 reference style check box.

Exploring the Excel Interface

■ You might want to review the Ribbon with students. Most commands are available as buttons on the Ribbon. The Ribbon is organized into tabs based on activities, such as formatting data or entering formulas. On each tab, commands are organized into groups. Contextual tabs are only available in certain situations. For example, if you select a picture, the Picture Tools tab becomes available. You can minimize the Ribbon to display on the tabs if you want to see more of a file, and expand it when you need to use the commands. When you point to a button on the Ribbon with the mouse, the button is highlighted and a ScreenTip displays information about the command. If there is a drop-down arrow on a button, it means that when you click the arrow, a menu or gallery displays so you can make a specific selection. You can rest the mouse pointer on a gallery item to see a Live Preview of the way your worksheet will look if you select that item. You can scroll a gallery or click the More button to view the entire gallery.

■ Some Ribbon groups have a dialog box launcher button. Click the dialog box launcher to display a dialog box, task pane, or window where you can select additional options, or multiple options.

Navigating the Worksheet

■ Have students practice activating different cells and scrolling through the worksheet. Use Page Down or Alt + Page Up, for example, to move quickly down or to the right and then use the scroll bars to return to the top of the worksheet.

■ Instruct students to click each sheet tab to display the three default worksheets in the workbook.

■ Prepare a workbook that has many sheet tabs. Demonstrate how to use the tab scrolling buttons to bring worksheet tabs into view.

■ If time permits, show students how to rename a sheet tab and how to apply a color to it. They will learn more about this in Lesson 19 of Chapter 2.

- **CUSTOMIZED INSTRUCTION: Less Advanced Students:** Have less advanced students practice navigating the worksheet using the mouse and keyboard. Then ask them to press Ctrl+Home to return to cell A1.

Changing Worksheet Views

- Review options on the View tab and have students practice turning View features on or off. Make sure the Formula bar and status bar are in view.
- Review use of Full Screen view and the Zoom slider to change the worksheet view, and allow students to practice using these features.
- Demonstrate how to change the view using options in the Zoom group on the View tab.
- **QUICK QUIZ:** If you had Excel available at home, for what purposes would you use it?

  Answers will vary but might include purposes such as personal budgets, grade tracking, tracking of running or swimming times, etc.
- **CUSTOMIZED INSTRUCTION: Special Needs Students:** Visually challenged students may find it helpful to work at a zoom percentage greater than 100%. Help students find a zoom percentage comfortable for their needs.

Exiting Excel

- Point out that commands to close a worksheet or exit Excel are the same as those in Word.
- **SKILLS EXTENSION:** Have students click the Microsoft Excel Help button at the right end of the Ribbon and explore one of the topics discussed in this lesson.

Project 1--Navigate

- In the Create It projects in this course, students are provided with specific instructions on how to execute each step. In most cases, figures are provided so they can see what their results should look like. The projects are designed to give them practice using the skills they learned in the lesson. Tips for many of the individual steps in the project are provided below for your convenience. You can share with students as you think is necessary.

Data/Solution Files

Data file: EProj02.xlsx
Solution files: ETry01_solution.xlsx
                  EProj02_solution.xlsx

- Step 4: Remind students that the active cell has a dark border surrounding it.
- Step 6: Point out that you can type a lowercase or uppercase "t" for cell addresses.

Project 2—Tour Data

- In the Apply It projects in this course, students are provided with instructions on what to execute, but not specific details on how to do it. In many cases, figures are provided so they can see what their results should look like. The projects are designed to challenge them to apply what they have learned in the lesson. Tips for many of the individual steps in the project are provided below for your convenience. You can share with students as you think is necessary.
- Step 1: Make sure students know how to access the data files for this lesson and where they are to save their work.
- Step 2: Click the File tab and click Save As. Enter the file name and select the location where you are saving files as instructed.
- Step 4: Click the Zoom In button on the slider until the display reaches 150%.
- Step 5: Click the View tab and click the check boxes for the Formula Bar and Gridlines. To hide and redisplay the Ribbon, double-click the active tab name.
- Step 6: Click the Page Layout button next to the zoom slider.
- Step 7: Click the Sheet3 tab and then click the Zoom In button until the display reaches 150%.
- Step 8: Click the cell, click the Home tab, and then click the Copy button.
- Step 9: Click the Sheet1 tab, click cell F5, and click the Paste button on the Home tab.
- Step 10: Click the Sheet2 tab, click cell B11, and click the Copy button.
- Step 11: Click the Sheet1 tab, click cell G8, and click the Paste button.
- Step 12: Click the File menu and click Print.

Lesson 2   Worksheet and Workbook Basics

What You Will Learn

- ✓ Creating a New (Blank) Workbook
- ✓ Entering Text and Labels
- ✓ Editing Text
- ✓ Using Undo and Redo
- ✓ Clearing Cell Contents
- ✓ Inserting a Built-in Header or Footer
- ✓ Previewing and Printing a Worksheet
- ✓ Closing a Workbook

Words to Know

Blank workbook	Label
Clear	Preview
Default	Redo
Footer	Text
Header	Undo

Tips, Hints, and Pointers

- Discuss each of the skills listed in the What You Will Learn section, and ask students if they have used any of these skills before.
- Discuss the scenario covered in the Application Skills section, and preview the tasks students will perform for Serenity Health Club.
- Key skills covered in this lesson include creating a new workbook, entering labels, using Undo and Redo, clearing cell contents, inserting a header and footer, and saving and closing workbooks.

Creating a New (Blank) Workbook

- Show students how to create a new workbook using the New tab on the File tab. Remind students that these procedures are the same as those used to create new Word documents.
- Have students create a new workbook using the New tab and the Blank Workbook option in Backstage view.
- Point out to students the similarities between the Backstage view and Word's New Backstage view.
- **SKILLS EXTENSION:** Have students explore the types of templates available on their computers. On the New tab in Backstage view, have them click Sample templates. If students have an active Internet connection, have them explore the templates available on Office.com.
- **CUSTOMIZED INSTRUCTION: More Advanced Students:** On the New tab in Backstage view, have students click Sample templates, click the Personal Monthly Budget template, and then click Create. Have them click on various cells and determine if the cell entry is a label or text, number, or formula. Ask them to explain how they identified the cell entries as they did. For example, label and text entries are aligned left in the cell; number values are aligned right, and formulas begin with an equal sign.

Entering Text and Labels

- Have students enter several labels on a worksheet, such as month names. Point out the default label alignment (left), font (Calibri), and font size (11 point).
- Have students enter a label such as *Year End Data* in a cell to see what happens when an entry is wider than the cell. If the cell to the right is empty, the data will run over. If the cell is not empty, the data will not display fully.
- Have students practice entering and correcting labels both before finalizing the entry and after.

- Point out that edits can also be made in the formula bar at any time.
- Demonstrate how data appears in the cell as well as in the formula bar as you enter it.
- **Try It! Entering Labels (Text):** Remind students that they can use the Backspace and Delete keys to correct errors. They can also edit data in the formula bar.
- **Steps 3-5:** Remind students to use the figure as a guide on where to enter data.

Editing Text

- Review how to Undo and Redo actions and encourage students to practice using these commands.
- Review the various methods for selecting cell data and editing it.
- In a sample worksheet, use the Escape key and the Cancel button on the formula bar to cancel an entry that has not been finalized yet. Use the Backspace key to demonstrate how to delete characters to the left of the insertion point, and the Delete key to delete characters to the right of the insertion point.
- Double-click a cell entry to activate in-cell editing. Again, you can use the Backspace and Delete keys to edit in the cell.
- Click a cell and make changes to it in the formula bar. Point out that you must press Enter or click the Enter button to the left of the formula bar in order to finalize edits.
- **QUICK QUIZ:** You have made edits to cell data using the formula bar but the corrections are not showing up in the worksheet cell. What could be causing this to happen?

  You have not pressed Enter or clicked the Enter key to the left of the formula bar to finalize the edits.

Using Undo and Redo

- Students were introduced to the Undo and Redo commands in Basics Chapter 1 and Word Chapter 1. These buttons are on the Quick Access Toolbar. The buttons are available in all the Office applications.
- In a sample Excel workbook, demonstrate how to use the Undo and Redo buttons on the Quick Access Toolbar.
- **QUICK QUIZ:** What is the difference between the Undo and Redo commands?

  The Undo command enables you to reverse a single action made in error, whereas the Redo command reinstates any action that you reversed with Undo.

Clearing Cell Contents

- Explain that in addition to using the Escape, Backspace, and Delete keys to delete data from a cell, you can also use the Clear option on the Home tab. When you click the Clear button, you can choose to clear the content of the cell as well as any formatting, comments, or hyperlinks that have been applied to it.

Inserting a Built-In Header or Footer

- Introduce headers and footers. A header appears at the top of each page, and a footer displays at the bottom of each page. Headers and footers usually contain useful information such as the file's name or the date.
- Add a header and footer to a sample workbook and demonstrate how to create different headers and footers for each of the different sections.
- Demonstrate how to move from the header to the footer.
- Click the File tab and then click Print to show students how the headers and footers appear in the Preview window.
- **Try It! Inserting a Built-in Header or Footer:** Students will be instructed to print various worksheets throughout this course. They will be instructed to insert their name and other information in a header or footer to help them identify their printouts.
- **Try It! Previewing and Printing a Worksheet, step 2:** To print a file, click the File tab and then click Print. In Backstage view, encourage students to carefully review the preview of the worksheet. You might also discuss the other print and page layout options that can be set from Backstage view.
- **Step 5:** Students are instructed to get your permission before printing any files in this course. Provide any special instructions for printing their worksheets.
- **WORKPLACE SKILLS:** Customer surveys, like the one students work on in this lesson, can be a powerful tool in a company's sales and marketing strategy. Ask students if they've ever filled out a survey or answered one conducted in person or over the telephone. Discuss the following three tips on developing effective surveys.
  - Timing is everything. Determining the best time to survey customers depends on many things, from the weather to the economy to global politics. For example, during economic

downturns, consumers are less likely to complete surveys and if they do, will probably be negative in their responses.

- Ask the right questions. These are the ones that help you identify what customers value in you.
- Follow up. If possible, contact each respondent in some manner to thank them, even if their responses were not all that positive.

Closing a Workbook
- Remind students that they should periodically save their files as they work on them to eliminate the risk of losing data due to a power failure or computer malfunction.
- You should always close files and exit programs when you are done working on them. This minimizes the risk of someone else working in your files or seeing data that may be sensitive or confidential.

Project 3—Basic Invoice
- Refer students to Figure 2-1. Their worksheets should look like this when they have completed them.
- Step 7: Instruct students to click in the left corner of the header area to activate the left header box.
- Step 28: Instruct students on whether or not they are allowed to print their worksheets.
- **WORKPLACE SKILLS:** Explain that an invoice is a business document prepared by a seller of goods or services listing all such items sold, and presented to the buyer for payment. Many companies create invoices using Excel worksheets because they can insert formulas to instantaneously calculate the amounts due, sales tax, shipping charges, and other fees.

Most invoices include columns for an item or service number, description, the unit price, the quantity ordered, and the line total. Invoices should also include the name, address, and contact numbers for both the seller and the buyer.

Project 4—Member Invoice
- Step 3: Click the Insert tab and click the Header & Footer button. Click in the left corner of the header area to activate the left header box and enter your name. Press Tab and click the Current Date button. Press Tab and click the Page Number button.
- Step 4: Press Escape, click the View tab, and then click the Normal button.
- Step 6: Click the cell and type No.
- Step 8: Click cell B10, click the Home, click the Clear button, and then click Clear Formats.
- Step 13: Remind students to carefully check their cell entries.
- Step 17: Instruct students on whether or not they are allowed to print their worksheets, and what they are to submit for grading.

Data/Solution Files

Data file: EProj04.xlsx
Solution files: ETry02_solution.xlsx
                   EProj03_solution.xlsx
                   EProj04_solution.xlsx

Lesson 3 Adding Worksheet Contents

What You Will Learn

- ✓ **Opening an Existing Workbook and Saving It with a New Name**
- ✓ **Entering and Editing Numeric Labels and Values**
- ✓ **Using AutoComplete**
- ✓ **Using Pick From List**
- ✓ **Using AutoCorrect**
- ✓ **Checking the Spelling in a Worksheet**

Words to Know

AutoComplete
AutoCorrect
Numeric label

Pick From List
Spelling checker
Value

Tips, Hints, and Pointers

- Discuss each of the skills listed in the What You Will Learn section, and ask students if they have used any of these skills before.
- Discuss the scenario covered in the Application Skills section, and preview the tasks students will perform for Whole Grains Bread.
- Key skills covered in this lesson include opening workbooks; using AutoComplete, Pick From List, and AutoCorrect; and checking spelling in a worksheet.

Opening an Existing Workbook and Saving It with a New Name

- Discuss with students reasons a saved workbook might need to be opened. Further revisions may be necessary, or the worksheet may not yet be finished. When you save a workbook with a new name, the original file remains unchanged.
- Remind students how to use the Open dialog box to locate a previously saved file. The Open dialog box in Excel looks the same as the Open dialog box they used to open Word documents.
- Have students display the File tab in Backstage view and locate the name(s) of recently saved workbooks. Point out that when you click a folder in the Recent Places section, the Open dialog box appears, displaying the contents of the selected folder.
- Have students display the Open dialog box and use the Views button to change the display of saved workbooks in the folder where they are saving their work for this class.
- Have students open a previously saved workbook and a new workbook and practice switching from one to the other using the Windows taskbar.
- **QUICK QUIZ:** Why might you use the Recent tab in Backstage view instead of the Open dialog box to open a file?

   You can more quickly access workbooks you've recently worked on through the Recent tab. This saves you the steps of opening the Open dialog box and navigating through levels of folders to find the file.

Entering and Editing Numeric Labels and Values

- Discuss the difference between text labels and numeric labels. Numeric labels and values are used in calculations.
- Point out that some numeric labels, such as Social Security numbers or phone numbers, will not be used in calculations and therefore are treated as text labels. Excel automatically recognizes these types of values as text labels. For other such values, such as a year used as a column heading, you may want to manually identify it as a text label by typing an apostrophe at the beginning of the entry.
- Have students practice entering numeric values. They should type numbers with the thousands

separator, dollar sign, percentage sign, and using an apostrophe at the beginning of a year entry.

- Point out how numeric values align to the right of the cell and the year entry, like other text labels, aligns to the left of the cell.
- **CUSTOMIZED INSTRUCTION: ESOL Students:** Have students list the denominations of money in their country of origin by spelling out the names and writing in currency format; for example, 1 yen and ¥1; 5 yen and ¥5; 10 yen and ¥10; and so on.
- **Try It! Entering and Editing Numeric Labels and Values:** Point out how numeric values to be used in calculations are aligned to the right. This ensures that decimal places in values are aligned down the column. Also, note the Error button's drop-down menu. Excel flagged the cell value as an error because it identified the value as a number that could be used in a calculation instead of a text label.
- **SKILLS EXTENSION:** Have students enter an apostrophe and then a numeric value. Click the Error button and then click Error Checking Options. Have them explore the settings in the Excel Options dialog box.

Using AutoComplete

- In a sample worksheet, have students type labels, such as the days of the week or the names of their teachers, in a blank worksheet and then repeat them to see how AutoComplete suggests a label that has already been entered in the column.
- Demonstrate that to accept the AutoComplete suggestion, you press Enter or Tab.

Using Pick From List

- In a sample worksheet, have students right-click in the next empty cell below their list of labels, select Pick From Drop-down List, and then choose an entry from the supplied list.
- Point out to students that the Pick From List feature works only with contiguous cells.
- **QUICK QUIZ:** You have created a list of billing codes in a worksheet column. You skip three cells and then try to use Pick From List to insert a billing code, but no options display on the list. Why?

Because cells were skipped between the previous list and the current cell; Pick From List works only for contiguous cells.

Using AutoCorrect

- Demonstrate how the AutoCorrect Options button displays, giving you options for correcting certain types of entries.

- Have students type an Internet address such as *www.microsoft.com* in a cell and then click the AutoCorrect button to undo the hyperlink.

Checking the Spelling in a Worksheet

- Have students enter some obviously misspelled data and run a spell check. Point out that each worksheet in a workbook must be checked separately.
- **SKILLS EXTENSION:** Have students review the entries in Excel's AutoCorrect list. To do this, they can click the Spelling button on the Review tab. In the Spelling dialog box, click the Options button. The Excel Options dialog box opens with the Proofing options displayed. Click the AutoCorrect Options button and then scroll through the list of entries at the bottom of the dialog box. Have students write down a few entries, close out of the Excel Options dialog box, and then enter the incorrectly spelled entries in the worksheet to see how AutoCorrect automatically corrects them.
- **CURRICULUM CONNECTION:** The United Nations Educational, Scientific and Cultural Organization (UNESCO) maintains a list of more than 800 protected World Heritage Areas, which are natural and cultural locations around the globe. The areas are selected based on cultural or natural significance. For example, the Statue of Liberty is a cultural World Heritage Site and the Grand Canyon is a natural one. Have students make a list of at least five World Heritage Sites and create a worksheet about them. They should include statistics such as the location, what year the site was added to the World Heritage List, and which of the 10 criteria it meets. They might also want to include a site they think should be included.
- **CUSTOMIZED INSTRUCTION: More Advanced Students:** Have advanced students create an AutoCorrect entry in the AutoCorrect dialog box (Proofing section of the Excel Options dialog box). Ask them to test the entry in the worksheet and then delete the entry from the AutoCorrect list.

Project 5—Bakery Schedule Entries

- Refer students to Figure 3-1. Their worksheets should look like this when they have completed them.
- Step 4: Click the Insert tab and click the Header & Footer button. Click in the left corner of the header area to activate the left header box and enter your name. Press Tab and click the Current Date button. Press Tab and click the Page Number button. Press Escape, click the View tab, and then click the Normal button.

- Step 5: Students should type the text exactly as shown. They will correct errors later.
- Step 23: Instruct students on whether or not they are allowed to print their worksheets, and what they are to submit for grading.

Project 6—Finishing the Bakery Schedule

- Refer students to Figure 3-2. Their worksheets should look like this when they have completed them.
- Step 3: Click the Insert tab and click the Header & Footer button. Click in the left corner of the header area to activate the left header box and enter your name. Press Tab and click the Current Date button. Press Tab and click the Page Number button. Press Escape, click the View tab, and then click the Normal button.
- Step 4: Right-click cell A12 and click Pick From Drop-down List on the shortcut menu. Click Village Green.
- Steps 5-6: Remind students that they can press Enter or Tab to accept the AutoComplete suggestion.
- Step 13: Click the Review tab and then click the Spelling button.

- Step 19: Instruct students on whether or not they are allowed to print their worksheets, and what they are to submit for grading.
- **WORKPLACE SKILLS:** Remind students that the bakery schedule they worked on in Projects 5 and 6 was the responsibility of the team leader at Whole Grains Bread. Point out that more and more companies today organize their employees into teams made up of people from different departments. For example, a team might include representatives from research, development, design, marketing, and finance. The goal is to bring different thoughts and ideas together from the start to produce higher quality products and services.

  Reinforce the idea of how teamwork gives individual team members access to valuable resources. You might discuss your school's parent/teacher association and provide examples of how individual members contribute different thoughts and ideas toward achieving the team's common goal. Or, ask students to comment on a team on which they participate.

Data/Solution Files

Data files: ETry03.xlsx
                EProj06.xlsx
Solution files: ETry03_solution.xlsx
                EProj05_solution.xlsx
                EProj06_solution.xlsx

Lesson 4   Worksheet Formatting

What You Will Learn
- ✓ Choosing a Theme
- ✓ Applying Cell Styles
- ✓ Applying Font Formats
- ✓ Merging and Centering Across Cells
- ✓ Applying Number Formats

Words to Know

Accounting format
Cell style
Comma format
Currency format
Fill
Font
Font size

Format
Live Preview
Merge and Center
Number format
Percent format
Theme

Tips, Hints, and Pointers

- Discuss each of the skills listed in the What You Will Learn section, and ask students if they have used any of these skills before.
- Discuss the scenario covered in the Application Skills section, and preview the tasks students will perform for Voyager Travel Adventures.
- Key skills covered in this lesson include applying a theme and cell styles, formatting data, and merging and centering data across cells.

Choosing a Theme

- You might want to take a few minutes now to review with students how to select portions of a worksheet for easy formatting. Select rows and columns by clicking their headers. Show students the Select All button to select the entire worksheet. You can select a range of contiguous or adjacent cells by simply dragging over them with the mouse. You can select noncontiguous cells by clicking or dragging over them and holding down the Ctrl key as you click on other cells.
- Introduce themes. Themes supply coordinated colors, fonts, and effects to give worksheets a distinctive look. Discuss the advantages of using themes to enhance the worksheet and save a great deal of time when formatting a worksheet.
- All of the Office 2010 applications offer the same set of themes. Discuss how this kind of consistent formatting could make it easy to create coordinated communications across applications.
- Point out the Themes gallery on the Page Layout tab. Have students open or create a sample worksheet that has several levels of headings, a block of data, and a total row. Have them practice previewing themes to see how the worksheet's appearance changes.
- In a sample worksheet, have students select a theme, and then make other changes to theme colors, fonts, or effects. When they are done, they should close the workbook without saving their changes.

Applying Cell Styles

- Remind students of the Quick Styles and Style Sets they applied to Word documents. Cell styles in Excel workbooks function in much the same way.
- Cell styles can be found by clicking the Cell Styles button in the Styles group on the Home tab.
- Review the Cell Styles gallery with students. In a sample worksheet, demonstrate how to apply various styles.
- **DESIGN FORUM:** The use of styles and themes can give worksheets a professional look. Many businesses find that they can also create continuity among their internal and external documents by using the same themes, styles, and formatting on

10 | Learning Microsoft Excel 2010 | Teacher's Manual

all of them. This applies to brochures and other marketing materials, the corporate logo, letterhead, financial documents, and even envelopes and mailing labels. The consistent use of formats on all documents can help a business enhance its image and strengthen corporate identity.
- **CUSTOMIZED INSTRUCTION: Special Needs Students:** Styles can save a great deal of formatting time and minimize the number of keystrokes a physically challenged person has to make. Create new styles to allow easier text formatting.

Applying Font Formats
- Review buttons on the Home tab for applying text formats such as font, size, style, and color. Have students open the Format Cells dialog box and display the Font tab. Point out similarities to the Font dialog box in Word. Remind students that it is faster to use the Font tab in the Format Cells dialog box when applying more than one font format.
- Provide students with a sample worksheet. Have students select the entire worksheet and change its font to 12 point Cambria.
- Compare the process of applying font and fill color to that used to apply color to Word table text and cells. Remind students that they have the option of choosing theme colors or standard colors in the palettes.
- Allow students to practice using the Format Cells dialog box or the Font Color and Fill Color buttons to apply color in their sample worksheet.
- **QUICK QUIZ:**
- How can font and fill color make a worksheet more useful as well as more attractive?

  Font and fill color can be used to group areas of a worksheet for easy reading or to emphasize portions of the worksheet such as total columns or rows.
- **CUSTOMIZED INSTRUCTION: Special Needs Students:** Remember that students with visual challenges may have difficulty reading text with certain combinations of font and background colors. It is generally best to use dark text on a light background, or light text on a dark background.

Merging and Centering Across Cells
- Students should be familiar with the merge and center feature from their work on Word tables in Lesson 16 of Word Chapter 2. Merging is useful for creating a header row across a table.

- You can merge horizontally or vertically adjacent cells using the Merge & Center button on the Home tab.
- **Try It! Merging and Centering Across Cells:** Have students check their worksheets against that shown in the figure to ensure they have correctly merged the cells and applied the Total cell style.

Applying Number Formats
- Remind students that in previous exercises they viewed values with a differing number of decimal points and inserted currency data without dollar signs. Number formats can make data such as this more meaningful to the user.
- Explore number formats available on the Number Format button's drop-down menu on the Home tab.
- Explore the number formats on the Number tab of the Format Cells dialog box. Urge students to pay attention to the examples given when a format is selected to ensure they choose the format they want.
- Have students enter several values in a sample worksheet and practice formatting using the Percent Style and Comma Style buttons on the Home tab. Stress that a decimal value must be entered to display a percent less than 100.
- Have students use the Format Cells dialog box to format one value with the Currency format and one with the Accounting format to see the difference in the way these formats display values.
- **CURRICULUM CONNECTION:** Have students use a math or business textbook to define the terms, percentage, fraction, and exponentiation. Answers are:
  - Percentage: A proportion stated in terms of one-hundredths that is calculated by multiplying a fraction by 100.
  - Fraction: A number that is not a whole number, formed by dividing one quantity into another.
  - Exponentiation: Multiplication of a number or quantity by itself a given number of times, the number of times being the power to which the number or quantity is to be raised.

Project 7—Inventory Sheet Entries and Formatting
- Refer students to Figure 4-1. Their worksheets should look like this when they have completed them.
- Step 3: Click the Insert tab and click the Header & Footer button. Click in the left corner of the header area to activate the left header box and enter your name. Press Tab and click the Current Date

button. Press Tab and click the Page Number button. Press Escape, click the View tab, and then click the Normal button.
- Step 4: Remind students that to select the headings, they must hold down the mouse button as they drag over them.
- Step 7: Remind students that the dialog box launcher is the small arrow in the lower right corner of the group.
- Steps 24-25: Point out that students will be entering the values down the column as shown in Figure 4-1.
- Step 29: Instruct students on whether or not they are allowed to print their worksheets, and what they are to submit for grading.
- **JOB FOCUS:** Many companies employ an inventory manager to order, track, and manage the business's inventory of products. The responsibilities of an inventory manager vary depending on the type of business, but in general, they include the following:
  - Manages the storage and distribution of a company's products as well as materials it uses in the production of products.
  - Oversees the bookkeeping of accounts and financial control of the department's budget.
  - Maintains all inventory records.
  - Establishes and maintains good communication between the department and other departments in the company, such as Production, Engineering and Maintenance, Quality Control, Purchasing and Sales.
  - Logs the receipt of stock and notifies all interested departments of the arrival of stock.
  - Inspects and checks all deliveries and the return to the supplier of rejected stock.
  - Manages the distribution of products as well as production materials.

Project 8—Finishing the Inventory Worksheet
- Refer students to Figure 4-2. Their worksheets should look like this when they have completed them.
- Step 3: Click the Insert tab and click the Header & Footer button. Click in the left corner of the header area to activate the left header box and enter your name. Press Tab and click the Current Date button. Press Tab and click the Page Number button. Press Escape, click the View tab, and then click the Normal button.
- Step 4: Click the Page Layout tab, click the Themes button, and then click Clarity.
- Step 5: Click the Home tab and click the Number dialog box launcher. Click the Percentage option and enter 2 for Decimal places.
- Step 6: Click the Home tab, click the Number Format drop-down arrow, and click Accounting.
- Step 7: Click the Home tab, click the Cell Styles button, and click Accent 3. Then, click the Center button in the Alignment group.
- Step 8: Click the Home tab, click the Cell Styles button, and click the specified style.
- Step 9: Click the Home tab, click the Number Format drop-down arrow, and click Long Date.
- Step 11: Instruct students on whether or not they are allowed to print their worksheets, and what they are to submit for grading.

Data/Solution Files

Data files: ETry04.xlsx
                EProj07.xlsx
                EProj08.xlsx
Solution files: ETry04_solution.xlsx
                EProj07_solution.xlsx
                EProj08_solution.xlsx

Lesson 5 More on Cell Entries and Formatting

What You Will Learn

- ✓ Entering Dates
- ✓ Filling a Series
- ✓ Aligning Data in a Cell
- ✓ Wrapping Text in Cells
- ✓ Changing Column Width and Row Height
- ✓ Using Keyboard Shortcuts

Words to Know

Auto Fill
Date
Wrap text
Default column width
Fill handle

Key Tips
Keyboard shortcuts
Series
Wrap text

Tips, Hints, and Pointers

- Discuss each of the skills listed in the What You Will Learn section, and ask students if they have used any of these skills before.
- Discuss the scenario covered in the Application Skills section, and preview the tasks students will perform for Serenity Health Club.
- Key skills covered in this lesson include entering dates; creating a series; changing data alignment; and changing the column width.

Entering Dates

- Discuss the different formats you can apply to dates. Note that dates are often used in calculations; for example, to determine the date when an item was ordered and the date it arrived.
- Explain that dates entered in a worksheet are stored as a number code. This allows for them to be used in calculations.
- Review the keyboard shortcuts for entering the current date and time. Press Ctrl + : to enter the current date. Press Ctrl + Shift + : to enter the current time.
- Point out that you can quickly apply the Short Date (8/21/2012) or Long Date (Tuesday, August 21, 2012) formats using the Number Format drop-down menu.
- You can apply other date formats from the Number tab in the Format Cells dialog box.

Filling a Series

- Explain that the fill handle can be used to quickly copy the data in one cell to adjacent cells.
- The fill handle also can be used to complete a series. Excel recognizes some series, such as days of the week, months of the year, and consecutive numbers.
- For other more specific series, you must first enter two to three values to establish the pattern.
- Show students how to use the fill handle to copy data from one cell to adjacent cells. Then, start a series, such as for the years 2010 to 2016. Enter the first two years (2010, 2011), select the cells, and then drag the fill handle to continue the series.
- Point out the ScreenTip that displays to indicate the increment in the series that each cell represents.
- **QUICK QUIZ:** When would you want to fill a column or row with identical values?

    When preparing a budget, for example, where income or an expenditure is the same in all weeks or months.

Aligning Data in a Cell

- Remind students of the default alignments of labels (left) and values (right). Have students use alignment buttons on the Home tab to change alignments of both labels and values.

Chapter 1 | 13

- Point out that the alignment buttons in Excel are similar to those students used in tables they created in Word documents. These include horizontal and vertical alignment options.
- The horizontal alignment options are Align Text Left, Center, and Align Text Right buttons.
- Demonstrate how to use the Top Align, Middle Align, and Bottom Align buttons on the Home tab.
- Have students open the Format Cells dialog box and click the Alignment tab. Explore options in this dialog box for aligning cell contents both horizontally and vertically, controlling text in a cell, and changing text orientation.

Wrapping Text in Cells
- On the Alignment tab in the Format Cells dialog box, point out the Wrap text option in the Text control section. Wrapping text in a cell is ideal for headings that are longer than the data that falls under them.

Changing Column Width and Row Height
- Point out that Excel will automatically widen the cell to accommodate the entire entry if there is no data in the next cell to the right.
- Demonstrate methods for adjusting column width. Have students insert some long entries in column A and then practice methods for adjusting the column's width. These include dragging a column or row border, double-clicking a border, or by clicking options on the Format drop-down menu on the Home tab.
- Point out the ScreenTip that displays when you drag a border. The ScreenTip identifies the row height or the column width as you drag.

Using Keyboard Shortcuts
- Students learned about access keys and keyboard shortcuts in Lesson 3 of Basics Chapter 1.
- Ask students how many of them have used keyboard shortcuts in Office programs or other applications. Stress that such shortcuts can be an efficient way to issue commands because a user does not have to remove his or her hands from the keyboard.
- Explain the Office 2010 access key system and allow students to practice accessing tabs and commands on tabs.
- Have students press the access key for a tab of their choice. They will see access keys assigned to the various options on that tab.
- Explain that becoming familiar with keyboard shortcuts can help you work more quickly and efficiently.

- **CUSTOMIZED INSTRUCTION: Less Advanced Students:** Have students make flash cards of commonly used keyboard shortcuts. Starting with the Home tab on the Ribbon, have students point to a button or command to determine if it has a keyboard shortcut. For example, the shortcut for the Cut command is Ctrl + X; the shortcut for the Bold command is Ctrl + B. Have them write the command name on one side of the flash card and the keyboard shortcut on the other side. You can assign a tab to each student or have each student identify the shortcuts on all the tabs.

Project 9—Client Account Tracking Worksheet
- Refer students to Figure 5-1. Their worksheets should look like this when they have completed them.
- Step 22: Make sure students drag over the column letters.
- Step 24: Remind students that Ctrl + z is the keyboard shortcut for the Undo Typing command on the Undo button.
- Step 31: Instruct students on whether or not they are allowed to print their worksheets, and what they are to submit for grading.
- Step 32: Note that the keyboard shortcut opens the File tab and selects the Close command.
- **JOB FOCUS:** Point out that Serenity Health Club's accounts receivable supervisor was responsible for the client account tracking worksheet shown in Figure 5-1. Many companies employ a billing manager or accounts receivable supervisor to issue invoices and oversee billing practices. In addition to preparing, verifying, and processing invoices, this individual may also be responsible for coordinating and resolving sales tax issues, tracking payments, developing payment plans, and collecting unpaid bills, and maintaining the company's general ledger.
- **CURRICULUM CONNECTION:** On a sheet of paper, have students use an arithmetic operation of their choice to manually calculate the total payments by month and the total payments by client ID using the data on the worksheet shown in Figure 5-1.

Project 10—Extra Services Tracking Worksheet
- Refer students to Figure 5-2. Their worksheets should look like this when they have completed them.
- Step 7: Click the Home tab and click the Wrap Text button. Click the Alight Text Right button in the Alignment group.

- Step 8: Click the Home tab and click the Top Align button.
- Step 9: Click the row 1 header to select the row, click the Home tab, click the Format button, and then click AutoFit Row Height.
- Step 10: Click the fill handle and drag to cell F6.
- Step 17: Click the Home tab and click the Wrap Text button.
- Step 19: Click the Home tab, click the Format button, and then click Column Width. In the Column Width dialog box, enter the specified width.
- Step 20: Click the Home tab, and click the Center button.
- Step 21: Click the row 7 header to select the row, click the Home tab, click the Format button, and click Row Height. In the Row Height dialog box, enter the specified height.
- Step 24: Instruct students on whether or not they are allowed to print their worksheets, and what they are to submit for grading.

Data/Solution Files

Data files: ETry05.xlsx
EProj09.xlsx
EProj10.xlsx

Solution files: ETry05_solution.xlsx
EProj09_solution.xlsx
EProj10_solution.xlsx

Lesson 6 Working with Ranges

What You Will Learn
- ✓ Selecting Ranges
- ✓ Entering Data by Range
- ✓ Making a Range Entry Using a Collapse Dialog Box Button

Words to Know
Collapse Dialog box button Noncontiguous range
Contiguous range Range

Tips, Hints, and Pointers
- Discuss each of the skills listed in the What You Will Learn section, and ask students if they have used any of these skills before.
- Discuss the scenario covered in the Application Skills section, and preview the tasks students will perform for Overview Academy.
- Key skills covered in this lesson include selecting ranges, entering data by range, and using the Collapse Dialog button.

Selecting Ranges
- Introduce a range as a block or group of cells in a worksheet and discuss the advantages of identifying ranges for purposes of formatting or creating formulas.
- Have students open a new workbook and practice selecting both contiguous and noncontiguous ranges. Discuss how ranges are designated by the first and last cell in the range, such as A1:B3.
- Point out how the first cell in a range (the active cell) is not highlighted but other cells in the range are highlighted.
- **QUICK QUIZ:** For what purposes would you select a range of cells in a worksheet?

    To delete the contents of the selected cells, to apply the same formats to a group of cells, to include the entire group in a formula, etc.

Entering Data by Range
- Remind students that the fill handle can be used to quickly copy the data in one cell to adjacent cells. If necessary, show students how to use the fill handle to copy data from one cell to adjacent cells.
- Show students how to use the options on the Fill drop-down menu. Select a cell containing the value you want to repeat, drag across the range to which you want to copy, click the Fill button, and then select the desired option.
- Use the Series option when you want to fill the range with a series of values that increment, or "step," by a designated number. This is referred to as the "step value."

Making a Range Entry Using a Collapse Dialog Box Button
- In a dialog box, show students what the Collapse Dialog button looks like. You can use the Page Setup dialog box, which is used in the Try It exercise, or another one, such as the Function Arguments dialog box.
- Click the Collapse Dialog button, select a range on the worksheet, and then click the Expand Dialog button to redisplay the dialog box.
- Students may wonder why the cell references include dollar signs when a range is selected using the Collapse Dialog button. Explain that the dollar signs designate absolute cell references. Students will learn about cell references in Lesson 8.

Project 11—Starting the Instructor Performance Ratings Worksheet
- Refer students to Figure 6-1. Their worksheets should look like this when they have completed them.
- Step 26: Instruct students on whether or not they are allowed to print their worksheets, and what they are to submit for grading.
- **WORKPLACE SKILLS:** Explain to students that a performance review or job review is a report that rates how well an employee does his or her job.

    A performance review rating, like that shown in Figure 6-1, is similar to a report card in that it provides a measure of how an employee is performing. The main difference between the two is that a performance review rating is often largely dependent on the way an individual behaves on the job, his or her attitude, and his or her work ethic. The grades you get on a report card are measures of your performance on tests, quizzes, and assignments; they usually are not indicative of your behavior, attitude, and ethics.

Explain that a performance review is also an opportunity for an employee to share ideas about their future with the company or organization. Ask students who have gone through a performance review what they gained from the process. If you think it is appropriate, discuss your own experiences in performance reviews.

Project 12—Completing the Instructor Performance Ratings Worksheet

- Step 4: Click the column A column header, click the Home tab, click the Format button, and click AutoFit Column Width.

- Step 6: Click the Home tab and click the Alignment dialog box launcher.
- Step 8: Remind students to hold down the Ctrl key as they select the noncontiguous cells.
- Step 12: Select the range E11:E14, click the Home tab, click the Fill button, and then click Down.
- Steps 13-14: Encourage students to use the options on the Fill drop-down menu and in the Series dialog box to fill in the ranges.
- Step 15: Click the Page Layout tab, click the Page Setup dialog box launcher, and click the Sheet tab. Click the Collapse Dialog button at the end of the Print area text box. On the worksheet, select the range A1:E26. Click the Expand Dialog button to return to the dialog box.
- Step 16: Instruct students on whether or not they are allowed to print their worksheets, and what they are to submit for grading.

Data/Solution Files

Data files: ETry06.xlsx
                  EProj11.xlsx
                  EProj12.xlsx
Solution files: ETry06_solution.xlsx
                  EProj11_solution.xlsx
                  EProj12_solution.xlsx

Lesson 7 Creating Formulas

What You Will Learn
- ✓ Entering a Formula
- ✓ Using Arithmetic Operators
- ✓ Editing a Formula
- ✓ Copying a Formula Using the Fill Handle
- ✓ Using the SUM Function

Words to Know
Arithmetic (mathematical) operators
Formula
Order of precedence
SUM function

Tips, Hints, and Pointers

- Discuss each of the skills listed in the What You Will Learn section, and ask students if they have used any of these skills before.
- Discuss the scenario covered in the Application Skills section, and preview the tasks students will perform for Serenity Health Club.
- Key skills covered in this lesson include entering and editing formulas.

Entering a Formula
- Introduce formulas as calculations performed in a worksheet. Explain the parts of a formula (cell references or values and mathematical operators).
- Demonstrate how to create a formula, pointing out the equal sign that begins the formula and how the formula displays in both the cell and the formula bar.
- Have students enter some values in a new worksheet and practice creating formulas to add, subtract, multiply, and divide the values, making sure to use cell references in the formulas. Then have them change some values to see the formulas recalculate.
- Stress the importance of using cell references in a formula rather than cell values. When cell references are used, Excel will correctly update the formula when values in those cells change.

Using Arithmetic Operators
- Review the order of precedence, or order of operations, as discussed in the text. Write several equations on the board that incorporate the different operators as well as parentheses and have students explain the order in which the operations will be calculated.
- **CUSTOMIZED INSTRUCTION: Special Needs Students:** Show special needs students where to find the mathematical operators on the keyboard and on the numeric keypad.
- **CUSTOMIZED INSTRUCTION: ESOL Students:** On a sheet of paper, have students write the names of the standard arithmetic operations in English and in their primary language.
- **TROUBLESHOOTING:** Advise students that if they forget the equal sign at the beginning of a formula, the formula itself will appear in the cell instead of the result.

Editing a Formula
- Demonstrate how to edit a formula by double-clicking it to enter edit mode or by clicking it and making changes in the formula bar.
- Point out the color coding of parts of a formula. These identify cell references.

Copying a Formula Using the Fill Handle
- You can copy a formula in a cell using the Fill handle just as you copied a cell entry. Demonstrate how to copy a formula using the fill handle.

Using the SUM Function
- Introduce students to the SUM function, which is used to add or total the values in a selected range of cells. The SUM function enables you to total a range of cells without having to click individual cell references.

- Remind students that they worked with the SUM function in Word tables they created in Lesson 17 of Word Chapter 2.
- In a sample worksheet, have students enter the SUM function using the different methods discussed in the text.
- Point out that you must press Enter or Tab to complete the SUM function.

Project 13—Entering First Formulas in the Extra Services Worksheet

- Refer students to Figure 7-1. Their worksheets should look like this when they have completed them. Explain to students not to worry about the error message that appears in cell B14. The total values will be calculated in the next project, which will be used to compute the percentages.
- Step 10: Instruct students on whether or not they are allowed to print their worksheets, and what they are to submit for grading.

Project 14—Completing the Formulas in the Extra Services Worksheet

- Refer students to Figure 7-2. Their worksheets should look like this when they have completed them.
- Step 4: Students may press Alt + = to quickly sum the values above.
- Step 5: Remind students how to use the fill handle, if necessary.
- Step 6: Remind students that double-clicking copies the formula down to the blank cells.
- Step 7: Explain that Excel changed the reference from cell G12 to the next corresponding cell to the right.
- Step 8: Select each cell, highlight the incorrect divisor cell reference, and type in G12. Note that you can type a lowercase or uppercase "G."
- Step 10: Instruct students on whether or not they are allowed to print their worksheets, and what they are to submit for grading.

Data/Solution Files

Data files:　　ETry07.xlsx
　　　　　　　EProj13.xlsx
　　　　　　　EProj14.xlsx
Solution files:　ETry07_solution.xlsx
　　　　　　　EProj13_solution.xlsx
　　　　　　　EProj14_solution.xlsx

Lesson 8   Copying and Pasting

What You Will Learn

- ✓ Copying and Pasting Data
- ✓ Copying Formats
- ✓ Copying Formulas Containing a Relative Reference
- ✓ Copying Formulas Containing an Absolute Reference

Words to Know

Absolute reference
Clipboard
Copy
Format Painter
Paste
Relative reference

Tips, Hints, and Pointers

- Discuss each of the skills listed in the What You Will Learn section, and ask students if they have used any of these skills before.
- Discuss the scenario covered in the Application Skills section, and preview the tasks students will perform for Voyager Travel Adventures.
- Key skills covered in this lesson include copying and pasting data, copying formats, and working with relative and absolute cell references.

Copying and Pasting Data

- Review the Copy and Paste process if you think students need a refresher on working with the Clipboard. Remind students that the fill handle can also be used to copy cell data.
- Explain that Copy and Paste can be used between sections on a worksheet, between worksheets in the same workbook, or between worksheets in different workbooks.
- Have students practice copying cell data or ranges in a sample worksheet using the Copy and Paste process. Have students practice using the fill handle to copy data. Encourage them to click the Auto Fill Options button to select different options for copying cells, fill with formatting, and fill without formatting.
- **QUICK QUIZ:** How does copying and pasting help a user create an accurate worksheet?

  Use Copy and Paste to insert similar or identical data to reduce the chance of data entry errors.

Copying Formats

- Students worked with the Format Painter in Lesson 23 of Word Chapter 2. Point out that the Format Painter works in the same way on Excel data.
- Remind students that the Format Painter copies formats from one selection to other selections. Students should understand that the Format Painter not only saves a great deal of formatting time but also ensures consistency in the formats of headings and ranges of numeric values.
- Demonstrate how to use the Format Painter to copy formats once or to multiple selections. To copy to multiple selections, double-click the Format Painter button.
- A shortcut for turning off the Format Painter is to click Esc.

Copying Formulas Containing a Relative Reference

- In a blank sample worksheet, have students enter any values in the range A1:B4. In cell C1, insert a formula to multiply A1*B1 and then copy the formula down to C4. Have students click in cell C2 to see how the relative cell references have adjusted automatically.

Copying Formulas Containing an Absolute Reference

- In a sample worksheet, demonstrate how to change a relative cell reference to an absolute cell reference.

- Point out to students that the $ must be entered before the column letter and the row number to set an absolute cell reference.
- Demonstrate how to use a mixed cell reference. You use a mixed reference to retain a certain column letter or row number as a formula is copied.
- You can set an absolute cell reference by typing the $ sign as you type in a reference, or you can press the F4 key.

Project 15—Copying Between the Trip Budget and Profit Worksheets

- Refer students to Figure 8-1. Their worksheets should look like this when they have completed them.
- Step 7: Point out to students that they should click the top portion of the Paste button, not the drop-down arrow.
- Step 13: Instruct students on whether or not they are allowed to print their worksheets, and what they are to submit for grading.

Project 16—Finishing the Trip Profit worksheet

- Refer students to Figure 8-2. Their worksheets should look like this when they have completed them.
- Step 5: Click cell E9, click the Copy button on the Home tab, select the specified range, and click the Paste button.
- Step 6: Click the Undo button on the Quick Access Toolbar.
- Step 8: Double-click cell E9, type a $ before the G and the 4 in the cell reference.
- Step 10: Click cell F9 and drag the fill handle down to F19.
- Step 12: Click cell E9, click the Home tab, click the Number Format button, and click Currency.
- Step 13: Click cell E9, click the Home tab, double-click the Format Painter button, and then select the ranges specified.
- Step 14: Click the Home tab, click the Cell Styles button, and then click Total.
- Step 16: Instruct students on whether or not they are allowed to print their worksheets, and what they are to submit for grading.
- **WORKPLACE SKILLS:** A worksheet that shows estimated profits like the one in Figure 8-2 can be a valuable tool to a company like Voyager Travel Adventures. By estimating costs, a business can determine if their pricing structure will allow them to make a profit on the product or service. Profit can be defined simply as the money left over after all the bills are paid.

Review the columns of data shown in the figure. Explain that the values in the "Our" columns represent the actual costs of each item to Voyager Travel Adventures. The values in the "Their" columns represent the actual costs plus Voyager's markup. The difference between the two represents the profit for the company.

Data/Solution Files

Data files:	ETry08.xlsx
	EProj15.xlsx
	EProj16.xlsx
Solution files:	ETry08_solution.xlsx
	EProj15_solution.xlsx
	EProj16_solution.xlsx

Lesson 9 Techniques for Moving Data

What You Will Learn
- ✓ Inserting and Deleting Columns and Rows
- ✓ Cutting and Pasting Data
- ✓ Using Drag-and-Drop Editing

Words to Know
Cut
Drag-and-drop

Tips, Hints, and Pointers
- Discuss each of the skills listed in the What You Will Learn section, and ask students if they have used any of these skills before.
- Discuss the scenario covered in the Application Skills section, and preview the tasks students will perform for Whole Grains Bread.
- Key skills covered in this lesson include inserting and deleting columns and rows, cutting and pasting data, and using drag-and-drop editing.

Inserting and Deleting Columns and Rows
- Emphasize that one of the great benefits of using a spreadsheet application to create files is that data can be easily rearranged without having to completely retype it.
- Discuss how the process of inserting and deleting rows and columns in Excel is very similar to inserting and deleting rows in Word tables.
- Caution students that they are not warned about data loss when deleting a column or row. If they delete data unintentionally, they can use Undo to restore it.
- Have students open a sample worksheet or a workbook file they have worked on previously. Have them click in any cell containing data. On the Home tab, click the Insert drop-down arrow and click Insert Sheet Columns. A new blank column is inserted to the left of the column containing the active cell. Have them click a column heading and then click the top portion of the Insert button. Because a column is selected, Excel automatically assumes you want to insert a column.
- Have students click in a different cell containing data. Have them click the Insert drop-down arrow and click Insert Sheet rows. A row is inserted above the selected cell. Have them drag across two or three row headings to select the rows. Then, have them click the top portion of the Insert button. The same number of rows as they selected is inserted above.
- Click the Insert Options button to see formatting options for the new column or row.
- Instruct students to delete the new rows and column they inserted.
- **TROUBLESHOOTING:** Stress that Excel does not warn that a deletion may result in data loss, so if a row or column is accidentally deleted, the user should immediately click Undo. Also, warn students that if they paste cut data in a cell that already contains data, Excel may overwrite the original data. Use Undo to restore lost data.
- **SKILLS EXTENSION:** Have students investigate the Hide and Unhide commands. You can hide columns or rows of data by using the commands on the Format button on the Home tab. Or, you can right-click a column or row heading and click Hide on the shortcut menu. Ask students when they might want to hide columns or rows. For example, you may want to hide sensitive or confidential data before you print a worksheet.

Cutting and Pasting Data
- Excel allows the user to control the formatting of data pasted from another location. Pasted data can keep its original formatting or accept the formats of the destination location.
- Discuss with students situations in which users might choose to keep original formatting and situations when it would be preferable to apply destination formatting.
- Demonstrate the Cut and Paste process. This process can be used to move data from one

location to another and from one file to another. Review how to cut and paste using buttons on the Home tab or keyboard shortcuts and instruct students to practice cutting a portion of the worksheet and pasting it in empty cells at the bottom of the worksheet.

- Stress the difference between the Cut command and the Delete or Backspace command. Cut places the highlighted data on the Clipboard, from which location it can be pasted elsewhere. The other two commands simply remove the highlighted data.

Using Drag-and-Drop Editing

- Demonstrate how to drag and drop data using the four-headed pointer. If necessary, review how to drag data by first selecting it, then holding down the mouse button, then moving the mouse pointer to the location where the moved data is to appear.
- Display the Clipboard task pane and show students how cut or copied data is stored in the task pane. Also demonstrate how to insert an item from the task pane.
- Point out that having the task pane open can make editing more efficient because a user can collect more than one item to copy or move and then paste the stored items as required.

Project 17—Working with Columns and Rows in the Payroll Worksheet

- Step 5: Remind students to click the top portion of the Insert button.
- Step 7: Make sure students move the mouse pointer over the border of the selected row and not the row heading.
- Step 11: Instruct students on whether or not they are allowed to print their worksheets, and what they are to submit for grading.

Project 18—Moving and Copying Data in the Payroll Worksheet

- Refer students to Figure 9-1. Their worksheets should look like this when they have completed them.
- Steps 4-5: On the Home tab, click the Cut button, click in the cell to the top left of the selection, and click the Paste button.

Data/Solution Files

Data files: ETry09.xlsx
               EProj17.xlsx
               EProj18.xlsx

- Step 6: Remind students to double-click the border of a column heading to widen it to accommodate the longest entry.
- Step 7: Move the mouse pointer over the border of the selection, hold down the Ctrl key, and drag the selection to the range specified.
- Step 8: On the Home tab, click the Insert button.
- Step 9: Select the range, click the Cut button on the Home tab, click in cell A12, and click the Paste button.
- **CUSTOMIZED INSTRUCTION: Special Needs Students:** Remind special needs students that they can use keyboard shortcuts for copying (Ctrl + C), cutting (Ctrl + X), and pasting data (Ctrl + V) to save the number of keystrokes they need to make.
- Step 10: Students are to complete the row of data for Vicki Helms. Remind them to click the cell above in each column and drag its fill handle down to Vicki's row.
- Step 11: Click the row 22 row heading and click the Delete button on the Home tab.
- Step 12: Instruct students on whether or not they are allowed to print their worksheets, and what they are to submit for grading.
- **JOB FOCUS:** Remind students that the worksheets they prepared in Projects 17 and 18 are the responsibility of the Payroll Manager. Payroll is simply the total sum of money that a company pays to employees at a given time. Companies employ a payroll manager to ensure that the payroll department operates as efficiently as possible.

  The payroll department may be responsible for two main functions: timekeeping (tracking employee time cards, hours worked, salary, and overtime) and payroll processing. The payroll manager oversees employee benefits processing and payroll tax reporting. These responsibilities require the manager to work closely with the company's accounting and finance department as well as human resources. In addition, the payroll manager must ensure the payroll system functions appropriately. This requires him or her to work closely with the company's information technology department.

Solution files: ETry09_solution.xlsx
                   EProj17_solution.xlsx
                   EProj18_solution.xlsx

Lesson 10 Chart, Sheet, Display, and Print Operations

What You Will Learn

- ✓ Creating a Column Chart
- ✓ Deleting Unused Sheets in a Workbook
- ✓ Displaying, Printing, and Hiding Formulas
- ✓ Previewing and Printing a Worksheet

Words To Know

Chart
Chart sheet
Column chart
Show Formulas

Tips, Hints, and Pointers

- Discuss each of the skills listed in the What You Will Learn section, and ask students if they have used any of these skills before.
- Discuss the scenario covered in the Application Skills section, and preview the tasks students will perform for Hyland Manufacturing.
- Key skills covered in this lesson include creating a column chart, working with formulas, deleting worksheets, and previewing and printing a worksheet.

Creating a Column Chart

- Discuss basic chart types and the best uses for each. Column charts, for example, show comparisons; line charts show trends over time; pie charts compare parts to the whole.
- Note that Excel Chapter 3 provides more information on creating and formatting charts.
- Discuss how the use of charts can illustrate complex data and make it easier to interpret. Charts are also useful for illustrating significant amounts of data that can take up many rows and columns in a worksheet.
- Using a sample worksheet, show students how to select data and use the buttons on the Insert tab to create a chart.
- Show students a worksheet with data and an embedded chart. Point out how the chart makes the data easier to understand because of its graphic format.
- **SKILLS EXTENSION:** Have students use a sample worksheet or a workbook they have used in a previous exercise to experiment with the different chart types. Also have them try using different chart styles on the Chart Tools Design tab.
- **CUSTOMIZED INSTRUCTION: Less Advanced Students:** Have students cut out a sample of a chart used in a newspaper or magazine and bring it in to share with the class. Discuss the type of chart and how it is used to illustrate data.

Deleting Unused Sheets in a Workbook

- Demonstrate the methods for deleting worksheets from a workbook.

Displaying, Printing, and Hiding Formulas

- Discuss how displaying formulas can help you identify errors in the calculation of data.
- You can view formulas on-screen and also print worksheets with formulas displayed.
- You display formulas by clicking the Formulas tab and then clicking the Show Formulas button in the Formulas Auditing group. You can also toggle formulas on and off by pressing Ctrl + ~. Point out to students where the tilde (~) character is on their keyboards.

Previewing and Printing a Worksheet

- Remind students of the importance of previewing before printing. Have students preview a sample worksheet in Backstage view.
- Students will notice that Backstage view looks much different than the Print dialog box they used in previous versions of Office programs.

- Demonstrate how to change the number of copies to print.
- Under Settings, click the drop-down arrow on each option and explain what each is for.
- Point out the Preview screen, and how you can use the Previous Page and Next Page buttons to navigate through the file's pages. Note that the Preview screen replaces the Print Preview in previous versions of Office.
- Note the Page Setup link, which you can click to open the Page Setup dialog box.
- **CUSTOMIZED INSTRUCTION: More Advanced Students:** Have more advanced students explore the settings on the Print tab in Backstage view (without making any changes), including the Properties for the current printer.

Project 19—Adding a Chart in the Balance Sheet Worksheet

- Step 4: Students will select two noncontiguous ranges that will be used for charting.
- Step 8: Remind students to replace "Student Name" with their own first and last names.
- Step 9: Instruct students on whether or not they are allowed to print their worksheets, and what they are to submit for grading.

Project 20—Reviewing and Printing the Balance Sheet Worksheet

- Step 4: Right-click each sheet tab and then click Delete on the shortcut menu.

Data/Solution Files

Data files: ETry10.xlsx
                EProj19.xlsx
                EProj20.xlsx
Solution files: ETry10_solution.xlsx
                EProj19_solution.xlsx
                EProj20_solution.xlsx

- Step 5: Click the Formulas tab and then click the Show Formulas button in the Formula Auditing group.
- Step 6: Click the File tab and then click Print. Under Settings, click the Scaling drop-down arrow and click Fit Sheet on One Page.
- Step 7: Instruct students on whether or not they are allowed to print their worksheets, and what they are to submit for grading.
- **WORKPLACE SKILLS:** A balance sheet is an essential financial record for any type of business. It shows a business's financial situation at a particular time, such as the end of a quarter. A balance sheet shows the relationship between the business's assets, liabilities, and owner's equity.
  - Assets include cash on hand, checking or other money accounts, accounts receivable, real estate that the business owns, office equipment, and vehicles such as company cars or trucks.
  - Liabilities include all debts that the business must pay to creditors, suppliers, or banks. These are also called accounts payable.
  - Owner's equity is the amount of money invested in the business by its owners or shareholders.

  In a financially healthy business, assets equal liabilities plus owner's equity; that is, the liabilities and owner's equity must balance with the assets, which is why this financial document is called a balance sheet.

Chapter Assessment and Application
Project 21   Safety Consulting Services

Tips, Hints, and Pointers

- In the Make It Your Own project, students will apply the skills they have learned in this chapter to a real-world activity. In this project, they will create a worksheet to track, report, and bill work for their safety consulting company's clients.
- Refer students to Illustration A. Their worksheets should look like this when they have completed them.
- Step 5: Click cell A9 and drag the fill handle through cell A15.
- Step 6: Click cell B9 and drag the fill handle through cell B15.
- Steps 7-8: Click cell E9 and drag the fill handle through cell E15.
- Step 9: Students may use the Sum button on the Home tab or Formulas tab to total the data.
- Step 11: Remind students to start the formula with an = sign.
- Step 12: Click the Page Layout tab, click the Themes button, and then click the specified theme.
- Step 13: Click the cell, click the Home tab, click the Cell Styles button, and click the Title style. Click the Merge & Center button on the Home tab.
- Step 14: Click cell A3, click the Home tab, click the Cell Styles button, and click the specified style. Click cell A3 again, if necessary, double-click the Format Painter button on the Home tab, and then select the other labels as instructed.
- Step 15: Select the cells, click the Home tab, click the Wrap Text button, and then click the Center button.
- Step 16: Hold down the Ctrl key to select the cells. Click the Home tab, click the Number Formats drop-down arrow, and click More Number Formats. Click Currency and specify 0 decimal places.
- Step 17: Select the cells, click the Number Format button, and click Currency.
- Step 19: Click the Number Format button, click More Number Formats, click Percentage, and then specify 1 decimal place.
- Step 21: Instruct students on whether or not they are allowed to print their worksheets, and what they are to submit for grading.
- **WORKPLACE SKILLS:** Explain to students the concept of a retainer. A retainer fee is a fixed amount of money that a client agrees to pay, in advance, to secure the services of a consultant. In many cases, the fee is not associated with the success of a project or the consultant's ability to achieve certain results. A retainer is often paid in a single lump sum at the outset of the project, or if the consultant will be working on a longer-term basis, it may be paid at regular intervals, such as monthly or quarterly.

Data/Solution Files

Data file: None
Solution file: EProj21_solution.xlsx

Project 22   Personal Budget

Tips, Hints, and Pointers

- In the Master It project, students will use the skills they have learned in this chapter to build a personal budget worksheet.
- Step 4: Click cell B7 and drag the fill handle through G7.
- Step 5: Students may use the addition operator and reference the specified cells or use the SUM function to total the cells.
- Step 6: Click the row heading containing the Expenses label, click the Home tab, and click the Insert button.
- Step 8: Click the row 6 row heading, click the home tab, and click the Insert button. Click the row heading for the Gifts row, position the mouse pointer on the border of the selection, and drag to the new row 6. Click the row 13 row heading, click the Home tab, and click the Delete button.
- Step 10: The formula should subtract the subtotal in B14 from the subtotal in B8.
- Step 11: Click the row heading for the Surplus row, click the Home tab, and click the Insert button.
- Step 12: Click the Page Layout tab, click the Themes button, and click a desired theme.
- Step 13: To apply the Accounting format, select the data, click the Number Format button, click More Number Formats, click Accounting, and then specify 0 decimal places.
- Step 14: Remind students to hold down the Ctrl key to select noncontiguous ranges. They should press the F11 key to place the chart on its own worksheet.
- Step 15: Click the Chart Tools Layout tab, click the Legend button, and click None. Click the Chart Title button, click Above Chart, and enter the chart title.
- Step 16: Right-click the sheet tab and click Delete on the shortcut menu.
- Step 17: Click the Formulas tab and click the Show Formulas button.
- Step 18: Click the File tab and click Print. Under Settings, click the Scaling drop-down arrow and click Fit Sheet on One Page.
- Step 19: Instruct students on whether or not they are allowed to print their worksheets, and what they are to submit for grading.

Data/Solution Files

Data file: EProj22.xlsx
Solution file: EProj22_solution.xlsx

Chapter 2: Working with Formulas, Functions, and Worksheet Tasks

Lesson 11 Getting Started with Functions

What You Will Learn

- ✓ Using Functions (SUM, AVERAGE, MEDIAN, MIN, and MAX)
- ✓ Inserting a Function
- ✓ Using AutoCalculate

Words to Know

Argument
AutoCalculate
Formula AutoComplete
Function
Function name
Nest

Tips, Hints, and Pointers

- Discuss each of the skills listed in the What You Will Learn section, and ask students if they have used any of these skills before.
- Discuss the scenario covered in the Application Skills section, and preview the tasks students will perform for Restoration Architecture.
- Key skills covered in this lesson include learning about common functions, inserting functions, and using AutoCalculate.

Using Functions (SUM, AVERAGE, MEDIAN, MIN, and MAX)

- Introduce functions as predefined formulas that perform specific types of calculations based on values the user specifies. Excel offers hundreds of functions that perform financial, statistical, mathematical, and logical calculations.
- Review the common functions discussed here and make sure students understand the purpose of each.
- Review the mathematical concepts behind common functions, such as summing, averaging, and rounding.
- Write a simple function such as =SUM(B2:B10) on the board or an overhead and point out the function elements. Stress that functions have no spaces between elements.
- Point out that when a function allows multiple arguments, the arguments are separated by commas. Do not insert a space after the commas.

- Demonstrate how to use Formula AutoComplete in Excel to type functions faster.
- Note that function names do not have to be typed in all capital letters. They can also be typed in lowercase letters.
- In a new workbook, have students enter a column of values and then use the Sum button on the Formulas tab to quickly sum the values.
- Instruct students to delete the function and then use the other functions on the AutoSum drop-down menu.
- **Try It! Using Functions (SUM, AVERAGE, MEDIAN, MIN, and MAX):** Note that in this exercise, students practice typing in commonly used functions and inserting them using the Sum button drop-down menu. Explain that for more complex functions, they will find it easier to insert functions using the Insert Function dialog box.
- **QUICK QUIZ:** What functions may be useful to you in a worksheet you create for school or work?
  Answers will vary. SUM and AVERAGE are probably the most widely used functions for many applications.
- **CUSTOMIZED INSTRUCTION: ESOL Students:** Have students write the names of common functions (SUM, AVERAGE, COUNT, MAX, MIN, and ROUND) in both English and their primary language

Inserting a Function

- Have students display the Insert Function dialog box and explore the options for selecting a function. Have students select a function such as SUM or COUNT and step through the process of selecting the range for the argument.
- Encourage students to select other functions and practice inserting function names and arguments to perform specific calculations.
- Using the Insert Function dialog box, remind students how to select a range using the Collapse button; they may need to identify ranges this way when inserting functions.
- **Try It! Inserting a Function, step 8:** Remind students to click cell C10 and show them where the fill handle is located, if necessary.
- **Step 9:** Remind students that they can double-click a column's border to change the width so it accommodates the longest entry in the column. Or, they can click the border and drag it until the column is the desired width.
- **CUSTOMIZED INSTRUCTION: Special Needs Students:** Remind physically challenged students how to use Key Tips to access specific functions from the Formulas tab. They can press Alt+M, F to quickly open the Insert Function dialog box.
- **CUSTOMIZED INSTRUCTION: Less Advanced Students:** Give students practice finding the average, median, maximum, and minimum numbers in a data set. You can have them figure these on paper or using a calculator.

Using AutoCalculate

- Demonstrate the use of AutoCalculate.
- Show students how to display the Customize Status Bar menu and how to add or remove AutoCalculate functions from the status bar.
- Have students enter values in the cells of several rows and columns so the values are contiguous. Have them select several values and view the AutoCalculate sum on the status bar. Encourage students to try all of the functions on the Customize Status Bar shortcut menu.

Data/Solution Files

Data files: ETry11.xlsx
                  EProj23.xlsx
                  EProj24.xlsx
Solution files: ETry11_solution.xlsx
                  EProj23_solution.xlsx
                  EProj24_solution.xlsx

Project 23—Type Functions in Formulas

- Step 3: Remind students how to enter a header. Click the Insert tab, click the Header & Footer button. Enter the header in the sections as instructed.
- Step 4: Remind students that they can type in the cell references or click the individual cells to reference them.
- Step 11: Instruct students on whether or not they are allowed to print their worksheets, and what they are to submit for grading.

Project 24—Insert Functions in Formulas

- Step 4: Right-click the status bar, click the AutoCalculate options that do not have check marks beside them, and then press Escape.
- Step 8: Click the cell, click the Sum drop-down arrow, and then click Min. If necessary, edit the range to include only the cells that contain data. Drag the fill handle across the row.
- Step 10: Click the Formulas tab, click the More Functions button, point to Statistical, and then scroll to and click the MAX function. In the Function Arguments dialog box, verify the range and click OK.
- Step 12: Click the Formulas tab and click the Insert Function button. In the Search for a function text box, type "Find the median" and press Enter. The MEDIAN function should be selected. Click OK. In the Function Arguments dialog box, verify the range and click OK.
- Step 14: Right-click the status bar and remove the check mark for the Min, Max, and Numerical Count AutoCalculate options.
- Step 15: Instruct students on whether or not they are allowed to print their worksheets, and what they are to submit for grading.
- **CUSTOMIZED INSTRUCTION: Less Advanced Students:** Less advanced students may require help constructing the MEDIAN function in step 12 of the project. Direct them to Help information on this function or provide additional assistance if needed.

Lesson 12   Using Excel Tables

What You Will Learn

- ✓ Creating an Excel Table
- ✓ Sorting and Filtering an Excel Table
- ✓ Converting a Table to a Range

Words to Know

Column specifier
Criterion
Excel table
Filter
Sort
Structured references
Total row

Tips, Hints, and Pointers

- Discuss each of the skills listed in the What You Will Learn section, and ask students if they have used any of these skills before.
- Discuss the scenario covered in the Application Skills section, and preview the tasks students will perform for Restoration Architecture.
- Key skills covered in this lesson include working with Excel tables and sorting and filtering data.

Creating an Excel Table

- Discuss the advantages of formatting a range as an Excel table and demonstrate how to convert a range to an Excel table.
- Show students an example of a structured reference in a formula and discuss how this type of formula could be easier to construct and understand (no need to interpret the cell ranges or references in the formula).
- Have students enter data similar to that shown in the illustration. Show them how to turn on the option that allows labels in formulas and then try creating formulas with structured references.
- Have students use one of their column labels as a row label and then create a structured reference formula to practice selecting the correct cell for the label.
- **QUICK QUIZ:** Why would column specifiers make formulas easier to understand?
  Column specifiers assign a name to the column of data that more clearly identifies it as opposed to a range address that uses the beginning and ending cell addresses.
- Point out that Excel will automatically identify the proper range for a table if there are no blank columns or rows within the data and the column headers are contiguous to the range of data.
- Demonstrate how to create a table in a range that does have a blank row or column, such as a range with a blank row between the column headings and data.
- Point out the drop-down arrows that appear on the column headings in a table. Explain that clicking the arrow displays a drop-down menu with options for sorting and filtering the data in the table according to criteria set for that column.

Sorting and Filtering an Excel Table

- Review with students the difference between an ascending sort and a descending sort. An ascending sort orders data alphabetically from A to Z, from largest to smallest, and from oldest to newest. A descending sort orders data alphabetically from Z to A, from smallest to largest, and from newest to oldest.
- As in a Word table, you can sort an Excel table using more than one column. For example, in a payroll table, you might sort first by department name, and then by salary.
- Explain that a filter is a tool for limiting the display of rows in a table.
- Demonstrate how to apply the various filters on the drop-down menu.
- Show students how to remove the filter and reset the table.
- **Try It! Sorting and Filtering an Excel Table:** Point out that when you filter data, the total is recalculated based on only the data that is displayed.

- In a sample worksheet, create a table with several rows of numeric data. Click the Filter drop-down arrow on any column and point to the Number Filters option. Discuss the various options for filtering numeric data. Apply the various number filters to demonstrate the results.

Converting a Table to a Range

- Show students how to convert a table to a range. On the Table Tools Design tab, click the Convert to Range button. A dialog box displays, asking if you want to convert the table to a normal range.
- **QUICK QUIZ:** What is the difference between sorting and filtering?

  Sorting allows you to re-order data according to a specified column or columns in a table. Filtering allows you to specify criteria that limit which rows in a table display.
- **CUSTOMIZED INSTRUCTION: More Advanced Students:** Have students create an Excel table that lists 12 to 15 items on the menu in your school cafeteria and their prices. Have them filter the price column using the top 10 filtering option

Project 25—Revenue Table

- Step 4: Remind students that they can type in the cell references or click the specified cells.
- Step 11: Instruct students on whether or not they are allowed to print their worksheets, and what they are to submit for grading.

Project 26—Enhance the Revenue Table

- Step 4: Click the Formulas tab, click the Sum drop-down arrow, and click Average. Edit the formula to average the data for July through September.

- Step 5: Click the cell and type the new column heading.
- Step 6: Click the Table Tools Design tab and click the Total Row check box.
- Step 8: Click cell D12, click the drop-down arrow, and click Average. Do the same for E12:G12.
- Step 9: Click the drop-down arrow on the Type column heading and click Sort A to Z.
- Step 10: Click the drop-down arrow on the Project Manager column heading and deselect all the check boxes except for Jansen's.
- Step 12: Instruct students on whether or not they are allowed to print their worksheets, and what they are to submit for grading.
- **JOB FOCUS:** Remind students that revenue worksheets like those they modified in Projects 25 and 26 are often generated by a company's chief financial officer. The CFO typically has three areas of responsibility:
  - Controllership duties, in which they compile and report the company's historical financial information. This is sometimes referred to as "past performance" data. It is used by the company to make important decisions about the future.
  - Treasury duties, in which they assess the company's present financial condition and determine the best mix of debt, equity, and internal financing.
  - Economic strategy and forecasting, in which they identify areas of a company that are most efficient and financially sound and recommend how the company can capitalize on them.

Data/Solution Files

Data files:	ETry12.xlsx
	EProj25.xlsx
	EProj26.xlsx
Solution files:	ETry12_solution.xlsx
	EProj25_solution.xlsx
	EProj26_solution.xlsx

Lesson 13 The NOW Function and Named Ranges

What You Will Learn
- ✓ Using the NOW Function to Display a System Date
- ✓ Using Named Ranges

Words to Know
Name Box
Range name
Volatile

Tips, Hints, and Pointers

- Discuss each of the skills listed in the What You Will Learn section, and ask students if they have used any of these skills before.
- Discuss the scenario covered in the Application Skills section, and preview the tasks students will perform for Restoration Architecture.
- Key skills covered in this lesson include working with the NOW function and using named ranges.

Using the NOW Function to Display a System Date

- Explain that the NOW function displays the current date and time based on the computer's internal clock and calendar. It is useful for worksheets that are reused or updated on a regular basis because the date and time automatically update each time the workbook file is opened.

Using Named Ranges

- Remind students of the structured references and column specifiers they used in Excel tables. Named ranges function in much the same way in that they more clearly identify the data contained in a range as compared to a range address.
- Remind students that a range is a group of contiguous or noncontiguous cells and point out that ranges are usually related in some way, such as the expenses entries in a budget worksheet.
- In a sample workbook, have students enter a few columns of data. Have them select each column and in the Name Box to the left of the formula bar, enter a range name.
- Discuss rules for naming ranges, with special emphasis on avoiding row or column labels, which can cause problems when using formulas with structured references.

- Show students a worksheet that contains named ranges and demonstrate how to use a range in a formula or print only a range. Point out that a named range can consist of a single cell or many cells.
- Have students practice naming several ranges in a sample worksheet using both the Define Name command and the Name Box. Remind them to use Go To (F5) to move quickly to a named range.
- Show students how to open the Define Names dialog box. On the Formulas tab, click the Define Name button and click Define Name.
- Show students how the range name displays on the Name Box drop-down menu.
- Demonstrate how to open the Name Manager dialog box where you can edit and delete named ranges.
- **Try It! Using Named Ranges:** Have students watch how Excel outlines the named range when they type it in the formula.
- **QUICK QUIZ:** Is the range name *2ndquarter* a legal name? Why not?
  It is not because it begins with a number.

Project 27—Revenue Worksheet Preparation
- Step 4: Students can type =NOW() in the cell.
- Step 11: Instruct students on whether or not they are allowed to print their worksheets, and what they are to submit for grading.

Project 28—Creating and Using Range Names in the Revenue Worksheet
- Refer students to Figure 13-2 on page 437. Their worksheets should look like this when they have completed them.

- Steps 4-5: Remind students to simply click in the Name Box and type the name.
- Steps 9-10: Type =sum(jan, press the down arrow to select the specified range, and then press Tab.
- Step 11: Follow the procedure for steps 9 and 10, but substitute the first letters of the other project managers' names.
- Steps 12-13: Remind students that they can reference a range by clicking the drop-down arrow on the Name Box and selecting the range name.
- Step 14: Instruct students on whether or not they are allowed to print their worksheets, and what they are to submit for grading.

Data/Solution Files

Data files: ETry13.xlsx
             EProj27.xlsx
             EProj28.xlsx
Solution files: ETry13_solution.xlsx
             EProj27_solution.xlsx
             EProj28_solution.xlsx

Lesson 14 Working with IF Functions

What You Will Learn

- ✓ Understanding IF Functions
- ✓ Nesting Functions
- ✓ Using =SUMIF() and SUMIFS() Functions
- ✓ Using =COUNTIF() and COUNTIFS() Functions

Words to Know

Expression
Nesting

Tips, Hints, and Pointers

- Discuss each of the skills listed in the What You Will Learn section, and ask students if they have used any of these skills before.
- Discuss the scenario covered in the Application Skills section, and preview the tasks students will perform for Whole Grains Bread.
- Key skills covered in this lesson include understanding IF functions; using nested IF functions; and using the SUMIF, SUMIFS, COUNTIF, and COUNTIFS functions.

Understanding IF Functions

- IF functions are complex logical functions used to display labels or values based on the evaluation of a condition. The function allows a user to test for values in a worksheet and perform specific actions based on the result of the test. The function requires three arguments: the condition to be tested, the answer to return if the test is true, and the answer to return if the test is false.
- Answers returned can be values, formulas, or text. Rather than mathematical operators, the IF function uses conditional operators such as > (greater than), < (less than), and >= (greater than or equal to).
- The best way to help students understand IF functions is to demonstrate their use with an example such as the following: =IF(B5>=93, "A", "Sorry! "). Explain that B5 might indicate an average score for math tests. If the value in B5 is greater than or equal to 93, the cell will display the grade A. If B5's value is less than 93, the cell will display Sorry!.
- Discuss ways a business might use an IF function. For example, they might provide a discount to customers *if* their purchase exceeds a certain amount. Or, they might pay a different hourly rate to employees *if* they work weekends.
- Discuss the conditional operators listed in the text. These operators are required to set up the condition in the function. Stress the difference between > and >= or < and <=.
- Remind students that they can enter a function either by typing it manually or by using the Insert Function feature. The Function Arguments dialog box can help students set up a complex IF function correctly.
- **CURRICULUM CONNECTION:** Boolean algebra is used to express logic in mathematical terms; in other words, to solve equations made up of logical operators. Boolean operators are used to define the relationship between terms. The most common Boolean operators are AND, OR, and NOT, although there are others, such as IF...THEN. Boolean algebra is used in computer programming because results are always either true or false.

  Have students use a worksheet to list and define common Boolean operators, such as AND, OR, and NOT. They should also provide examples of how each might be used in an equation.

Nesting Functions

- Demonstrate how to create nested IF functions to test for more than one condition. A nested IF function could be used to return grades of B, C, etc., in the example discussed on the previous page.
- Work through the syntax of this function shown at the bottom of the page under the Nesting Functions heading. If the condition in the first IF

Chapter 2 | 35

statement is true (if C3 is greater than 92), then the cell displays A. If the condition is not true, then the second IF statement's condition will be evaluated, and so on. Point out the proper use of parentheses to contain the arguments.

Using SUMIF() and SUMIFS() Functions

- Show students how to construct SUMIF statements and COUNTIF statements to total or count values based on the result of the IF condition.
- Work through the syntax of the SUMIF function. The user must first specify the range in which to check the condition, then establish the condition, then specify the range in which to sum values.
- **QUICK QUIZ:** How does the Insert Function feature help with functions such as IF or SUMIF?

  The Function Arguments dialog box makes it easy to select each argument.
- If necessary, review how to enter a SUMIF function: =SUMIF(range, criteria,sum_range)
  - The range is the range of cells you want to review.
  - The criteria is an expression that is either true or false, and defines which cells should be added to the total.
  - If you specify an optional sum_range, values from the sum-range on the rows where the range data results in a true result for the criteria are added to the total. If you do not specify a sum_range, the formula adds the values from the range rows that evaluate as true.
- **Try It! Using SUMIF() and SUMIFS() Functions:** Make sure students carefully check their entries in the Function Arguments dialog box against those shown in the figure.

Using COUNTIF() and COUNTIFS() Functions

- Work through the syntax of the COUNTIF function. This is similar to SUMIF, but the statement merely counts items in the specific range that meet the condition.
- If necessary, review how to enter a COUNTIF function: =COUNTIF(range, criteria). The range is the range of cells holding the values to test (and count). The criteria is an expression that is either true or false, defining which cells should be counted.
- Point out that you must enclose the condition (a text label, for example) in quotation marks if it is not a cell reference.
- **Try It! Using COUNTIF() and COUNTIFS() Functions:** Make sure students carefully check their entries in the Function Arguments dialog box against those shown in the figure.

Project 29—Setting Up Monday Discounts in the Bread Sales Workbook

- Step 3: Make sure students enter the header information on both worksheets in the workbook.
- Step 5: Have students click on various cells in column B to see the range names assigned to each.
- Step 6: Students should end up with the following formula in B3: =IF(WEEKDAY('Daily Sales'!B4)=2,2,2.55).
- Step 7: Students should end up with the following formula in B4: =IF(WEEKDAY('Daily Sales'!B4)=2,2,2.6).
- Step 10: Remind students that to undo the change, they can click the Undo button on the Quick Access Toolbar.
- Step 11: To show formulas, click the Formulas tab and click the Show Formulas button.
- Step 12: Instruct students on whether or not they are allowed to print their worksheets, and what they are to submit for grading.

Project 30—Counting in the Bread Sales Workbook

- Step 3: Make sure students enter the header information on the Daily Sales sheet only.
- Step 4: In C36, students should enter the formula, =COUNT(N7:N30).
- Step 5: In C37, students should enter the formula, =COUNTBLANK(N7:N30).
- Step 6: In C38, students should enter the formula, =COUNTIF(Q7:Q30,"x").
- Step 7: In C39, students should enter the formula, =COUNTIF(R7:R30,"x").
- Step 8: In C40, students should enter the formula, =COUNT(P7:P30).
- Step 9: In C41, students should enter the formula, =COUNTIFS(P7:P30, "<10",Q7:Q30,"x").
- Step 10: In D36, students should enter the formula, =SUMIF(N7:N30, ">0",P7:P30).
- Step 11: In D37, students should enter the formula, =SUMIF(N7:N30,"",P7:P30).
- Step 12: In D38, students should enter the formula, =SUMIF(Q7:Q30,"x",P7:P30).
- Step 13: In D39, students should enter the formula, =SUMIF(R7:R30,"x",P7:P30).
- Step 14: In D40, students should enter a formula to total the cash sales and credit sales.

- Step 15: In D41, students should enter the formula, =SUMIFS(P7:P30,Q7:Q30,"x",P7:P30,"<10").
- Step 16: To apply the Currency style, click the Home tab, click the Number Format button, and click Currency.
- Step 17: Instruct students on whether or not they are allowed to print their worksheets, and what they are to submit for grading.

Data/Solution Files

Data files: ETry14.xlsx
 EProj29.xlsx
 EProj30.xlsx
Solution files: ETry14_solution.xlsx
 EProj29_solution.xlsx
 EProj30_solution.xlsx

Lesson 15 Using Frozen Labels and Panes

What You Will Learn
- ✓ **Freezing Labels While Scrolling**
- ✓ **Splitting a Worksheet into Panes**

Words to Know
Freeze
Panes

Tips, Hints, and Pointers

- Discuss each of the skills listed in the What You Will Learn section, and ask students if they have used any of these skills before.
- Discuss the scenario covered in the Application Skills section, and preview the tasks students will perform for Voyager Travel Adventures.
- Key skills covered in this lesson include freezing labels while scrolling and splitting a worksheet into panes.

Freezing Labels While Scrolling
- Remind students that they have worked with some worksheets that require them to scroll up and down to select ranges for formulas or functions. Discuss how scrolling may take time and effort in large worksheets.
- Show students how to freeze row and column labels to keep them in view while scrolling.
- Discuss the organization of the options in the Window group on the View tab of the Ribbon.
- Remind students that If a workbook is saved with labels frozen, they will still be frozen the next time the workbook is opened.
- Have students open a previously created worksheet and ask them to click in the cell just below column labels and to the right of row labels and issue the Freeze Panes command. Ask them to scroll to the right and down to see how column and row labels stay in view. Then instruct students to unfreeze panes.
- Have them practice freezing other portions of the worksheet. This will help them become familiar with where they are to position the insertion point in order to freeze the desired labels.
- Point out that to freeze only rows, you must click in a cell in column A. To freeze only columns, click a cell in row 1. You can choose to freeze the top row only by clicking that option on the Freeze button drop-down menu; you can choose to freeze the first column only by clicking its option on the drop-down menu.

Splitting a Worksheet into Panes
- Demonstrate how to split a worksheet into panes and point out how the top and bottom panes and the left and right panes can be scrolled separately to bring different portions of a worksheet into view at the same time.
- In a previously created worksheet, have students click anywhere in row 1 and then issue the Split command. The vertical split bar displays to the left of the selected cell. Point out how both panes scroll vertically but can be scrolled separately horizontally. Have them remove the split bar by dragging it off the worksheet.
- Show students where to find the horizontal and vertical split boxes and have them drag both split bars into place to split the screen into four panes.
- **QUICK QUIZ**
- Which feature (freezing titles or splitting panes) do you think gives you the most flexibility when working with a large worksheet?

  Answers will vary. Students may find the freeze labels feature easier to control.
- **CUSTOMIZED INSTRUCTION: Special Needs Students:** Spend some extra time with visually challenged students to demonstrate how freezing worksheet labels and working with panes can help them more effectively view their worksheets. Encourage them to use a larger zoom as necessary when working in these views.

Project 31—Finishing the Data in the Inventory Worksheet

- Step 4: Make sure students enter the data in the cells specified.
- Step 5: Note that pressing Ctrl + Home moves you to cell A1 of the worksheet.
- Step 8: Again, remind students to pay careful attention to which cells they are entering data in.
- Step 9: Instruct students on whether or not they are allowed to print their worksheets, and what they are to submit for grading.

Project 32—Using Panes to Finish the Inventory Worksheet

- Refer students to Figure 15-1. Their worksheets should look like this when they have completed them.
- Step 3: Panes have been frozen in this data file. When students switch to Page Layout view to enter the header information, a message box will appear telling them that the panes will be unfrozen if they proceed. Instruct them to click OK.
- Step 4: Click the View tab and click the Split button.
- Step 5: The title is in cell B48.
- Step 6: In C49, students should enter the formula, =SUM(F7:F34).
- Step 7: In C50, students should enter the formula, =SUM(G7:G34).
- Step 8: In C51, students should enter the formula, =0.025*C50.
- Step 9: In C52, students should enter the formula, =AVERAGE(I7:I34).
- Step 10: Instruct students on whether or not they are allowed to print their worksheets, and what they are to submit for grading.
- In Figure 15-1, point out the four panes that make up the split window. Also, make sure students have the same results in cells C49:C52 as shown in the figure.
- Note that the panes are not visible in the Preview window in Backstage view.

Data/Solution Files

Data files:　　ETry15.xlsx
　　　　　　　EProj31.xlsx
　　　　　　　EProj32.xlsx
Solution files:　ETry15_solution.xlsx
　　　　　　　EProj31_solution.xlsx
　　　　　　　EProj32_solution.xlsx

Lesson 16 Using Conditional Formatting and Find and Replace

What You Will Learn
- ✓ Applying Conditional Formatting
- ✓ Using Find and Replace

Words to Know
Color scales
Conditional formatting
Data bars
Highlight cells rules
Icon sets
Top/Bottom rules

Tips, Hints, and Pointers

- Discuss each of the skills listed in the What You Will Learn section, and ask students if they have used any of these skills before.
- Discuss the scenario covered in the Application Skills section, and preview the tasks students will perform for Telson Tech.
- Key skills covered in this lesson include applying conditional formats and using Find and Replace.

Applying Conditional Formatting

- Discuss the use of conditional formatting to highlight cells whose contents meet certain conditions. Conditional formatting is often used to call out trends or identify positive or negative data.
- Discuss examples of when conditional formatting might be used on a worksheet. For example, you might have worksheet that tracks the sales for each salesperson. You could use conditional formatting to call out those who have exceeded a certain amount or those who have not met their sales quota.
- Review the different types of conditional formats that are available. These are:
  - Highlight cells rule, which applies specified formatting to cells whose contents meet a certain rule.
  - Top/bottom rule, which applies specified formatting to cells with the top or bottom values.
  - Data bars, which applies a horizontal bar that varies in length depending on the value in the cell.
  - Color scales, which applies different cell fill colors based on the values in the cells.
  - Icon sets, which applies a graphic to cells based on their values.
- Show students how to open the Conditional Formatting Rules Manager dialog box to make changes to a rule.
- **DESIGN FORUM:** Point out to students that while conditional formatting highlights important information and can add visual interest to a worksheet, you should be careful in the specific formats you select. Dark fill colors and data bars can make the values in the cells hard to read.

Using Find and Replace

- The Find and Replace commands in Excel are similar to those that students used in Word documents. Using Find and Replace, you can locate not only words or numbers, but specific formatting (such all bold text).
- Use the Find tab in the Find and Replace dialog box to find specified text or data. You can also set search options that find words that match case or are formatted in a certain way.
- Use the Replace tab to replace the text or data you find with replacement text or data. Again, you can set the options to replace the found data with data that is formatted a certain way.
- In Excel, you can use the Find & Select button to search for formulas, conditional formats, and even constants, which are values that do not change.
- **Try It! Using Find and Replace, step 3:** Make sure students are on the Replace tab in the Find and Replace dialog box.
- **SKILLS EXTENSION:** In the ETry 16 file, have students search for data with a specified format,

such as Accounting format with no decimal places. Have them use the Choose Format From Cell option on the Find tab to select a specific cell format and find all instances of that format.

Project 33—Replacing Terms in the P&L Worksheet

- Step 5: Make sure students are on the Replace tab in the Find and Replace dialog box.
- Step 8: Note that it is not necessary to close the Find and Replace dialog box while you are working in the worksheet.
- Step 13: Instruct students on whether or not they are allowed to print their worksheets, and what they are to submit for grading.

Project 34—Adding Conditional Formatting in the P&L Worksheet

- Step 4: Remind students to hold down the Ctrl key to select the noncontiguous cells.
- Step 5: Click the Home tab, click the Conditional Formatting button, click Color Scales, and then click the specified format.
- Step 8: Click the Home tab, click the Conditional Formatting button, click Highlight Cells Rules, and then click Less Than. In the Less Than dialog box, type 50% in the first text box, click the drop-down arrow on the With text box, and click the specified format.
- Step 9: Click the Home tab, click the Conditional Formatting button, click Highlight Cells Rules, and then click Greater Than. In the Greater Than dialog box, type 10% in the first text box, click the drop-down arrow on the With text box, and click the specified format.
- Step 10: Instruct students on whether or not they are allowed to print their worksheets, and what they are to submit for grading.
- **WORKPLACE SKILLS:** A profit and loss statement like the one students worked on Projects 33 and 34, is a financial document that summarizes a business's income and expenses over a given time period. Most are prepared once a month, quarterly, or once a year. A profit and loss statement has three parts:
  - Revenue. This is the money a company receives from selling its products, before taking into account how much money was spent on making and selling them.
  - Expenses. This is a list of everything a company pays to operate the business. It includes the cost of making, store, and selling its products, as well as rent for the company and wages for employees.
  - Net profit (or loss). Net profit is the amount of money a company actually makes, and net loss is the amount of money a company loses. Both are calculated by subtracting the expenses from the revenue.

The health of a company is reflected by the numbers on the profit and loss statement.

Data/Solution Files

Data files: ETry16.xlsx
                 EProj33.xlsx
                 EProj34.xlsx
Solution files: ETry16_solution.xlsx
                 EProj33_solution.xlsx
                 EProj34_solution.xlsx

Lesson 17 Rotating Entries and Resolving Errors

What You Will Learn
- ✓ Rotating Cell Entries
- ✓ Resolving a #### Error Message

Words to Know
Rotate

Tips, Hints, and Pointers

- Discuss each of the skills listed in the What You Will Learn section, and ask students if they have used any of these skills before.
- Discuss the scenario covered in the Application Skills section, and preview the tasks students will perform for Whole Grains Bread.
- Key skills covered in this lesson include rotating cell entries and resolving #### error messages.

Rotating Cell Entries

- Discuss instances when you might want to rotate data in a cell. For example, you might rotate heading labels to add visual interest or to shorten the width of the cell. Or, you might change the direction of data to save space. For example, if the column holds numeric data but the column headings are longer text labels, you can rotate the headings so they are closer to the width of the data, thereby enabling you to fit more columns across the page.
- In a sample worksheet, have students type column headings in several cells and use the options on the Orientation button's drop-down menu to practice rotating text in various ways.

Resolving a #### Error Message

- Remind students of the methods for adjusting column width: 1.) Double-click a column heading's right border to AutoFit the column width to the longest cell entry in the column; 2.) Drag a column heading to adjust the width as desired; 3.) click the Home tab, click the Format button, and select Column Width on the drop-down menu to enter a specific column width measurement; or, 4.) Click the Format button and select AutoFit Column Width to automatically adjust the width to accommodate the longest entry.

Project 35—Fixing Column Widths in the Payroll Worksheet

- Step 8: Instruct students on whether or not they are allowed to print their worksheets, and what they are to submit for grading.
- **SKILLS EXTENSION:** Ask those students who work and receive an employer-issued paycheck to review a recent pay stub and determine how much income is deducted for federal tax, FICA (Social Security and Medicare), state tax, and municipal tax (if applicable).

Project 36—Rotating Labels in the Payroll Worksheet

- Step 4: Click the row 4 row heading, hold down the Ctrl key, and click the row 16 row heading. Click the Home tab and then click the Delete button.
- Step 5. Click the column A column heading, click the Home tab, and click the Insert button. Select B1:B2, position the mouse pointer on the border of the selection, and drag to cell A1:A2.
- Step 6: Click the Home tab, click the Merge & Center drop-down arrow, and click Merge Cells.
- Step 7: Click the Home tab, click Cell Styles, click Accent1, and then click the Font Size drop-down arrow and click 24.
- Step 8: Click the Home tab, click the Orientation button, and click Rotate Text Up.
- Step 11: Instruct students on whether or not they are allowed to print their worksheets, and what they are to submit for grading.
- **WORKPLACE SKILLS:** Discuss the data shown on the payroll worksheet in Figure 17-2.
  - Gross Pay is the amount the employee earns before deductions are applied.
  - Net Pay is the amount earned after taxes and other deductions are made.

- Fed Tax is the amount of tax you pay to the federal government
- SS Tax refers to Social Security and Medicare tax that every employee must pay.
- State Tax is the amount you pay to the state government.
- State and federal taxes are used by the government to pay for public resources, such as streets, sidewalks, parks, schools, and libraries.

Data/Solution Files

Data files: ETry17.xlsx
                 EProj35.xlsx
                 EProj36.xlsx
Solution files: ETry17_solution.xlsx
                 EProj35_solution.xlsx
                 EProj36_solution.xlsx

Lesson 18 Adding Print Titles and Scaling a Printout

What You Will Learn
✓ Printing Titles
✓ Changing Orientation
✓ Scaling to Fit

Words to Know
Orientation
Print titles
Scaling

Tips, Hints, and Pointers

- Discuss each of the skills listed in the What You Will Learn section, and ask students if they have used any of these skills before.
- Discuss the scenario covered in the Application Skills section, and preview the tasks students will perform for Cleen-R Systems.
- Key skills covered in this lesson include printing titles, changing orientation, and changing other page setup options.

Printing Titles
- Discuss the new ways of accessing the Print commands in Excel 2010 — including Quick Print — and the options for printing in Backstage view.
- Show students an example of a printed worksheet with titles and without. Point out that titles make it easier for the reader to identify the data on every page of the printout.
- Show students different methods for accessing the Page Setup dialog box: Click the File tab and then click Print. In Backstage view, click Page Setup. Or, click the Page Layout tab and then click the Page Setup dialog box launcher.
- To display the Sheet tab in the Page Setup dialog box, click the Page Layout tab and then click the Print Titles button.
- **SKILLS EXTENSION:** Have students distinguish the difference between printing titles and printing row and column headers. Have them print a worksheet that displays both.

Changing Orientation
- Remind students of the difference between landscape and portrait orientation. Use portrait orientation when you want data displayed across the shorter length of a page. Use landscape orientation when you want data displayed across the wider length of a page.
- By default, worksheets are set up in portrait orientation. Ask students to suggest situations when landscape orientation would be appropriate, such as for worksheets with many columns or containing a wide table.
- **QUICK QUIZ:** How can changing print orientation save resources and time?
  Landscape orientation can often print a wide worksheet on one page rather than two, saving paper and printing time.

Scaling to Fit
- Demonstrate how to set scaling on a printout.
  - In the Page Setup dialog box, on the Page tab, you can use the options in the Scaling section.
  - You also can set options in the Scale to Fit group on the Page Layout tab.
  - Click the File tab and click Print. In Backstage view, under Settings, you can set the desired scaling option.

Project 37—Add Print Titles on the Water Data Worksheet
- Step 6: Students will need to click the Expand Dialog button to redisplay the Page Setup dialog box before they click OK.
- Step 7: Instruct students on whether or not they are allowed to print their worksheets, and what they are to submit for grading.

Project 38—Change Orientation and Scale the Water Data Worksheet
- Step 4: Click the Page Layout tab, click the Orientation button, and click Landscape.

- Step 5: Click the Page Layout tab, and in the Scale to Fit group, click the Height increment arrow to change it to 4.
- Step 6: In Backstage view, have students click the Next Page button to preview all the pages in the printout.
- Step 7: Instruct students on whether or not they are allowed to print their worksheets, and what they are to submit for grading.

Data/Solution Files

Data files:	ETry18.xlsx
	EProj37.xlsx
	EProj38.xlsx
Solution files:	ETry18_solution.xlsx
	EProj37_solution.xlsx
	EProj38_solution.xlsx

Lesson 19 Managing Worksheets and Performing Multi-worksheet Operations

What You Will Learn

- ✓ Inserting, Deleting, Copying, Moving, and Renaming Worksheets
- ✓ Changing the Color of a Worksheet Tab
- ✓ Hiding Sheets
- ✓ Grouping Worksheets for Editing and Formatting

Words to Know

Orientation
Print titles
Scaling

Tips, Hints, and Pointers

- Discuss each of the skills listed in the What You Will Learn section, and ask students if they have used any of these skills before.
- Discuss the scenario covered in the Application Skills section, and preview the tasks students will perform for Serenity Health Club.
- Key skills covered in this lesson include inserting, deleting, copying, moving, and renaming worksheets; changing the color of a worksheet tab; and hiding and grouping sheets.

Inserting, Deleting, Copying, Moving, and Renaming Worksheets

- Explain that Excel users often work with a number of worksheets in a workbook and challenge students to think of situations when this might happen (each sheet represents a quarter of the year, for example).
- Have students open a new workbook and identify the three sheet tabs at the bottom of the window.
- Remind students how to display another worksheet by clicking its sheet tab.
- Have students right-click the Sheet1 tab and explore with them the options on the shortcut menu.
- Insert a new sheet and then move it to its logical position by dragging it to the right of Sheet3. Then have students rename the sheets Qtr 1, Qtr 2, etc.
- Show students how to create a copy of a sheet and specify where it will be positioned in relation to the other sheets.

- Have students delete the last sheet in the workbook.
- **QUICK QUIZ:** Why would you want to copy a worksheet?
  If a worksheet contains data very similar to that you intend to create in a new worksheet, copy it to avoid having to reenter data.

Changing the Color of a Worksheet Tab

- In a sample workbook containing several worksheets, have students assign a different color to each sheet.

Hiding Sheets

- You can hide rows and columns as an alternative to deleting rows and columns that contain sensitive or confidential data.
- You may want to hide a sheet or sheets in a workbook for the same reason. For example, you may want to hide a sheet that contains confidential data before you print a workbook.
- **CUSTOMIZED INSTRUCTION: More Advanced Students:** Have students explore the options for locking cells and protecting a worksheet. Have them prepare a short report in Word that summarizes these features and discusses the difference between using them and hiding a worksheet.

Grouping Worksheets for Editing and Formatting

- In a sample workbook, have students rename the three sheets and apply a different color to each. Then have them group the sheets.
- On the first sheet, have them enter labels and values; they can make up the data or copy from a worksheet they've previously worked on (see Figure 14-2, for example).
- Have them apply a theme and cell styles as appropriate to the data.
- Have students check the other sheets in the group to see how the same data was entered and formats applied.
- **QUICK QUIZ:** How can grouping worksheets save time when entering data for several worksheets?

    If the worksheets will have identical entries, grouping the worksheets allows the user to enter the data only once and have it appear on all grouped sheets.

Project 39—Setting Up Sheets in the Services Tracking Worksheet

- Refer students to Figure 19-1. Their worksheet tabs should look like this when they have completed them.
- Step 12: Instruct students on whether or not they are allowed to print their worksheets, and what they are to submit for grading.

Project 40—Formatting and Editing Sheets in the Services Tracking Worksheet

- Step 3: Note that you may instruct students to group the sheets first and then add the header information, which will apply it to all the sheets in the group.
- Step 4: To group, click the first sheet tab, hold down the Shift key, and click the other sheet tabs.
- Step 9: To ungroup, right-click a sheet tab and click Ungroup Sheets. Point out that the sheet you right-clicked will be the active sheet.
- Step 11: Instruct students on whether or not they are allowed to print their worksheets, and what they are to submit for grading.

Data/Solution Files

Data files: ETry19.xlsx
                      EProj39.xlsx
                      EProj40.xlsx
Solution files: ETry19_solution.xlsx
                      EProj39_solution.xlsx
                      EProj40_solution.xlsx

Lesson 20 Summary Worksheets and Advanced Printing

What You Will Learn

- ✓ Constructing Formulas that Summarize Data from Other Sheets
- ✓ Changing Values in a Detail Worksheet to Update a Summary Worksheet
- ✓ Printing a Selection
- ✓ Printing All the Worksheets in a Workbook

Tips, Hints, and Pointers

- Discuss each of the skills listed in the What You Will Learn section, and ask students if they have used any of these skills before.
- Discuss the scenario covered in the Application Skills section, and preview the tasks students will perform for Hyland Manufacturing.
- Key skills covered in this lesson include using 3-D formulas and setting the print area.

Constructing Formulas that Refer to Cells in Another Worksheet

- Remind students that they have worked with several workbooks containing data on multiple sheets. Point out that they can use 3-D formulas to summarize data from multiple sheets on a summary sheet. Stress that these formulas use the same cells or range of cells on each worksheet.
- Show students a worksheet that contains 3-D formulas to sum or average data across several worksheets. Stress that these formulas require the user to select the same cell or range of cells on all sheets.
- Have students open a new workbook, assign sheet names, and practice creating 3-D formulas. They should try referencing consecutive and nonconsecutive sheets.
- Creating 3-D formulas can be simplified by displaying multiple sheets from the same workbook. Demonstrate how to display duplicate workbook windows to display a workbook's worksheets. (On the View tab, click the New Window button.)

Changing Values in a Detail Worksheet to Update a Summary Worksheet

- In the sample workbook they created on the previous page, have students click in a detail worksheet, change a value in one or more cells, and then check the summary worksheet to see that the data was updated.
- **QUICK QUIZ:** How would sheet names speed the operation of creating 3-D formulas?

  Sheet names that relate to their data are easier to distinguish from each other than the default sheet names.

Printing a Selection

- Review with students how to access the Print Backstage view.
- In Backstage view, under Settings, click the first drop-down arrow to review the options for what you can print. To print a selected range, use the Print Selection option.
- Remind students that naming ranges enables them to quickly select a range to print.

Printing All the Worksheets in a Workbook

- Explain that by default, only the active sheet will print. You can print all the pages in a workbook by selecting the Print Entire Workbook option in Backstage view.
- Emphasize the importance of previewing all the sheets in the workbook before printing them.
- Demonstrate how to set Page Setup options on grouped sheets.

Project 41—Adding Summary Formulas in the Balance Sheet Workbook

- Steps 8 and 11: The total assets and total liabilities during both years were the same, so no values will be entered in the summary sheet. Students will change values in a detail sheet in the next project.

48 | Learning Microsoft Excel 2010 | Teacher's Manual

- Step 12: Select the range, click the Home tab, click the Cell Styles button, and then click the specified style.
- Step 13: Instruct students on whether or not they are allowed to print their worksheets, and what they are to submit for grading.

Project 42—Printing a Selection and All Sheets in the Balance Sheet Workbook
- Step 3: Click the first sheet tab, then press Shift and click the other sheet tabs.
- Step 5: To ungroup, right-click a sheet tab and click Ungroup Sheets. Point out that the sheet you right-clicked will be the active sheet.
- Step 9: Click the File tab and then click Print. In Backstage view, click the top option under Settings, and click Print Selection.
- Step 10: Click the File tab and then click Print. In Backstage view, click the top option under Settings and click Print Entire Workbook. Make sure students preview the workbook pages before clicking the Print button.

Data/Solution Files

Data files: ETry20.xlsx
                 EProj41.xlsx
                 EProj42.xlsx
Solution files: ETry20_solution.xlsx
                 EProj41_solution.xlsx
                 EProj42_solution.xlsx

- **WORKPLACE SKILLS:** Students worked with a balance sheet in Project 20 of Lesson 10 in Excel Chapter 1. Remind them that a balance sheet shows a business's financial situation at a particular time, such as the end of a quarter. A balance sheet shows the relationship between the business's assets, liabilities, and owner's equity.
  - Assets include cash on hand, checking or other money accounts, accounts receivable, real estate that the business owns, office equipment, and vehicles such as company cars or trucks.
  - Liabilities include all debts that the business must pay to creditors, suppliers, or banks. These are also called accounts payable.
  - Owner's equity is the amount of money invested in the business by its owners or shareholders.

  In a financially healthy business, assets equal liabilities plus owner's equity; that is, the liabilities and owner's equity must balance with the assets, which is why this financial document is called a balance sheet.

Chapter Assessment and Application
Project 43   Client Activity Worksheet

Tips, Hints, and Pointers

- In this project, students will develop a worksheet to evaluate client activity for their landscaping business.
- Refer students to Illustration A. Their worksheets should look like this when they have completed them.
- Step 4: Click the Insert tab and click the Table button.
- Step 5: Click the Table Tools Design tab, click the Table Styles More button, and click the specified style.
- Step 6: Click the Table Tools Design tab and click the Total Row check box. Click cell C33, click the drop-down arrow, and click Sum.
- Step 7: In cell G5, students should enter the formula, =SUMIF(Table1[Paid],"Yes",Table1[Fee]).
- Step 8: In cell G7, students should enter the formula, =SUMIFS(Table1[Fee],Table1[Service],"Mowing",Table1[Paid],"Yes"). They should copy the formula to the remaining cells, but modify the service name.
- Step 9: Right-click the sheet tab, click Rename, and enter the new name.
- Step 10: Right-click the Version1 sheet, click Move or Copy, and click the Create a copy box.
- Step 11: Right-click Sheet3 and click Delete. Right-click Sheet 2 and click Hide.
- Step 12: Click a cell in the table, click the Table Tools Design tab, and click Convert to Range.
- Step 13: Select the Fee column, click the Home tab, click the Conditional Formatting button, click Highlight Cells Rules, and click Greater Than. Type 100 and then click the With drop-down arrow and click the specified format.
- Step 14: Select the Paid column, click the Home tab, click the Conditional Formatting button, click Highlight Cells Rules, and click Equal To. Type No and then click the With drop-down arrow and click the specified format.
- Step 15: Select the range, click the Home tab, click the Conditional Formatting button, click Data Bars, and click the specified format.
- Step 16: Click in cell A1, click the Home tab, click the Find & Select button, and then click Replace. Enter the find and replace text as instructed.
- Step 17: Click the Page Layout tab and click the Print Titles button. On the Sheet tab, enter the range for row 4. Repeat on the other sheet.
- Step 18: Instruct students on whether or not they are allowed to print their worksheets, and what they are to submit for grading.
- Have students check their work carefully against the worksheet shown in Illustration A.
- **SKILLS EXTENSION:** Have students do further evaluation of the client worksheet. Instruct them to save their **EProj43** workbook file with a different name. Have them determine the following by entering formulas where appropriate in the worksheet:
  - How much in fees are still outstanding? *Answer:* $875
  - What percentage of the total do the outstanding fees represent? *Answer:* 30%
  - Which service generated the most income? *Answer:* Mowing with $1,200
  - Which service generated the least income? *Answer:* Trimming with $170
  - Which customer bought the most services? *Answer:* Tyler, who spent $310

Data/Solution Files

Data file: EProj43.xlsx
Solution file: EProj43_solution.xlsx

Project 44   Fundraising Worksheet

Tips, Hints, and Pointers

- In this project, students will use the skills they have learned in this chapter to evaluate a budget worksheet for Crossmont Services.
- Step 3: Click the Sheet1 tab, press Shift, and click the Sheet3 tab.
- Steps 5-6: Click the Home tab, click the Cell Styles button, and click the specified style.
- Step 7: Click the Home tab, click the Cell Styles button, and click the specified style. To rotate the cell data, click the Home tab, click the Orientation button, and click Angle Counterclockwise.
- Step 8: Type =NOW().
- Step 9: Right-click a sheet tab and click Ungroup Sheets.
- Step 10: Right-click a sheet tab, click Rename, and enter the new sheet name.
- Step 14: In cell B5, students should enter the formula, =Income!B9-Expenses!B14. In cell C5, students should enter =Income!C9-Expenses!C14.
- Step 16: Students should check their Summary worksheet against that shown in Illustration B.
- Step 17: Click the File tab and then click Print. In Backstage view, click the top option under Settings and click Print Entire Workbook. Make sure students preview the workbook pages before clicking the Print button. Instruct students on what they are to submit for grading.

Data/Solution Files

Data file: EProj44.xlsx
Solution file: EProj44_solution.xlsx

Chapter 3: Charting Data
Lesson 21 Building Basic Charts

What You Will Learn

- ✓ Understanding Chart Basics
- ✓ Selecting Chart Data
- ✓ Reviewing Chart Elements
- ✓ Creating a Chart
- ✓ Changing Chart Types
- ✓ Selecting a Chart
- ✓ Resizing, Copying, Moving, or Deleting a Chart

Words to Know

Categories
Chart
Chart sheet
Data marker
Data points
Data series
Embedded chart

Tips, Hints, and Pointers

- Discuss each of the skills listed in the What You Will Learn section, and ask students if they have used any of these skills before.
- Discuss the scenario covered in the Application Skills section, and preview the tasks students will perform for Whole Grains Bread.
- Key skills covered in this lesson include learning about types of charts and their elements, creating a chart, changing the chart type, and working with charts.

Understanding Chart Basics

- Discuss basic chart types and the best uses for each. Line charts, for example, show trends over time; pie charts compare parts to the whole. Remind students that they created a simple column chart in Lesson 10 of Excel Chapter 1.
- **CUSTOMIZED INSTRUCTION: ESOL Students:** Have students make flash cards of the terms in the Words to Know list. They should write the term in both English and their primary language on one side and the definition in English only on the other side.

Selecting Chart Data

- Using a sample worksheet, show students how to select data and use the buttons on the Insert tab to create a chart.
- Show students a worksheet with data and an embedded chart. Point out how the chart makes the data easier to understand because of its graphic format.
- Discuss the guidelines offered for selecting data to chart and demonstrate ways to select data.
- Remind students how to hide rows and columns. Right-click the column or row heading and then click Hide on the shortcut menu.
- **CUSTOMIZED INSTRUCTION: Less Advanced Students:** Allow students extra time to practice selecting data to be charted. Have them use the Ctrl key to select noncontiguous ranges. Remind them how to hide rows and columns. Encourage them to experiment with different types of charts.

Reviewing Chart Elements

- Use a handout or slide of the illustration in Figure 21-1, with chart elements marked. Discuss the data series, data labels, data table, category labels, legend, and axes. Or, you can print this same chart from the Example sheet in the ETry21_solution file and make copies for all students. Call out the various chart elements identified in Figure 21-1 and have students label them on their copies.

- Have students create sample data in a worksheet for expenditures over the past four weeks. List expenditure items in column A and expenditures in columns B through E. Use Week 1, Week 2, etc., as column headers in cells B1, C1, etc. Have students select the data and create a default column chart. Remind students that to create a column chart, they select the data and then press the F11 key.
- **QUICK QUIZ:** What is the difference between the plot area in a chart and the chart area?

    The plot area contains the charted data only; it is contained within the chart area along with the chart title, legend, axes labels, and data table.

Creating a Chart

- Remind students that you can quickly create a default column chart on its own chart sheet by selecting the data and pressing the F11 key.
- You can create a default column chart embedded on the same sheet as the data by selecting the data and pressing Alt + F1.
- Review that Excel refers to the X-axis as the Category axis because it displays the categories for the chart and calls the Y-axis the Value axis because it shows the values being plotted.
- Explain that to create an effective chart, you must select the appropriate chart type. For example, when you want to compare parts of a whole, such as sales by salesperson relative to total sales, you use a pie chart. When you want to show trends over time, such as how total sales change from month to month, you use a line chart. Here are some common chart types.
    - A column chart shows data changes over a period of time or illustrates comparisons among items.
    - A bar chart illustrates comparisons among individual items.
    - A line chart shows trends over time.
    - A circle—or pie—chart shows the relationship of parts to a whole.
    - A scatter chart compares pairs of values.
    - An area chart displays the magnitude of change over time.

Changing Chart Types

- Review the chart types discussed with students. Have them open a workbook and on the Insert tab, point to each of the chart types in the Chart group to display its ScreenTip.
- **CURRICULUM CONNECTION:** Theodor Seuss Geisel, commonly known as Dr. Seuss, wrote more than 40 books, which combined have sold more than half a billion copies. His first blockbuster was *The Cat in the Hat*, which he wrote in response to a request for a fun, interesting book designed to teach children how to read using a limited number of vocabulary words. Amazingly, *The Cat in the Hat* uses only 220 new-reader vocabulary words. Have students pick their favorite Dr. Seuss book and use an Excel worksheet to analyze the use and distribution of vocabulary words. They should record the number of times a word is used, and perform calculations to determine such statistics as the total number of words, the number of times a word is used, and the number of words per page. Encourage students to create a chart based on their data.
- **SKILLS EXTENSION:** Have students create a chart either by hand or on the computer that illustrates personal data or data they have collected for a certain purpose. For example, if a student swims for a swim team, he might use a line chart to illustrate how his times in a certain event have changed during the course of the season. If a student has a collection of music CDs, she might create a pie chart that illustrates the breakdown of each genre (rock, country, rap, etc.). Encourage students to be creative with the design of their charts. Have them share their charts with the class.
- **CUSTOMIZED INSTRUCTION: Less Advanced Students:** Review the common chart types covered in this exercise with less advanced students and discuss when each is best used. Caution students that not all charts are interchangeable.
- Demonstrate how to change the chart type.
- Review the options on the Chart Tools Design, Layout, and Format tabs. Allow students time to get familiar with the options on each, as this will help them work more quickly and efficiently with charts.

Selecting a Chart

- Show students how to select the chart. Make sure they know how to select the whole chart and not a single part of it. Point out the Chart Elements button in the Current Selection group on the Chart Tools Layout tab.

Resizing, Copying, Moving, or Deleting a Chart
- Demonstrate how to resize, copy, move, and delete a chart.
- Point out that you cannot resize a chart that's on a chart sheet.

Project 45—Add the First Chart
- Refer students to Figure 21-3. Their charts should look like this when they have completed them.
- Step 3: Remind students how to group sheets—click the first sheet tab, press Shift, and click the other sheet tabs. To ungroup, right-click a sheet and click Ungroup Sheets on the shortcut menu. To insert a header, click the Insert tab and click the Header & Footer button. Enter the header in the sections as instructed.
- Step 12: Instruct students on whether or not they are allowed to print their worksheets, and what they are to submit for grading.

Project 46—Add and Change Charts
- Step 3: To group sheets, click the first sheet tab, press Shift, and click the other sheet tabs. To ungroup, right-click a sheet and click Ungroup Sheets on the shortcut menu. To insert a header, click the Insert tab and click the Header & Footer button. Enter the header in the sections as instructed.
- Step 5: Remind students to hold down the Ctrl key to select noncontiguous ranges.
- Step 6: Click the Insert tab, click the Pie button, and click the specified subtype.
- Step 7: Click the chart to select it, click the Cut button on the Home tab, click the Charts sheet tab, and click the Paste button.
- Step 8: Make sure the chart is selected and point to a border. When the pointer changes to a four-headed arrow, drag to the specified location.
- Step 9: Make sure the chart is selected and drag a sizing handle as instructed.
- Step 11: Click the Chart Tools Design tab and click the Change Chart Type button. Select the new chart type as instructed.
- Step 12: Instruct students on whether or not they are allowed to print their worksheets, and what they are to submit for grading.

Data/Solution Files

Data files:	ETry21.xlsx
	EProj45.xlsx
	EProj46.xlsx
Solution files:	ETry21_solution.xlsx
	EProj45_solution.xlsx
	EProj46_solution.xlsx

Lesson 22 Showing Percentages with a Pie Chart

What You Will Learn
- ✓ Calculating Percentages
- ✓ Creating a Pie Chart on a Chart Sheet

Tips, Hints, and Pointers

- Discuss each of the skills listed in the What You Will Learn section, and ask students if they have used any of these skills before.
- Discuss the scenario covered in the Application Skills section, and preview the tasks students will perform for Telson Tech.
- Key skills covered in this lesson include calculating percentages and creating pie charts that illustrate the percentages of a whole.

Calculating Percentages

- Remind students that pie charts are used to illustrate the relationship of parts to a whole. They are used to represent the individual values that comprise the whole as a percentage of that whole.
- Provide examples of pie charts and explain the data they illustrate.
- Remind students that percentages, such as 25% and 60%, are portions in relation to a whole. The "whole" is 100%. To find the percentage of a number, change the percentage to a decimal and then multiply that decimal by the number.
- For example, to find 25% of 165, change 25% to a decimal. You do this by replacing the percent sign with a decimal and moving the decimal two spaces to the left. So, 25% = 25. = .25. Then, multiply .25 by 165. When you multiply decimal numbers, you set up the problem like a whole number multiplication problem. To place the decimal point in the product, count the total number of decimal places in both factors. Then, insert the decimal point in the product so that it has the same total number of decimal places as the factors.

Creating a Pie Chart on a Chart Sheet

- **Try It! Creating a Pie Chart on a Chart Sheet, step 1:** Remind students to hold down the Ctrl key as they select noncontiguous ranges.
- **Step 4:** In the Move Chart dialog box, make sure students click the New sheet button.

Project 47—Add Percentage Calculations in the Q3 Sales Workbook

- Refer students to Figure 22-1. Their worksheets should look like this when they have completed them.
- Step 4: Make sure students enter the $ symbols to make the second cell reference absolute.
- Step 8: Instruct students on whether or not they are allowed to print their worksheets, and what they are to submit for grading.

Project 48—Add a Pie Chart on a Chart Sheet in the Q3 Sales Workbook

- Step 3: Remind students to hold down the Ctrl key as they select nonadjacent ranges.
- Step 4: Click the Insert tab, click the Pie button, and then click the specified subtype.
- Step 5: Click the Chart Tools Design tab and click the Move Chart button. In the Move Chart dialog box, click the New sheet button and type the name of the sheet as instructed.
- Step 6: Click the Insert tab and click the Header & Footer button. On the Header/Footer tab in the Page Setup dialog box, click Custom Header. In the Header dialog box, enter the header information as instructed.
- Step 7: Instruct students on whether or not they are allowed to print their worksheets, and what they are to submit for grading.
- **JOB FOCUS:** Discuss the job of a company's sales force. The goal of a business is to sell its goods or services. Personal selling is a type of promotion, accomplished by using a sales force. A sales force is another term for salespeople, or sales representatives. It is the group of employees responsible for contacting customers and arranging the terms of a sale.

Personal selling has a few advantages over other types of promotion. It helps build personal relationships, because the salespeople meet face-to-face with customers. It allows for customized communication, which means the salespeople can customize their message to each potential customer.

A sales person represents the company to the customer. It is likely that a customer will form an opinion about an entire company based on the attitude and behavior of the sales person. It is very important for sales representatives to be professional, well dressed, knowledgeable, ethical, and polite.

Data/Solution Files

Data files: ETry22.xlsx
               EProj47.xlsx
               EProj48.xlsx
Solution files: ETry22_solution.xlsx
               EProj47_solution.xlsx
               EProj48_solution.xlsx

Lesson 23 Enhancing a Pie Chart

What You Will Learn

- ✓ Applying 3-D to a Pie Chart
- ✓ Rotating Slices in a Pie Chart
- ✓ Exploding and Coloring a Pie Chart
- ✓ Formatting the Chart Area of a Pie Chart

Words to Know

Chart area
Explode

Tips, Hints, and Pointers

- Discuss each of the skills listed in the What You Will Learn section, and ask students if they have used any of these skills before.
- Discuss the scenario covered in the Application Skills section, and preview the tasks students will perform for Telson Tech.
- Key skills covered in this lesson include applying 3-D effects and other formats to a pie chart.

Applying 3-D to a Pie Chart

- Discuss the formats you can apply to a pie chart. Formats such as exploded pie slices and patterns or fills can emphasize certain data as well as add visual interest.
- Show how to adjust the amount of 3-D applied to a chart.

Rotating Slices in a Pie Chart

- Using a sample 3-D pie chart, demonstrate how to adjust the rotation. You might want to change the rotation to position important slices of the pie in a more prominent location, such as at the top or bottom.
- Remind students that they can drag a dialog box by its title bar so they can see the effects of their changes as they make them.

Exploding and Coloring a Pie Chart

- Have students practice applying formats to pie charts.
- Have them change a pie chart to a 3-D subtype of their choice.
- Have them adjust the rotation of pie slices. Click the chart, click the Chart Tools Layout tab, click the Chart Elements drop-down arrow, and select the series. On the Chart Tools Layout tab, click the Format Selection button. Adjust the rotation by dragging the slider.
- Have them explode a pie slice. Simply click a slice and drag it away from the pie. Then have them format the slide with a different fill color or pattern.
- Have them apply a different chart style to the chart. On the Chart Tools Design tab, click the Chart Styles More button and select from the gallery of styles.
- **CUSTOMIZED INSTRUCTION: More Advanced Students:** Have students create a pie chart that illustrates data of their choice. For example, they could create a chart that shows the percentage of each day they spend at school, at work, on leisure activities, and sleeping. Have them explode the largest pie slice. On each pie slice, have them insert a piece of clip art or picture that illustrates the pie slice data.

Formatting the Chart Area of a Pie Chart

- In a sample pie chart, point out the plot area and the chart area.
- Show students how to use the Chart Elements button on the Chart Tools Layout tab to help them identify the parts of a pie chart.
- Have them select each part on the Chart Elements drop-down menu to select the part on the chart.

Project 49—Q3 Sales Worksheet Data Changes

- Refer students to Figure 23-1. Their charts should look like this when they have completed them.

- Step 10: Instruct students on whether or not they are allowed to print their worksheets, and what they are to submit for grading.
- **WORKPLACE SKILLS:** Ask students to consider the expression, "A picture is worth a thousand words," and discuss in class what it means.

  Pictures and other graphical representations are a way of conveying information without words. They can be a great way of communicating ideas without saying them directly or writing them down. And there are times when this is the best way to communicate. For instance, visual aids can sometimes make us see ideas that would be difficult to explain otherwise. Graphs and charts like the ones you can create in Excel are excellent examples of this.

  Businesses often find that using visual aids is the most effective way to communicate. This includes putting a picture or graph in your presentation, making a chart instead of describing a trend in your data set, or drawing a picture to explain what you are talking about. Visual aids are often helpful in communicating ideas that you have so far been unsuccessful at communicating with words.

Project 50—Working with Slices and Chart Area on the Chart Sheet in the Q3 Sales Worksheet

- Step 4: Remind students that they can easily identify if they have selected the correct chart part by using the Chart Elements button on the Chart Tools Layout tab. When the chart is selected, "Chart Area" displays on the button.
- Step 5: Click the Chart Tools Layout tab and click the Format Selection button. In the Format Chart Area dialog box, click the 3-D Rotation option and change the settings as instructed.
- Step 6: Right-click a pie slice and click Format Data Series on the shortcut menu. Move the slider as instructed.
- Step 7: Click and drag the Parker pie slice down.
- Step 8: Right-click the exploded pie slice and click Format Data Series on the shortcut menu. In the Format Data Series dialog box, click the Fill option. Under Fill, click Picture or texture fill. Click the Texture drop-down arrow and click Granite.
- Step 9: Right-click the chart area and click Format Chart Area. In the Format Chart Area dialog box, click Fill. Click the Color drop-down arrow and select the specified fill color.
- Step 10: Instruct students on whether or not they are allowed to print their worksheets, and what they are to submit for grading.

Data/Solution Files

Data files:	ETry23.xlsx
	EProj49.xlsx
	EProj50.xlsx
Solution files:	ETry23_solution.xlsx
	EProj49_solution.xlsx
	EProj50_solution.xlsx

Lesson 24   Adding Special Elements to a Chart or Sheet

What You Will Learn

- ✓ Inserting a Text Box in a Chart
- ✓ Updating a Chart
- ✓ Inserting WordArt in a Worksheet

Words to Know

Text box
WordArt

Tips, Hints, and Pointers

- Discuss each of the skills listed in the What You Will Learn section, and ask students if they have used any of these skills before.
- Discuss the scenario covered in the Application Skills section, and preview the tasks students will perform for Telson Tech.
- Key skills covered in this lesson include inserting a text box in a chart, updating chart data, and inserting WordArt in a worksheet.

Inserting a Text Box in a Chart

- You can further enhance charts with text boxes and SmartArt graphics.
- Text boxes are useful for placing text embellishments at any position in the chart area. For example, you might want to highlight the best-selling product for the company by inserting a text box that says "Top seller!"
- Show students a chart in which a text box has been added to form a container for text.
- Point out that a user may want to position a block of text in a precise location on the chart. A text box can be used to contain text and can be moved, sized, or formatted like a drawing object.
- Have students insert a text box and type some text in it. Encourage them to format the text using text formatting options on the Home tab.
- **SKILLS EXTENSION:** Students should be familiar with formatting text boxes from their work with them in Word Chapter 1. When you select a text box inserted in a chart, the Drawing Tools Format tab becomes available. Have students insert a text box in a chart and experiment with the various formatting options available on the tab. Have them change the shape style, fill, outline, and other effects.

Updating a Chart

- Explain that one of the great things about charting worksheet data is that charts automatically update to reflect any changes made to the data.

Inserting WordArt in a Worksheet

- Show how to insert WordArt in a worksheet and in a chart.
- Demonstrate how to position the WordArt by dragging it to another location on the sheet.

Project 51—Add a WordArt Title to the Q3 Sales Workbook

- Step 8: Instruct students on whether or not they are allowed to print their worksheets, and what they are to submit for grading.
- **JOB FOCUS:** Explain that if you can create and interpret charts, you will be an asset in any career. Health care professionals use charts to track patient progress. Business managers use charts to display financial information. Human resources managers use charts to track employee data such as salary and staffing levels. Zookeepers use charts to schedule feedings, warehouse managers use charts to monitor inventory, and wholesalers use charts to track sales.

Project 52—Add a Text Box and Change the Charted Data in the Q3 Sales Workbook

- Step 4: Click the Home tab, click the Sort & Filter button, and click Custom Sort. In the Column Sort by box, click Total and, if necessary, select Smallest to Largest for the Order.

- Step 6: In the Select Data Source dialog box, edit the range addresses in the Chart data range box as instructed.
- Step 8: Click the Chart Tools Layout tab and click the 3-D Rotation button. Set the rotation as instructed. To explode the pie slice, click it and drag down.
- Step 9: Click the Insert tab and click the Text Box button. Click at the bottom of the chart area and enter the text as specified.
- Step 10: Click the text box to select it, click the Drawing Tools Format tab, click the WordArt Styles More button, and select the style as specified.
- Step 12: Instruct students on whether or not they are allowed to print their worksheets, and what they are to submit for grading.

Data/Solution Files

Data files:	ETry24.xlsx
	EProj51.xlsx
	EProj52.xlsx
Solution files:	ETry24_solution.xlsx
	EProj51_solution.xlsx
	EProj52_solution.xlsx

Lesson 25 Completing Chart Formatting

What You Will Learn

- ✓ Changing Data Series Orientation
- ✓ Formatting a Chart
- ✓ Resizing, Moving, or Deleting a Chart Element
- ✓ Changing Chart Text
- ✓ Enhancing the Chart Plot Area
- ✓ Formatting Category and Value Axes

Words to Know

Chart layout
Object
Tick marks

Tips, Hints, and Pointers

- Discuss each of the skills listed in the What You Will Learn section, and ask students if they have used any of these skills before.
- Discuss the scenario covered in the Application Skills section, and preview the tasks students will perform for Whole Grains Bread.
- Key skills covered in this lesson include working with data series and axes, and formatting and modifying other chart elements.

Changing Data Series Orientation

- Use a sample column or bar chart to illustrate how to change the data series orientation.
- Point out that changing the orientation provides a different way to interpret the data. Using the example in the text, if you have a worksheet that lists several branches of a store in rows and the monthly sales for each store in columns, a column chart should show each store's sales as a different color column for each month. This orientation allows you to compare store sales month by month. If you switch column and row data, the column chart would show each month's sales as a different color column for each store. This allows you to compare monthly sales store by store.

Formatting a Chart

- Have students open a previously created workbook and create a new chart from sample data.

- Instruct students to select the chart and then explore with them the tools on the Chart Tools tabs.
- Encourage students to click the Chart Elements down arrow on the Chart Tools Layout tab to see the various chart objects and try selecting objects. As they select an object on the list, it is also selected on the chart.

Resizing, Moving, or Deleting a Chart Element

- Allow students to practice selecting chart objects and resizing, moving, or deleting the objects. Have them delete a legend to see how the other chart objects change in size.
- Remind students that if they are unhappy with a formatting change, they can click the Undo button on the Quick Access Toolbar.
- **CUSTOMIZED INSTRUCTION: Special Needs Students:** Visually challenged students may find it necessary to change the colors of chart text or backgrounds so they can more easily read the text. Remind them how to change these chart settings as necessary.

Changing Chart Text

- Demonstrate how to edit chart text and use the options in the Labels group on the Chart Tools Layout tab to add and modify label text.

Enhancing the Chart Plot Area
- Remind students of the difference between the plot area and the chart area. The plot area contains the charted data; the chart area contains the plot area as well as the chart title, legend, axes titles, etc.
- Demonstrate how to fill the plot area and the chart area with a fill color, a texture or pattern, or a picture or piece of clip art.
- Remind students of the shapes and pictures they formatted in Lessons 9 and 10 of Word Chapter 1. You can apply similar formatting and effects to parts of a chart.
- Review the various formats you can apply from the Chart Tools Format tab.

Formatting Category and Value Axes
- Show students how to adjust formatting of axis labels using the Format Axis dialog box.
- Have students select an axis and display the Format Axis dialog box to see all available options. Encourage them to change axis formats to see how the chart is modified.

Project 53—Changing the Data Orientation and Layout on a Daily Sales Chart
- Refer students to Figure 25-1. Their charts should look like this when they have completed them.
- Step 10: Instruct students on whether or not they are allowed to print their worksheets, and what they are to submit for grading.

Project 54
- Refer students to Figure 25-2. Their charts should look like this when they have completed them. Ask students which chart in Figure 25-2 they think is most useful in illustrating each item's sales. Most will say that the top chart provides a clearer indication. In the bottom chart, you are forced to constantly refer to the legend to determine the sales for individual items.
- Step 5: Click the Chart Tools Layout tab, click the Axes button, click Primary Horizontal Axis, and click None.
- Step 6: Click the Chart Tools Layout tab, click the Data Labels button, and click More Data Label Options. In the Format Data Labels dialog box, click Label Options if necessary, and click Category Name.
- Step 7: With the Format Data Labels dialog box still open, click the Alignment option, click the Text direction drop-down arrow, and click the specified option.
- Step 8: Make sure students select only the specified data label.
- Step 9: Click to select the legend and press the Delete key.
- Step 10: Click the Chart Tools Layout tab, click the Chart Title button, click Above Chart, and type in the chart title as instructed.
- Step 11: Click to select the plot area, and on the Chart Tools Layout tab, click the Format Selection button. Click the Solid fill option, click the Color drop-down arrow, and click the specified color.
- Step 12: Right-click the data point, click Fill in the Format Data Point dialog box, click Solid fill, click the Color drop-down arrow, and click the specified color.
- Step 14: Click the Chart Tools Design tab and click the specified style in the Chart Styles gallery.
- Step 15: Drag a sizing handle to widen the chart.
- Step 16: Click to select the Horizontal (Category) Axis and then press Delete.
- Step 17: Click the Chart Tools Layout tab, click the Axis Titles button, click Primary Vertical Axis Title, and click Rotated Title. On the Home tab, click the Font Size drop-down arrow and click 16.
- Step 18: Right-click the chart area and click Format Chart Area on the shortcut menu. Click Fill and then click Picture or texture fill. Click the Texture drop-down arrow and click Pink tissue paper; then drag the Transparency slider to 25%.
- Step 20: Instruct students on whether or not they are allowed to print their worksheets, and what they are to submit for grading.

Data/Solution Files

Data files: ETry25.xlsx
  EProj53.xlsx
  EProj54.xlsx

Solution files: ETry25_solution.xlsx
  EProj53_solution.xlsx
  EProj54_solution.xlsx

Lesson 26   Comparing and Analyzing Data

What You Will Learn

- ✓ Using Parentheses in a Formula
- ✓ Calculating a Value After an Increase
- ✓ Performing What-If Analysis
- ✓ Creating a Line Chart to Compare Data

Words to Know

What-if analysis

Tips, Hints, and Pointers

- Discuss each of the skills listed in the What You Will Learn section, and ask students if they have used any of these skills before.
- Discuss the scenario covered in the Application Skills section, and preview the tasks students will perform for Cantrell Resources.
- Key skills covered in this lesson include using parentheses to control the order of calculations in a formula, calculating a percentage increase, and performing what-if analyses to determine future values.

Using Parentheses in a Formula

- Discuss how parentheses are used in formulas to control the order of calculations. Review the order of operations and operator precedence.
- Remind students of the standard arithmetic operators used in formulas:
  - + Addition
  - – Subtraction
  - * Multiplication
  - / Division
  - ^ Exponentiation
- Review the order of precedence, or order of operations. The order in which Excel calculates is operations enclosed in parentheses first; exponentiation next; multiplication and division next; and addition and subtraction last.
- When a formula has multiple operators of the same precedence level, such as multiple multiplication operations, Excel performs the calculations from left to right. When a formula contains multiple nested pairs of parentheses, Excel starts with the innermost pair, working outwards.

- Write several equations on the board that incorporate the different operators as well as parentheses and have students explain the order in which the operations will be calculated.

Calculating a Value After an Increase

- Provide students with common examples of calculating an increase in value. For example, you might want to determine how much sales tax will be added to the price of a new pair of shoes. If the sales tax is 6% and the shoes cost $40, you convert the percentage to a decimal (.06), add 1 (1.06) and multiply 1.06 by 40. The cost of the shoes with tax is $42.40.
- **CUSTOMIZED INSTRUCTION: Special Needs Students:** Make sure special needs students know where to find the mathematical operators and parentheses on the keyboard.
- **CUSTOMIZED INSTRUCTION: ESOL Students:** Have students write the names for the basic mathematical operations (addition, subtraction, multiplication, division, and exponentiation) in English and in their primary language.

Performing What-If Analysis

- Point out that what-if analysis is an Excel feature that allows a user to find solutions for specific situations by inputting variable data to create a data table. This tool and others, including Goal Seek and Solver, are discussed in more detail in Lesson 31 of Excel Chapter 4.
- Explain that what-if analyses involve looking at how future results might change based on varying inputs of data. Businesses use this type of analysis to forecast and plan for the future. They can then use a line chart to illustrate projections that result from what-if analyses.

Creating a Line Chart to Compare Data

- Discuss with students how a company might use the information illustrated by the line chart. For example, the data shows the average expenses per account are likely to increase in the third quarter. This signals that the company will need to do something to increase sales to cover the added expenses or find ways to reduce expenses. Being able to anticipate changes such as these helps a company better manage its cash flow.

Project 55—Calculating Tax Withholding in the Projections Workbook

- Refer students to Figure 26-1. Their worksheets should look like this when they have completed them.
- Step 8: Remind students they can use the F4 key or $ symbol to set an absolute reference.
- Step 10: Instruct students on whether or not they are allowed to print their worksheets, and what they are to submit for grading.

Data/Solution Files

Data files: ETry26.xlsx
      EProj55.xlsx
      EProj56.xlsx
Solution files: ETry26_solution.xlsx
      EProj55_solution.xlsx
      EProj56_solution.xlsx

Project 56—Calculating and Charting the What If Analysis in the Projections Workbook

- Step 4: In cell C8, students should enter the formula, =(1+C4)*B8.
- Step 5: In cell B15, students should enter the formula, =B13*1.019.
- Step 7: Remind students to hold down the Ctrl key as they select noncontiguous ranges.
- Step 8: Click the Insert tab, click the Line button, and click the specified subtype.
- Step 9: Click the Chart Tools Layout tab, click the Chart Elements drop-down arrow, and click Vertical (Value) Axis. In the Format Axis dialog box, click the Fixed button next to Minimum, and enter the specified value.
- Step 10: In the Format Axis dialog box, click the Number option and set the decimal places to 0.
- Step 13: Instruct students on whether or not they are allowed to print their worksheets, and what they are to submit for grading.

Lesson 27 Chart Printing and Publishing

What You Will Learn

✓ Printing a Chart
✓ Preparing and Printing a Chart Sheet
✓ Publishing a Chart to the Internet/Intranet

Words to Know

Intranet
Publish

Tips, Hints, and Pointers

- Discuss each of the skills listed in the What You Will Learn section, and ask students if they have used any of these skills before.
- Discuss the scenario covered in the Application Skills section, and preview the tasks students will perform for Restoration Architecture.
- Key skills covered in this lesson include printing a chart and a chart sheet and publishing a chart to the Internet or an intranet.

Printing a Chart

- Using a workbook that contains a chart, open the Page Setup dialog box, click the Chart tab, and discuss with students the options for printing the chart. Point out that large or full-page charts generally look better when printed in landscape orientation.
- **Try It! Printing a Chart:** In this exercise, students print the chart and the data on the worksheet. Point out that if you select the embedded chart, you can print the chart by itself.

Preparing and Printing a Chart Sheet

- **QUICK QUIZ:** Why would you print a chart without the worksheet data?

  The chart may show data trends more clearly than the worksheet data does, or the worksheet data may take up a lot of space on a printout.

Publishing a Chart to the Internet/Intranet

- Remind students that in Lesson 19 of Word Chapter 2, they published Word documents as Web pages. Publishing a chart or worksheet works in much the same way.
- Discuss reasons why a user would publish a chart (or worksheet data) to the Internet or an intranet. Stress that this process makes the chart available for viewing by many people, such as employees at a branch office.
- Explain that businesses often publish financial data and related charts on the Web for potential investors to review.
- **Try It! Publishing a Chart to the Internet/Intranet, step 4:** Point out that the title is the title of the page that appears in the Web browser when you open the page.
- **CUSTOMIZED INSTRUCTION: Special Needs Students:** Show visually challenged students how to enlarge the display of text in their Web browser, if this option is available.

Project 57—Print Data and a Chart

- Step 6: Instruct students on whether or not they are allowed to print their worksheets, and what they are to submit for grading.

Project 58—Publish a Chart Sheet for the Web

- Step 3: Students may group the Revenue Chart and Data sheets before they enter the header information. Make sure they ungroup them before proceeding with the rest of the steps.
- Step 4: Click the Revenue Sheet tab, if necessary, click the File tab, and click Print.
- Step 5: Instruct students on whether or not they are allowed to print their worksheets.
- Step 6: Click the File tab and click Save As. In the Save As dialog box, click the Save as type drop-down arrow and click Single File Web Page. Click the Change Title button, enter the title specified, and click OK. Click the Selection: Chart button and then click the Publish button.
- Step 8: Click the Publish button to finish publishing.

- Step 10: Instruct students on whether or not they are allowed to print their worksheets, and what they are to submit for grading.

Data/Solution Files

Data files: ETry27.xlsx
                EProj57.xlsx
                EProj58.xlsx

Solution files: ETry27_solution.xlsx
                ETry27_solution.mhtml
                EProj57_solution.xlsx
                EProj58_solution.xlsx
                EProj58_solution.mhtml

Lesson 28 Using Charts in Other Files

What You Will Learn

- ✓ Pasting a Picture of a Chart
- ✓ Embedding a Chart in a Word Document
- ✓ Linking a Chart
- ✓ Editing a Linked or Embedded Chart

Words to Know

Embed
Link

Tips, Hints, and Pointers

- Discuss each of the skills listed in the What You Will Learn section, and ask students if they have used any of these skills before.
- Discuss the scenario covered in the Application Skills section, and preview the tasks students will perform for Hyland Manufacturing.
- Key skills covered in this lesson include inserting an Excel chart in a Word document: pasting a picture of the chart, embedding the chart, linking the chart, and editing a linked or embedded chart.

Pasting a Picture of a Chart

- Remind students that Office 2010 is an integrated suite of applications designed to work together to facilitate data sharing. One of the most common types of data sharing is inserting worksheet data or charts in a word processing document. Doing so saves a user from recreating data in a Word table or a chart using Word's charting feature.
- Discuss with students that pasting a picture of a chart is the simplest operation. The pasted chart becomes part of the destination file and cannot be updated from either the source or destination application.

Embedding a Chart in a Word Document

- Remind students to select the correct object when using the Paste Special dialog box. When embedding a chart, for example, they should choose Microsoft Excel Chart Object rather than Picture.
- Have students open a new Word document and an Excel worksheet that contains a chart (or create a simple chart in a new worksheet). In the Word document, have students type *Picture of Chart* and press Enter.
- In the Excel worksheet, have them select the chart and copy it.
- In the Word document, have them click the Paste drop-down arrow and under Paste Options, click Picture. Have students press Enter twice in the Word document and type *Embedded Chart*. Then they should press Enter, click the Paste drop-down arrow, and under Paste Options, click the Keep Source Formatting & Embed Workbook button. Point out the differences in the two charts.
- **CUSTOMIZED INSTRUCTION: Special Needs Students:** Remind physically challenged students that they can use the familiar Ctrl+C, Ctrl+X, and Ctrl+V shortcuts to copy, cut, and paste data. However, the Ctrl+V shortcut only pastes a picture of the data; it doesn't work when you need to link or embed data.

Linking a Chart

- Students will learn more about linking and embedding Excel day in Lesson 36 of Excel Chapter 5.
- Explain that if the source data is likely to change, you should link the chart to its source, so that it will automatically update. This is especially useful when the source data is updated by several different people in your organization.
- In sample documents, have students press Enter twice in the Word document and type *Linked Chart*.
- In the Excel worksheet, they should copy the chart. In the Word document, click the Paste button. The Paste Options button should appear with the pasted chart. Have students click the Paste

- Options button and then click the Use Destination Theme & Link Data button.
- **TROUBLESHOOTING**
- It is a common problem that linked documents become separated from one another when the source document is moved or renamed. Show students how to change the source of a linked document to restore the connection.
- **QUICK QUIZ:** You want to use a Word report to circulate sales figures in your department every week. The sales figures are stored in an Excel worksheet with an accompanying chart. What option should you use to insert the chart in your report: pasting, linking, or embedding?

  Linking is appropriate because the report will be updated on a weekly basis.

Editing a Linked or Embedded Chart

- Demonstrate how to update an Excel chart linked to a Word document. Open the chart in Excel (double-click the chart in Word to open Excel) and make modifications. These changes are automatically shown in the chart in the Word document.
- In their sample Word document, have students double-click the linked chart to open the Excel Ribbon. They should switch to the Design tab, click Edit Data, make a change to the data to modify the chart, and then close the data window and return to Word to see the change in the linked chart.
- Have students double-click the embedded chart in Word to display the data in Excel. Ask them to change the color of one of the data series and save their changes. Have students switch to the Excel workbook to see that this change has not been made to the original chart.

Project 59—Paste a Picture of a chart in the Executive Summary Document

- Steps 1-4: The EProj59a file is an Excel workbook in which students copy an existing chart; the EProj59b file is a Word document in which they paste the chart as a picture.
- Step 10: Note that students may click the Paste drop-down arrow and click the Picture button under the Paste Options; or, they can use the Paste Options button that appears on the chart after it is pasted in the document.
- Step 11: Instruct students on whether or not they are allowed to print their worksheets, and what they are to submit for grading.
- **CUSTOMIZED INSTRUCTION: More Advanced Students:** Have students use the Paste Special dialog box to paste an Excel chart as an icon in a Word document. To do this, they should copy the chart. In the Word document, click the Paste drop-down arrow and then click Paste Special. In the Paste Special dialog box, click Microsoft Excel Chart Object, click Display as icon, and then click OK.

Project 60—Link and Embed Charts in the Executive Summary Document

- Steps 1-4: The EProj60a file is an Excel workbook in which students copy existing charts; the EProj60b file is a Word document in which they link the charts.
- Step 6: Double-click in the footer area of the page. On the Header & Footer Tools Design tab, click the Footer button, and then click Blank (Three Columns).
- Step 7: Click to select the chart and then press Delete.
- Steps 10-11: Click the Paste button. Click the Paste Options button and then click the Use Destination Theme & Link Data button.
- Step 17: Instruct students on whether or not they are allowed to print their worksheets, and what they are to submit for grading.
- **SKILLS EXTENSION:** In the EProj60b document, have students change the chart type for both charts to the Layout 1 type. In this layout, the data labels and their percentages appear on the slices. Ask students if they think this improves the charts.

Data/Solution Files

Data files:		Solution files:	
	ETry28a.xlsx		ETry28a_solution.xlsx
	ETry28b.docx		ETry28b_solution.docx
	EProj59a.xlsx		EProj59a_solution.xlsx
	EProj59b.docx		EProj59b_solution.docx
	EProj60a.xlsx		EProj60a_solution.xlsx
	EProj60b.docx		EProj60b_solution.docx

Lesson 29 Making Special Purpose Charts

What You Will Learn
- ✓ Creating Organization Charts
- ✓ Creating Other SmartArt Diagrams

Words to Know
Organization chart
SmartArt graphic

Tips, Hints, and Pointers

- Discuss each of the skills listed in the What You Will Learn section, and ask students if they have used any of these skills before.
- Discuss the scenario covered in the Application Skills section, and preview the tasks students will perform for Hyland Manufacturing.
- Key skills covered in this lesson include building an organization chart and creating other SmartArt graphics.

Creating Organization Charts

- Discuss organization charts as ways to show how people or objects in a hierarchy relate to one another. Show students an overhead or handout with terminology such as superior, subordinate, assistant, and coworker labeled so students understand the levels of an organization chart.
- Discuss the process of creating an organization chart. Make sure students understand the terminology and how chart levels relate to each other.
- In a new workbook, have students insert an organization chart and type their principal's name (or the name of the president of their company if they hold a job) and title in the top box. Encourage them to enter subordinates and assistants as necessary to create the school or company structure.
- Have students format the organization chart to improve its appearance. Then have students select the top box and apply different layouts to the chart to see how it changes.
- **CUSTOMIZED INSTRUCTION: Special Needs Students:** Remind students who are physically challenged that they can use KeyTips to quickly access the SmartArt diagrams by pressing Alt+N, M.

Creating Other SmartArt Diagrams

- Discuss various uses for SmartArt graphics. These graphics are used often to illustrate information, concepts, and ideas. For example, as students have learned, an organization chart illustrates the relationships between employees in an organization; a Venn diagram compares and contrasts concepts. Office has automated this process to make it simple for users to add text and change the appearance of the final diagram using SmartArt.
- In the Choose a SmartArt Graphic dialog box, click on each of the categories in the list on the left. For each category, click several of the SmartArt options and read through its description with the class. Ask students to think of an instance in which a company might use the selected option.
- If time allows, have students insert one of the graphics discussed in class and fill it in with sample data.
- Demonstrate how to enter data directly in the placeholder and using the Text pane. Then, show students how to edit and format the data. You can edit data directly in the placeholder or in the Text pane. To format data, simply select it as you would any other text and apply formats as desired.

Project 61—Creating the Process Diagram

- Refer students to Figure 29-1. Their SmartArt graphic should look like this when they have completed it.
- Step 7: If the Text Pane is not displayed, click the SmartArt Tools Design tab and click the Text Pane button.
- Step 13: Instruct students on whether or not they are allowed to print their worksheets, and what they are to submit for grading.

Project 62—Creating the Organization Chart and Formatting Diagrams

- Step 4: Click the Insert tab and click the SmartArt button. In the Choose a SmartArt Graphic dialog box, click Hierarchy, and then click the specified type.
- Step 5: The Assistant shape is the middle shape.
- Step 8: Make sure students use the ScreenTips to locate the Pentagon shape under the Block Arrows section of the gallery. They should not use the Regular Pentagon shape under Basic Shapes.
- Step 10: Click the SmartArt Tools Design tab, and in the SmartArt Styles gallery, select the specified style.
- Step 11: On the SmartArt Tools Design tab, click the Colors button and click the specified color.
- Step 13: Instruct students on whether or not they are allowed to print their worksheets, and what they are to submit for grading.
- **WORKPLACE SKILLS:** An organization chart identifies the organizational structure within a company. This is a system that assigns work, authority, and responsibility. An organizational structure is very important. It defines the chain of command, which is the path of authority and supervision among employees. A well-organized company clearly identifies the responsibilities of each employee, the relationship between employees, and the relationship between departments within the company.

Data/Solution Files

Data files: EProj61.xlsx
                 EProj62.xlsx
Solution files: ETry29_solution.xlsx
                 EProj61_solution.xlsx
                 EProj62_solution.xlsx

Chapter Assessment and Application
Project 63   Investment Portfolio

Tips, Hints, and Pointers

- In this project, students will develop a worksheet that tracks and charts stock market data.
- Step 3: Click the first sheet tab, hold down the Shift key, and click the other sheet tabs. After entering the header information, ungroup the sheets by right-clicking a sheet tab and clicking Ungroup Sheets.
- Step 5: Click the Chart Tools Design tab. Select the specified layout from the Chart Layouts gallery and the specified style from the Chart Styles gallery.
- Step 6: Click the Chart Tools Layout tab, click the Chart Elements drop-down arrow, and click Vertical (Value) Axis. Click the Format Selection button. On the Axis Options tab, click the Fixed button next to Minimum and enter 9.
- Step 7: Click the chart title and edit the name as instructed.
- Step 10: In cell E8, students should enter the formula, =(1+$D$4)*D8.
- Step 11: In cell F8, students should enter the formula, =(1-$D$5)*D8.
- Step 13: Click the Insert tab, click the Column button, and then click the specified subtype.
- Step 14: To delete the legend, click it and press Delete. To add a title, click the Chart Tools Layout tab, click the Chart Title button, click Above Chart, and enter the chart name as instructed.
- Step 16: Instruct students on whether or not they are allowed to print their worksheets, and what they are to submit for grading.

Data/Solution Files

Data file: EProj63.xlsx
Solution file: EProj63_solution.xlsx

Chapter Assessment and Application
Project 64 Sales Data Chart and Web Page

Tips, Hints, and Pointers

- In this project, students will chart sales data and publish it to the Web for Teesy Apparel.
- Steps 4-5: Select the ranges E4:H4 and E29:H29 and then press the F11 key.
- Step 6: Click the legend and press Delete. On the Chart Tools Layout tab, click Chart Title, click Above Chart, and enter the name as instructed. Select the chart and on the Chart Tools Design tab, click the Chart Styles More button and click the specified style.
- Step 7: Select the data as specified, click the Insert tab, click the Pie button, and click the specified subtype. Click the Move Chart button and in the Move Chart dialog box, specify a new sheet and enter the name for the sheet as specified.
- Step 8: Select each chart, click the Chart Tools Layout tab, and in the Chart Layout gallery, click the specified layout.
- Step 9: Select the chart area, click the Chart Tools Format tab, click the Shape Fill drop-down arrow, and click the specified color. Make sure students do this to both pie charts.
- Step 10: Click and drag the smallest slice to explode it. Make sure students do this to both pie charts.
- Step 11: Right-click the sheet tab, click Rename, and enter the new name.
- Step 12: Click the Insert tab, click the SmartArt button, click Matrix, and then click the specified SmartArt.
- Step 13: Click the SmartArt Tools Design tab and click the Text Pane button.
- Step 14: Click the Text Pane Close button. On the SmartArt Tools Design tab, click the Change Colors button, and click the specified color.
- Step 15: Right-click the sheet tab and click Delete.
- Step 16: Click the File tab and click Save As. Click the Save as type drop-down arrow and click Single File Web Page. Click the Change Title button and enter the title as instructed. Click the Publish button. In the Publish as Web Page dialog box, click the Choose drop-down arrow and click Entire workbook. Click Publish.
- Step 18: Instruct students on whether or not they are allowed to print their worksheets, and what they are to submit for grading.
- **SKILLS EXTENSION**
- Challenge students to write a report in Word that summarizes the data in the EProj64 workbook. Some of the items they should touch upon include:
  - Total quarterly sales and in which quarter the most sales occurred and the least sales occurred.
  - The product line that represents the most sales and the least sales.
  - The product size that represents the most sales and the least sales.
  - The item with the highest average sales and the lowest average sales (students will need to create a table of the sales data and sort it by the Average column).

Encourage students to paste, embed, or link charts as necessary to illustrate the information they write in their report.

Data/Solution Files

Data file: EProj64.xlsx
Solution files: EProj64_solution.xlsx
                 EProj64_solution.mhtml

Chapter 4: Advanced Functions, PivotCharts, and PivotTables

Lesson 30 Using Advanced Functions to Predict Trends

What You Will Learn

- ✓ Creating Predictions and Estimations
- ✓ Using FORECAST
- ✓ Using TREND
- ✓ Using GROWTH

Words to Know

Sparklines
Step
Trend

Tips, Hints, and Pointers

- Discuss each of the skills listed in the What You Will Learn section, and ask students if they have used any of these skills before.
- Discuss the scenario covered in the Application Skills section, and preview the tasks students will perform for Whole Grains Bread.
- Key skills covered in this lesson include creating predictions and estimations using the FORECAST, TREND, and GROWTH functions.

Creating Predictions and Estimations

- Explain how AutoFill can be used to identify trends.
- Discuss the difference between linear trends and growth trends. A linear trend determines the numerical increments at which a series of data will increase or decrease. A growth trend determines the percentage increments at which a series of data will increase or decrease.
- If necessary, remind students how to use AutoFill to create a series, such as days of the week, or numbers in a series.
- Use a simple series of numbers, such as 5, 10, to demonstrate how the linear and growth trends are calculated. If the existing data are 5 and 10, the linear trend will increase by increments of 5. So you'd have 5, 10, 15, 20, and so forth. The growth trend, on the other hand, will increase by 100 percent. So you would have 5, 10, 20, 40, 80, and so forth.
- Demonstrate how to display the AutoFill shortcut menu and point out the Linear Trend and Growth trend options on it.
- Point out the Sparklines identified in Figure 30-1. Sparklines are a tool you can use to graphically illustrate a trend within a single cell.
- **CUSTOMIZED INSTRUCTION: Special Needs Students:** The AutoFill feature can help minimize the amount of typing a physically challenged person has to do when calculating future values. Remind them to right-click and hold the AutoFill handle when dragging it to create a linear or growth trend.
- **Try It! Using AutoFill to Complete a Series and Create Trends, step 8:** Have students evaluate the predicted sales for July, August, and September. Note that the linear trend indicates sales decreasing slightly each month.
- **Step 12:** Again, discuss the predicted sales, noting that the growth trend indicates sales decreasing slightly each month.
- **Try It! Using the Fill button to Create a Linear Trend:** Point out to students that the Fill button and Series dialog box represent another way to calculate the Linear and Growth trends.

- **CURRICULUM CONNECTION:** When traveling abroad or conducting business internationally, it is important to know the exchange rate for converting American dollars to other currency. In some countries, the dollar will be worth more, and in others it will be less. Exchange rates change daily, but usually not by much.

  Have students look up the exchange rate of American dollars to Australian dollars. They should create a worksheet that lists the price of at least five items that they use on a regular basis and then use the conversion formula to list the equivalent cost of the same item in Australian dollars. Encourage them to expand the worksheet to include other foreign currency, such as the euro, or the Japanese yen.

- **Try It! Using Sparklines to Instantly Chart Trends, step 3:** Remind students that they can type the range address in the Data Range and Location Range text boxes, or they can click the Collapse Dialog buttons and reference the cells directly on the worksheet.

- **Step 4:** Have students assess what the Sparkline illustrates. In this case, it shows that sales peaked in February and then declined steadily in the following months.

Using FORECAST

- Demonstrate how Excel functions can help predict future values. The FORECAST function projects values that change over time. The TREND function helps analyze complex data on a chart. The GROWTH function predicts future values using an exponential growth formula, y=bmx.

- Mention that because it bases its estimates on a linear trend, the FORECAST function is a good function to use if you need to project values that change over time, such as sales, inventory, or employee turnover.

- **Try It! Using the FORECAST Function, step 10:** Students should end up with a value of $20,158.70 in cell D14.

- **SKILLS EXTENSION:** Have students click cell D14 in the ETry30 file. Click the Formulas tab and then click the Insert Function button. Have them review the syntax of the FORECAST function in the Function Arguments dialog box.

Using TREND

- **Try It! Using the TREND Function, step 7:** Students should end up with a value of $24,715.40 in cell D15.

- **SKILLS EXTENSION:** Have students click cell D15 in the ETry30 file. Click the Formulas tab and then click the Insert Function button. Have them review the syntax of the TREND function in the Function Arguments dialog box.

- **CUSTOMIZED INSTRUCTION: Less Advanced Students:** Provide additional real-world examples to help less advanced students understand the complex but powerful FORECAST, TREND, and GROWTH functions.

Using GROWTH

- **Try It! Using the GROWTH Function, step 11:** Step 11: Students should end up with a value of $30,917.56 in cell D16.

- **SKILLS EXTENSION:** Have students click cell D15 in the ETry30 file. Click the Formulas tab and then click the Insert Function button. Have them review the syntax of the GROWTH function in the Function Arguments dialog box.

- **QUICK QUIZ:** When would it be useful to use functions that attempt to predict future trends? *Analyzing marketing results, the stock market, the economy, or scientific data.*

- **SKILLS EXTENSION:** Have students look up FORECAST, GROWTH, and TREND in Excel Help to learn more about these advanced functions.

Project 65—Inventory Projections

- Refer students to Figure 30-2. Their worksheets should look like this when they have completed them.

- Step 18: Instruct students on whether or not they are allowed to print their worksheets, and what they are to submit for grading.

Project 66—Inventory Projections

- Refer students to Figure 30-3. Their worksheets should look like this when they have completed them.

- Step 4: In cell E12, students should enter the formula, =TREND(B12:D12).

- Step 5: Copy the formula in E12 to F12:G12.

- Step 6: In cell E13, students should enter the formula, =TREND($B13:$D13,$B$12:$D$12,E$12).

- Step 7: Click cell E13, click the Copy button, click F13:G13, click the Paste drop-down arrow, and click Formulas. Follow the same procedure to copy the formulas in E13:G13 to the rest of the inventory items.

- Step 8: In cell E12, students should enter the formula, =GROWTH(B12:D12).

- Step 9: Copy the formula in E12 to F12:G12.

- Step 10: In cell E13, students should enter the formula, =GROWTH($B13:$D13,$B$12:$D$12,E$12).
- Step 11: Click cell E13, click the Copy button, click F13:G13, click the Paste drop-down arrow, and click Formulas. Follow the same procedure to copy the formulas in E13:G13 to the rest of the inventory items.
- Step 12: To apply the format, select the specified range, click the Home tab, click the Number Format drop-down arrow, and click Accounting. Make sure students apply the formatting on both the TREND and GROWTH worksheets.
- Step 13: Click in cell A1, click the Review tab, and then click the Spelling button. Follow this procedure for each sheet.
- Step 14: Instruct students on whether or not they are allowed to print their worksheets, and what they are to submit for grading.

Data/Solution Files

Data files:
ETry30.xlsx
EProj65.xlsx
EProj66.xlsx

Solution files:
ETry30_solution.xlsx
EProj65_solution.xlsx
EProj66_solution.xlsx

Lesson 31 Using Advanced Functions for Data Analysis

What You Will Learn

- ✓ **Using the PMT Function**
- ✓ **Creating What-If Data Tables**
- ✓ **Solving a Problem with Goal Seek**
- ✓ **Using Solver to Resolve Problems**

Words to Know

Data table
Goal Seek
Input cell
Solver

Substitution values
Variable
What-if analysis

Tips, Hints, and Pointers

- Discuss each of the skills listed in the What You Will Learn section, and ask students if they have used any of these skills before.
- Discuss the scenario covered in the Application Skills section, and preview the tasks students will perform for Restoration Architecture.
- Key skills covered in this lesson include using the PMT function, creating what-if data tables, and solving a problem with Goal Seek or Solver.

Using the PMT Function

- Students of an age to be considering a car purchase should be able to relate to uses for the PMT function, which calculates loan payments. Older students who own or hope to own a home will also find this function particularly useful. Discuss these common uses for the PMT function.
- Demonstrate how to set up the PMT function, explaining each argument carefully. The PMT arguments can be confusing for students new to this type of calculation.
- Stress that the rate and the number of payment periods must be expressed in the same time intervals, either monthly or yearly. If the interest rate is annual, for example, it must be divided by 12 to match monthly payment periods.
- Students may also be thrown by a negative number result for a PMT function. Show them how to enter the PV argument as a negative to give a positive result.

- In a new workbook, have students enter the following data: in cell A1, $50,000; in cell A2, 10; in cell A3, 6%. These values represent the principal, number of payment periods (years), and interest rate. In cell A5, have students enter the formula =PMT(A3/12,A2*12,A1).
- Discuss why the interest rate is divided by 12 and the number of payments multiplied by 12 in students' sample function.
- Point out that the red color and parentheses for the students' results indicates a negative number. Have them insert a minus sign in front of the A1 cell reference in the formula to change the negative result to a positive one.
- **Try It! Using the PMT Function, step 3:** Remind students to use the worksheet navigation buttons to bring sheets tabs into view, if necessary.

Creating What-If Data Tables

- Discuss what-if analysis, an Excel feature that allows a user to find solutions for specific situations by inputting variable data to create a data table.
- Demonstrate how to set up both one-input and two-input data tables. Use a sample worksheet with a one-input data table to introduce the basics of what-if analysis. Point out the formula cell that contains the formula that will be calculated using each variable; the input cell to which the formula refers; and the variables that will be substituted in the formula to give a series of results.

- Stress that the user enters only the variables (substitution values) in the data table. Excel calculates the other results when the user issues the Data Table command from the What-If Analysis button on the Data tab.
- **QUICK QUIZ:** You want to find out what your monthly loan payment would be at several current interest rates. What data analysis tool would give you the answer most efficiently?

  A what-if data table.

Solving a Problem with Goal Seek

- Stress the differences between Goal Seek and Solver. Goal Seek can change only one variable to achieve desired results. Solver can change several variables (and also meet constraints) to obtain the desired results.
- Demonstrate how to use both the Goal Seek and Solver features. Point out that in contrast to a what-if data table, the user already knows the result when using these features. Excel satisfies the result by changing input values until the result is correct.
- **Try It! Using Goal Seek, step 2:** Have students note the value in cell D9 before they start the Goal Seek.
- **Steps 3 and 5:** Remind students that they can also click the Collapse Dialog button and click the cell reference directly on the worksheet. They click the Expand Dialog button to redisplay the entire Goal Seek dialog box.
- **Step 7:** Note the difference in the value in cell D9. Point out that you can click Cancel to retain the existing values.

Using Solver to Resolve Problems

- Show students how to enter Solver constraints such as a minimum or maximum value.
- **TROUBLESHOOTING:** If you have not used Solver on your computers, you may need to install it or have students install it. Click the File menu and click Options. In the Excel Options dialog box, click Add-Ins. The CD is not required to add this feature.
- **Try It! Using Solver, steps 4-9:** Make sure students check the values they enter in the Solver Parameters dialog box against those shown in the figure.
- **SKILLS EXTENSION:** Have students determine if a what-if data table, Goal Seek, or Solver would be the best tool to use to solve the following problem.

  You have the following scores on tests in one of your classes: 93%, 90%, 88%, and 94%. You have one more test coming up. What score must you get on the test to achieve 93% overall?

  Answer: Students should determine that Goal Seek is the best tool to use. To solve the problem, they must enter the four known scores, plus zero for the unknown score, and then average them. They should then set the set cell to the cell containing the average, change that value to 93, and set the changing cell value to the cell containing zero. Goal Seek determines that you would have to get 100% on the last test in order to achieve 93% overall.
- **CUSTOMIZED INSTRUCTION: More Advanced Students:** Have advanced students set up a two-variable data table to display payment amounts for a typical car loan in their price range, over a period of four years. The variables in this example are the loan amounts and interest rates.

Project 67—Bid Projections

- Refer students to Figure 31-1. Their worksheets should look like this when they have completed them.
- Step 4: Have students jot down the current values in cells B20 and D7.
- Step 10: Remind students to hold down the Ctrl key to select the noncontiguous cells.
- Step 18: Instruct students on whether or not they are allowed to print their worksheets, and what they are to submit for grading.

Project 68—Bid Projections

- Refer students to Figures 31-2 and 31-3. Their worksheets should look like this when they have completed them.
- Step 5b: Select the data range, then click the Data tab, click the What-If Analysis button, and click Data Table.
- Steps 5c-5d: In the Data Table dialog box, enter the cell references as instructed and click OK.
- Step 6a: In cell A9, students should enter the formula, =PMT(C7/12,F6,-C6).
- Step 6b: Select the data range, click the Data tab, click the What-If Analysis button, and click Data Table.
- Steps 6c-6d: In the Data Table dialog box, enter the cell references as instructed and click OK.
- Step 8: You may want to instruct students to first group the sheets in order to run the spelling check on the entire workbook at once. Otherwise, they will need to run the spell check on each sheet. To group sheets, click the first sheet tab, press Shift, and click the last sheet tab. To check spelling, click

in cell A1 of the active sheet, click the Review tab, and click the Spelling button.
- Step 9: Instruct students on whether or not they are allowed to print their worksheets, and what they are to submit for grading.
- **WORKPLACE SKILLS:** Have students evaluate the data on the Labor worksheet, as shown in Figure 31-2. Have them compare the individual values in the range F20:F25 with the value in cell G16. Notice how the base cost increases dramatically with delays in the schedule. Discuss how projecting increased costs like this can help a company better manage their resources.

You might also want to discuss the payment information for the construction loan as shown in Figure 31-3. Explain that many business owners rely on loans to help start up and run their company. When you borrow money, you increase the company's debt, which is called debt financing.

Banks and credit unions are sources of debt financing. They issue business loans for a set amount of time—called the term—at a specific interest rate. The bank may ask for collateral against the loan. Collateral is property or other assets that you pledge to the bank. If you fail to repay the loan, the bank takes ownership of the collateral. For example, if you own a truck, you might use it as collateral. The bank may also ask for a co-signer for the loan. A co-signer is an individual who agrees to make the loan payments if you cannot.

Data/Solution Files

Data files:	ETry31.xlsx
	EProj67.xlsx
	EProj68.xlsx
Solution files:	ETry31_solution.xlsx
	EProj67_solution.xlsx
	EProj68_solution.xlsx

Lesson 32 Using LOOKUP Functions

What You Will Learn
✓ Creating Lookup Functions

Words to Know
Range name
Table

Tips, Hints, and Pointers

- Discuss each of the skills listed in the What You Will Learn section, and ask students if they have used any of these skills before.
- Discuss the scenario covered in the Application Skills section, and preview the tasks students will perform on their income tax worksheets.
- The key skill covered in this lesson is creating lookup functions.

Creating Lookup Functions

- Discuss how the VLOOKUP and HLOOKUP functions can be used to produce a value in a cell without calculating. The cell contents are looked up in a table and the answer is returned to the cell.
- Mention that creating a lookup table in a worksheet or workbook and then using lookup functions can make repetitive calculations easier to set up.
- Differentiate between the VLOOKUP and HLOOKUP functions. Use VLOOKUP to find values in a column or HLOOKUP to find values in rows.
- Discuss the format of the VLOOKUP and HLOOKUP functions and explain their arguments. Point out that the item argument can be either a value or a cell reference.
- Point out that the lookup table itself can appear anywhere on a worksheet. Identifying the table with a range name can save time when entering the function.
- Note that the data in the table must be arranged in ascending order.
- Demonstrate how a lookup function works. In a sample worksheet that has a lookup table inserted already, insert the formula. Use VLOOKUP to return a value in a column. Use HLOOKUP to return a value in a row.
- To give students some practice in using VLOOKUP, have them create a short lookup table in a worksheet with three Zip codes in one column and their corresponding city names in the next column (use real or made-up data and make sure Zip codes are in ascending order).
- Have students name the lookup table range Zips. In another cell, ask them to enter the function =VLOOKUP(zip,Zips,2), replacing zip with one of the Zip codes in the lookup table. The function should return the city name associated with the chosen Zip code.
- Continuing on their example worksheets, have students copy the lookup table and use Paste Special to transpose the data into rows. Name the range *Zips2*. Ask students to practice using the HLOOKUP function with another of the Zip codes in the lookup table.
- **QUICK QUIZ:** You have grades arranged in the first column of your lookup table column as 100, 95, 90, 85, 80. Why doesn't the VLOOKUP function return the correct grade?
  Values must be arranged in ascending order.

Project 69—Income Tax Calculations

- Refer students to Figure 32-1. Their worksheets should look like this when they have completed them.
- Step 5: Point out that the data on this worksheet is a copied 1040 tax form with line items numbered at the left. Make sure students do not confuse the line item numbers with the worksheet's row numbers.
- Step 8: Make sure students click the Tax Table sheet tab and then select the specified range.
- Step 10: In cell F50, students' formulas should be, =VLOOKUP(F49,'Tax Table'!A4:C304,2).
- Step 11: Instruct students on whether or not they are allowed to print their worksheets, and what they are to submit for grading.

Project 70—Income Tax Calculations

- Refer students to Figure 32-2. Their worksheets should look like this when they have completed them.
- Step 5: In cell F7, students should enter the formula, =IF(B7="married, filing jointly",HLOOKUP(2,B14:D15,2),HLOOKUP(1,B14:D15,2))
- Step 12: Instruct students on whether or not they are allowed to print their worksheets, and what they are to submit for grading.
- **WORKPLACE SKILLS:** Each year, you must file income tax returns for the income you earned the previous year. You must file the income tax returns by April 15th or the date specified by the government if the 15th is on a weekend or holiday. (That means on April 15, 2012, you file a return for the income you earned in 2011.) Income tax returns are forms on which you calculate the amount of income tax you owe. You file federal tax returns to the Internal Revenue Service (IRS), the agency responsible for collecting federal taxes, and you file state tax returns with your state's revenue department.

The minimum amount you have to earn to file a tax return changes every year, and depends on your age and whether or not you are married. Once you calculate the amount you owe based on your tax bracket, you subtract the amount that your employer withheld throughout the year. If it is more than the amount you owe, the government sends you a refund check. If it is less than the amount you owe, you must send the government a check for the difference.

Data/Solution Files

Data files:	ETry32.xlsx
	EProj69.xlsx
	EProj70.xlsx
Solution files:	ETry32_solution.xlsx
	EProj69_solution.xlsx
	EProj70_solution.xlsx
	EProj70_Tax_solution.xlsx

Lesson 33 Understanding PivotTables and PivotCharts

What You Will Learn

✓ Creating PivotTables
✓ Using the PivotTable Field List
✓ Enhancing PivotTables and Creating PivotCharts

Words to Know

Database
Field
PivotChart
PivotTable
Report filter

Tips, Hints, and Pointers

- Discuss each of the skills listed in the What You Will Learn section, and ask students if they have used any of these skills before.
- Discuss the scenario covered in the Application Skills section, and preview the tasks students will perform for Voyager Travel Adventures.
- Key skills covered in this lesson include creating PivotTables, creating PivotCharts, and using the PivotTable Field List.

Creating PivotTables

- Explain to students that PivotTables rearrange complex worksheet data to summarize and analyze it. The rearranged data is displayed in a report that allows the user to select different data categories to show only that data.
- Students who have never worked with PivotTables or PivotCharts may have difficulty grasping the concepts behind this feature, especially knowing how to reorganize the data in the PivotTable report. Use an example worksheet displaying sales information for several products by store location to demonstrate how to create a PivotTable.
- Explore the options available in the Create PivotTable dialog box and demonstrate how to use them.
- Show students a PivotTable created from data in a worksheet so they will begin to understand how the data has been reorganized.
- **Try It! Creating PivotTables with Excel Data, step 3:** Students should select A5 on the Sheet1 worksheet.
- **Step 4:** Point out to students how the table data is outlined in a dashed marquee and the table range appears in the Select a table or range box in the Create PivotTable dialog box.
- **CUSTOMIZED INSTRUCTION: ESOL Students:** Ask students if they have terms for PivotTable and PivotChart in their primary language. If not, ask them to "create" the term

Using the PivotTable Field List

- Discuss the three areas into which columns (fields) can be dragged into the report structure from the PivotTable Field List: the row area, column area, and body. Show students how to drag more than one column into an area.
- Point out the report filter area of a PivotTable, into which you also can drag items from the PivotTable Field List.
- More than one PivotTable can be created for each worksheet to allow the user to view different aspects of the data.
- Point out the down arrows next to the PivotTable items. Show students how to rearrange the data displayed in a PivotTable.
- Review the parts of the worksheet shown in Figure 33-2. The PivotTable3 report area on the left displays the results of the changes you make in the PivotTable Field List task pane on the right. The fields listed at the top of the task pane represent the columns in the selected table range. Remind students of the basic areas into which you can drag fields.

- Report Filter: Applies a filter arrow to the specified field that you can click to display data related to particular category.
- Column Labels: Fields that you drag to this section appear as columns in the PivotTable.
- Row Labels: Fields that you drag to this section appear as rows in the PivotTable.
- Values: Fields: Numerical fields that you drag to this section are summarized according to the corresponding rows and columns.

- **QUICK QUIZ:** Why would anyone want to create a PivotTable of a complex worksheet?

  A PivotTable can help the user look at the data in different ways to identify trends or patterns in the data.

- **Try It! Using the PivotTable Field List, step 5:** Have students drag the Customer field to the Report Filter area. In the PivotTable, have them click the cell B3 filter arrow and select each of the customers to display the data specific to that customer. Students will also do this in the next Try It exercise.

- **Step 6:** Allow students time to experiment with rearranging the fields in the PivotTable. To remove a field from one of the field areas, they can drag it out of the area or deselect its box at the top of the task pane.

- **CUSTOMIZED INSTRUCTION: More Advanced Students:** Have advanced students create a sample PivotTable and examine and experiment with the buttons and commands available on the PivotTable Tools Options and PivotTable Tools Design tabs on the Ribbon.

Enhancing PivotTables and Creating PivotCharts

- Show students how to format a PivotTable report using the PivotTable Styles list on the PivotTable Tools Design tab. Explore the other options in the Layout group on that tab.
- Demonstrate how to create a PivotChart from a PivotTable report. A PivotChart can be created from a PivotTable to display data in a graphic format.
- Show students how to customize the PivotChart by changing chart type or other chart formats.
- **Try It! Creating a PivotChart from a PivotTable, step 4:** Have students click the Customer filter arrow and select A-1 Pharmacy. Notice how the chart changes. Have them click the Drug Purchased filter arrow and deselect one of the drugs. Note how the chart changes.

- **Try It! Moving a PivotChart, step 2:** Point out to students that they can drag the chart to another location on the same sheet the same way they would any other Excel chart.

Project 71—Inventory Analysis

- Refer students to Figure 33-3. Their worksheets should look like this when they have completed them.
- Step 10: Instruct students on what they are to submit for grading.

Project 72—Inventory Analysis

- Refer students to Figure 33-4. Their worksheets should look like this when they have completed them.
- Step 6a: Click the PivotTable Tools Design tab, click the PivotTable Styles More arrow, and click PivotStyle Dark 5.
- Step 6b: Select B13:D17, click the Home tab, click the Number Format button, and click More Number Formats. Select Accounting with no decimal places.
- Step 7: Group the sheets by clicking the first sheet tab, pressing Shift, and clicking the last sheet tab. Click cell A1 on the active sheet, click the Review tab, and then click the Spelling button. Students do not need to correct the spelling of abbreviations, nor should they add any terms to the custom dictionary.
- Step 8: Instruct students on whether or not they are allowed to print their worksheets, and what they are to submit for grading.
- Step 9: Refer students to Figure 33-5. Their charts should look like this when they have completed them. To create the chart, click in the data table, click the PivotTable Tools Options tab, and click the PivotChart button. Click Bar and then the Clustered Bar chart type. To move the chart to the PivotChart sheet, click the PivotChart Tools Design tab and click the Move Chart button. In the Move Chart dialog box, click Object in, click the drop-down arrow, and click PivotChart. Click OK.
- Step 10: Instruct students on whether or not they are allowed to print their chart sheets, and what they are to submit for grading.
- **WORKPLACE SKILLS:** Discuss with students the importance of inventory management for a business, particularly a retailer like the stores operated by Voyager Travel Adventures. Inventory management is the function of tracking and managing the stocks of finished products, semi-finished products, and raw materials. Proper

inventory management can lead to lower costs and increased revenues for a business.

How high or low the inventory depends on the type of business. A car dealer, for example, has very high inventories, sometimes as high as 50 percent of the total assets, whereas in the hotel industry it may be as low as 2 to 5 percent.

The inventory management process begins as soon as the company orders the raw materials, semi-finished product, or finished product from a supplier. If you are a retailer like the store operated by Voyager Travel Adventures, then this process begins as soon you place an order with a wholesaler, which is a business that buys goods in large quantities, typically from manufacturers, and resells them in smaller batches to retailers.

Once the order is placed, you must decide where the products will be stored. Like the Logan store where storage space is limited, you must determine well in advance of ordering if you have the space to store the items. That's why many companies use software applications such as Excel and other inventory management programs to determine the volume of sales on specific items. With just-in-time inventory management, a computerized system is implemented that orders inventory at the exact right time and only for the exact right amount.

Data/Solution Files

Data files:	ETry33.xlsx
	EProj71.xlsx
	EProj72.xlsx
Solution files:	ETry33_solution.xlsx
	EProj71_solution.xlsx
	EProj72_solution.xlsx

Chapter Assessment and Application

Project 73 Revenue PivotTable

Tips, Hints, and Pointers

- In this project, students will develop PivotTable reports and use forecasting functions to analyze sales data for Whole Grains Bread.
- Refer students to Illustration A. Their PivotTables should look like this when they have completed them.
- Step 5a: Remind students to use the worksheet navigation buttons to bring the Revenue sheet into view if necessary. Click a cell in the table on the Revenue sheet. Click the Insert tab and click the PivotTable button. In the Create PivotTable dialog box, click Existing Worksheet and type Analysis!$A$10.
- Step 5b: In the PivotTable Field List task pane, drag the City field to the Row Labels section.
- Step 5c: Drag the Qtr field to the Column Labels section.
- Step 5d: Drag the Sales field to the Values section.
- Step 5e: Drag the State field to the Report Filter section.
- Step 5f: Select the range B12:F18, click the Home tab, click the Number Format button, and click More Number Formats. Click Currency with no decimal places.
- Step 5g: Click the filter arrow in cell B8 and click OR.
- Step 5h: Click in the PivotTable, click the PivotTable Tools Design tab, click the PivotTable Styles More button, and click the specified style.
- Step 5i: Group the sheets by clicking the first sheet tab, pressing Shift, and clicking the last sheet tab. Click cell A1 on the active sheet, click the Review tab, and then click the Spelling button.
- Step 5k: Instruct students on whether or not they are allowed to print their worksheets.
- Step 6a: Click the filter arrow in B8 and click All.
- Step 6c: Click the Paste drop-down arrow and click Paste Special. In the Paste Special dialog box, click Values and then click OK.
- Step 7: Refer students to Illustration B. Their worksheets should look like this when they have completed them.
- Steps 7a-7c: In cell F9, students should enter the formula, =GROWTH(B9:E9). Copy the formula as instructed.
- Step 10: Instruct students on whether or not they are allowed to print their worksheets.
- Step 11: Click a blank cell on the New Product sheet. Click the Data tab and click the Solver button. In the Solver Parameters dialog box, enter $C$19 in the Set Objective text box. Click Value Of and type 1200.
- Step 11a: Click the Collapse Dialog button on the By Changing Variable Cells box, click cell C15, hold down Ctrl, and click cell D18. Click the Expand Dialog button.
- Step 11b-c: Click the Add button and add the following constraints: C15>=3.75; C15<=4.25; D18<=.75; D18>=.5.
- Have students check their worksheet data against that shown in Illustration C.
- Step 13: Instruct students on whether or not they are allowed to print their worksheets, and what they are to submit for grading.

Data/Solution Files

Data file: EProj73.xlsx
Solution file: EProj73_solution.xlsx

86 | Learning Microsoft Excel 2010 | Teacher's Manual

Project 74 Lemonade Stand Projections

Tips, Hints, and Pointers

- In this project, students will collect and evaluate data for a lemonade stand.
- Step 5: Enter the first few values (1, 2, 3) and then use the fill handle to complete the numbering.
- Step 6: Enter Monday in cell B4, t0068en use the fill handle to complete the days of the week.
- Step 7: In cell J4, students should enter the formula, H4*I4 and copy it to the rest of the column.
- Step 8: In cell K4, students should enter the formula, =G4*0.25 and copy it to the rest of the column.
- Step 9: In cell L4, students should enter the formula, =E4*F4, and copy it to the rest of the column.
- Step 10: In cell M4, students should enter the formula, =J4-K4-L4, and copy it to the rest of the column.
- Step 12: In cell O4, students should enter the formula, =M5+N5.
- Step 13: In cell N5, students should enter the formula, =O4.
- Step 15: Click in the table, click the Insert tab, click the PivotTable button, click Existing Worksheet, and type PivotTable!$B$3.
- Step 16: In the PivotTable Field List task pane, drag the Charger per Glass field to the Row Labels section. Drag the Predicted Weather and Actual Weather fields to the Column Labels section. Drag the Glasses Sold field to the Values section. Drag the Day of Week field to the Report Filter section.
- Step 17: Click in the PivotTable, click the PivotTable Tools Design tab, click the PivotTable Styles More button, and click Pivot Style Medium 4. Refer students to Illustration D.
- Step 18: Click the Sales Data sheet and select the data as instructed. Click the Copy button. On the Forecast sheet, click the Paste drop-down arrow and click Paste Special. In the Paste Special dialog box, click Values and Formats. Copy the Day and Day of Week columns and paste in the Forecast sheet.
- Step 19: In cell C32 on the Forecast sheet, students should enter the formula, =TREND($C$2:C31). Copy the formula for the rest of the days in the column.
- Step 20, In cell D32, students should enter the formula, =FORECAST(C32,D2:D31,C2:C31). In cell E32, students should enter the formula, =FORECAST(C32,E2:E31,C2:C31).
- Step 21: In cell F32, students should enter the formula, =C32-D32-E32.
- Step 23: Instruct students on whether or not they are allowed to print their worksheets, and what they are to submit for grading.

Data/Solution Files

Data file: EProj74.xlsx
Solution file: EProj74_solution.xlsx

Chapter 5: Advanced Printing, Formatting, and Editing

Lesson 34 Working with Graphics and Saving a Worksheet as a Web Page

What You Will Learn
- ✓ Inserting and Formatting Graphics
- ✓ Saving a Worksheet as a Web Page

Words to Know

Clip	Pictures
Clip art	Publishing
Clip Art task pane	Shape
Cropping handle	Web browser
HTML	Web page
Intranet	World Wide Web

Tips, Hints, and Pointers

- Discuss each of the skills listed in the What You Will Learn section, and ask students if they have used any of these skills before.
- Discuss the scenario covered in the Application Skills section, and preview the tasks students will perform for Intellidata Services.
- Key skills covered in this lesson include inserting and formatting graphics and saving a worksheet as a Web page.

Inserting and Formatting Graphics

- Ask students to leaf through their text and point out pages in which figures helped them to better understand a concept.
- Bring examples to class that illustrate how the use of figures, graphics, and other images help communicate the message of the text. Newsletters and promotional brochures that you receive through the mail might provide good examples.
- Students worked with clip art and other graphics in Lesson 8 of Word Chapter 1. Explain clip art as predrawn pictures that can be inserted in any Office application. Users can insert clip art from collections on their computers or from Microsoft Office Online.
- Demonstrate how to search for pictures and insert them in a worksheet.

- Clip art is an object that can be selected, edited, resized, positioned, and formatted independently from the surrounding data on the worksheet.
- **Try It! Inserting Clips from the Clip Art Task Pane, step 6:** Make sure the Photographs, Videos, and Audio options on the Results should be menu are deselected. Also, review with students the options on the drop-down menu for each clip.
- **SKILLS EXTENSION:** If students have an active Internet connection, you might encourage them to click the Find more at Office.com link at the bottom of the Clip Art task pane and explore the images available there.

Formatting Graphics

- When you select an object, such as clip art or a picture, sizing handles display around its borders. In addition, tabs specifically for use in editing and formatting the object become available on the Ribbon. For example, when you select a picture, the Picture Tools Format tab becomes available.
- Many of the commands you use to edit or format one type of object are the same as or similar to those you use to edit or format other types of objects.
- **Try It! Changing One Picture for Another:** The purpose of this Try It is to demonstrate that you

can replace a graphic object the same way you replace or overwrite other cell data. Simply select it and insert the new object in place of it. Make sure students replace the clip art image they inserted in cell A1.

- **SKILLS EXTENSION:** Have students click the Crop drop-down arrow and explore the options on the menu. These are:
  - Crop to Shape: Displays a gallery of shapes to which you can crop the picture.
  - Aspect Ratio: Enables you to crop the image to a common aspect ratio, which is the ratio between the picture's height and its width.
  - Fill: This allows you to fill the selected shape with as much of the original picture as possible.
  - Fit: This allows you to fit all of the picture within the selected shape.
- **Try It! Resizing a Graphic Object:** Review how to resize an object to make it larger or smaller by dragging a sizing handle. When resizing a graphic, remind students that dragging a corner handle will maintain the graphic's aspect ratio. Dragging a side or top or bottom handle will distort the image.
- Drag the sizing handles to resize a picture using the mouse. Enter a precise size using the Shape Height and Shape Width boxes in the Size group on the Picture Tools Format tab of the Ribbon.
- **TROUBLESHOOTING:** Remind students that they can use the Undo button on the Quick Access Toolbar to undo sizing changes.
- **QUICK QUIZ:** What is the difference between cropping a graphic and resizing it?

  Cropping means to trim and remove unwanted portions of a picture whereas resizing means to change its overall size without removing any portion of it.
- When you select a graphic, commands for editing and formatting become available on the Picture Tools Format tab of the Ribbon.
- Each type of object has a gallery of styles you can use to apply a collection of formatting settings, such as outlines and fills. You can also apply outlines and fill settings independently.
- You can use effects such as 3-D and shadows to format objects.
- Use the buttons in the Adjust group on the Picture Tools Format tab to modify the appearance of a picture.
- Use the Corrections gallery to sharpen or soften a picture, or adjust the brightness and contrast.
- Use the Color gallery to change the color palette, saturation, or tone of the picture.
- Use the Artistic Effects gallery to apply an effect to make a picture look more like a sketch, drawing, or painting.
- **CUSTOMIZED INSTRUCTION: Less Advanced Students and Special Needs Students:** Have students start a blank workbook and insert a picture from clip art that represents one of their hobbies or interests. Have them experiment with the editing and formatting options on the Picture Tools Format tab to give the clip art different looks.
- **CUSTOMIZED INSTRUCTION: More Advanced Students:** Have students start a blank workbook and insert a picture from clip art that represents one of their hobbies or interests. Then, have them gather statistics on the hobby or interest, such as how many participants, how much money a person typically spends in a year on it, etc. Have them enter the data in the workbook and format it and the clip art attractively.

Saving a Worksheet as a Web Page

- Review the procedure for publishing to a Web page and describe the available formats. When worksheet data is saved as a Web page, Excel formats it with the HTML codes required to display the data correctly in a Web browser such as Internet Explorer. Web pages may be published to Internet or intranet servers.
- Have students open a previously saved workbook or create a sample worksheet in a new workbook and choose to save it as a Web page. Point out the options for saving the file in the Save As dialog box. Remind students of the importance of specifying a page title. Have students publish the worksheet and view the data in a Web browser.
- Figure Focus
- Discuss options in the Publish as Web Page dialog box. In workbooks with several sheets or charts, the user can select which to publish from the Choose drop-down list.
- **Try It! Republishing a Worksheet or Workbook:** Explain to students that if they make changes to the worksheet, they must republish the data. They can choose the AutoRepublish option in the Publish as Web Page dialog box if they want to have Excel automatically republish the data when changes are made.
- **Try It! Opening a Web Page File in a Web Browser:** Students will need Internet or intranet access and a Web browser to complete this Try It.

Project 75—Publishing to the Web

- Steps 6-8: Remind students that they will have to click the Crop button when they are done cropping in order to complete the procedure.
- Step 14: Students may select a different computer-related clip art if desired.
- Step 16: Instruct students on whether or not they are allowed to print their worksheets, and what they are to submit for grading.
- **DESIGN FORUM:** Ask students to comment on the colors used in Intellidata's corporate logo and the computer clip art image. Do they think the colors look good together? Discuss the concept of color harmony, which is a combination or scheme of colors that look good together. Three common color harmonies are:
  - Monochromatic: A color harmony that uses only one color. It can include different values of one color or include neutrals.
  - Analogous: A color harmony that includes two or more colors that are next to each other on the color wheel, such as orange, yellow-orange, and yellow.
  - Complementary: A color harmony that uses two colors that are direct opposites on the color wheel, such as yellow and violet or red and green.

Project 76—Publishing to the Web

- Step 3: Students should resize the image by dragging a corner handle. To apply the Oval picture style, they should click the Picture Tools Format tab and then click the More button on the Picture Styles gallery. They should select one of the Oval options in the gallery. To recolor the image, they should click the Color button on the Picture Tools Format tab and select the specified option.
- Step 6: Make sure students change the data specified on Figure 34-3.
- Step 8: Instruct students on whether or not they are allowed to print their worksheets, and what they are to submit for grading.
- **JOB FOCUS:** Explain to students what a hosting, management, and warehousing company such as the fictitious Intellidata might do. The services range but most companies provide businesses with information technology services that include software tools to manage business processes, online data backup and warehousing, and general Internet-related services, such as Web hosting.
- **CUSTOMIZED INSTRUCTION: More Advanced Students:** Have students research on the Web companies that provide similar services to the fictitious Intellidata. In either a Word document or a PowerPoint presentation, have them prepare a brief summary of one of the companies and the services it offers.

Data/Solution Files

Data files:
ETry34.xlsx
ETry34_photo.jpg
ETry34_toy.jpg
EProj75.xlsx
EProj75_Intellidata_logo.gif
EProj76.xlsx

Solution files:
ETry34_solution.xlsx
ETry34_solution.mhtml
ETry34_Web_solution.mht
EProj75_solution.xlsx
EProj76_Newprod_solution.mht
EProj76_solution.xlsx
EProj76_Usage_solution.mht

Lesson 35 Working with Web Data

What You Will Learn
- ✓ Copying Data from a Web Page
- ✓ Creating a Web Query

Words to Know
Refresh
Web query

Tips, Hints, and Pointers

- Discuss each of the skills listed in the What You Will Learn section, and ask students if they have used any of these skills before.
- Discuss the scenario covered in the Application Skills section, and preview the tasks students will perform for HelpNow MedCenter.
- Key skills covered in this lesson include copying data from a Web page and creating a Web Query.

Copying Data from a Web Page
- Discuss situations in which a user might want to copy data from a Web page into Excel. "Data" may consist of tabular data, text, hyperlinks, or even graphics.
- Caution students that Web page copyrights must be respected; no user should ever copy data from a Web page and pass it off as his or her own data. When data is copied for a report or other publication, proper permission should be secured and the source of the data should be indicated.
- If students have Internet access, have them log in to the browser's start page and practice copying information from this page and pasting it in an Excel worksheet. Or, you might have students visit your school's home page from which they can copy information.
- **Try It! Copying Data from a Web Page:** This exercise uses a Web simulation with existing Web pages provided with the data files for the lesson. No Internet access is required.
- **Step 2:** Note that a data file is required. Remind students if necessary where to find the data files for this lesson.
- **Try It! Changing the Format of Pasted Data:** Remind students that the Paste Options button appears below the data you've pasted. Click it to display the pasting options available.

- **QUICK QUIZ:** You have found on a Web page exactly the data you need for a report. What should your next step be?

    Contact the Web site's author and request permission to use the data. If permission is granted, you should also indicate the source of the data in your report.

- **CUSTOMIZED INSTRUCTION: ESOL Students:** Have students determine the currency exchange rate between the U.S. dollar and the currency from their country of origin. They can use an online currency conversion calculator, look up the information in the business section of the daily newspaper, or contact a local bank.

Creating a Web Query
- Introduce a Web query as a feature that retrieves data stored on the Internet or an intranet and imports it into a worksheet.
- Differentiate between copying and pasting data and using a Web query to import data into an Excel worksheet. A Web query allows for quick selection of tabular data on a Web page. External data imported by means of a Web query can also be refreshed to update the data when the page from which it was imported changes.
- Have students create a new Web query and display the Microsoft home page (www.microsoft.com) in the New Web Query dialog box. Have them navigate to any page on the site and click the yellow arrow next to a table. Next, they should click Import and choose a cell.
- **CUSTOMIZED INSTRUCTION: Less Advanced Students:** Review the process of creating Web queries with less advanced students. This topic may seem complex to some until they have practiced importing data a few times.

- Discuss the tools on the Data tab of the Ribbon and point out the Refresh All button that allows the user to update data from an outside source.
- **SKILLS EXTENSION:** Have students open a workbook that contains a Web query. Then ask them to click the Connections button on the Data tab of the Ribbon and examine the settings in the Workbook Connections dialog box. You may suggest that they also select the Properties and Add buttons and see what additional settings are shown there.
- **QUICK QUIZ:** When could a Web query be helpful in a worksheet?

  To allow viewers to read the latest information on a subject related to the worksheet; to post relevant contact information for help; to indicate sites of related information, etc.

Project 77—Updating Medication Infusion Rates

- This project uses a Web simulation with existing Web pages provided with the data files for this lesson. No Internet access is required.
- Step 5: Note that a data file is required. Remind students if necessary where to find the data files for this lesson. Make sure students read the note following this step for how to quickly copy the file's path.
- Step 9: Instruct students on whether or not they are allowed to print their worksheets, and what they are to submit for grading.

- **CURRICULUM CONNECTION:** Students may be familiar with the effects of drugs on the human system through their science class studies. Discuss labeling on over-the-counter drugs and cautions about side effects and exceeding the recommended dosage.
- **WORKPLACE SKILLS:** Explain to students that an infusion rate (or dosing rate) is a medical term that refers not just to the rate at which a drug is administered, but the desired rate at which a drug should be administered to achieve a steady state of a fixed dose which has been demonstrated to be therapeutically effective. Nurses and other medical professionals may perform complex calculations to determine the rate of infusion for a particular drug, or they may use infusion rate calculators.

Project 78—Copying Web Data

- This project uses a Web simulation with existing Web pages provided with the data files for this lesson. No Internet access is required.
- If you think it might be helpful to students, print out the worksheet page from the EProj78 solution file (shown in Figure 35-2) showing gridlines and row and column headings. To do this, open the Page Setup dialog box, click the Sheet tab, and select Gridlines and Row and column headings.
- Step 7: Instruct students on whether or not they are allowed to print their worksheets, and what they are to submit for grading.

Data/Solution Files

Data files:
    ETry35.xlsx
    ETry35_Table.htm
    EProj77.xlsx
    EProj77_Medication.htm
    EProj78.xlsx
    EProj78_Fees.mht

Solution files:
    ETry35_solution.xlsx
    EProj77_solution.xlsx
    EProj78_solution.xlsx

Lesson 36   Linking and Embedding Data

What You Will Learn

- ✓ Linking and Embedding Excel Data
- ✓ Embedding Data
- ✓ Linking Data
- ✓ Editing Embedded Data
- ✓ Editing Linked Data

Words to Know

Embed
Link

Tips, Hints, and Pointers

- Discuss each of the skills listed in the What You Will Learn section, and ask students if they have used any of these skills before.
- Discuss the scenario covered in the Application Skills section, and preview the tasks students will perform for Whole Grains Bread.
- Key skills covered in this lesson include linking and embedding Excel data, pasting a picture, and editing linked and embedded data.

Linking and Embedding Excel Data

- Discuss with students how Office 2010 applications are designed to make data sharing easy and efficient: Paste worksheet data in another application such as Word to avoid retyping the data. Link data to maintain a connection to the original worksheet. Embed worksheet data to preserve the ability to edit data using Excel tools.
- Students learned how to link and embed an Excel chart in Lesson 28 of Excel Chapter 3. Linking and embedding Excel data works in the same manner.
- You can link or embed worksheet data into another document, such as a Word document or PowerPoint presentation.

Embedding Data

- You can embed the data to ensure that your changes will not affect the original data.
- You may want to show students how to link or embed data as an icon. This is a good way to make data available without taking up a lot of space in a document. It is useful only in a document that will be viewed onscreen, however.

- **QUICK QUIZ:** If you change the formatting to Excel worksheet data that has been embedded in a PowerPoint slide, why doesn't the embedded data also show the formatting changes in the PowerPoint file?

   The embedded data does not maintain a connection to the original Excel worksheet data. It is stored in the PowerPoint file.

Linking Data

- If the source data is likely to change, you should link the data to its source, so that your data will automatically update. This is especially useful when the source data is updated by several different people in your organization.
- Spend some time discussing linking options. It is a common problem that linked documents become separated from one another when the source document is moved or renamed. Show students how to change the source of a linked document to restore the connection.
- **CURRICULUM CONNECTION:** Ask students to explain how they would manually calculate the average scores for tests and quizzes for the entire class. Then, ask them how they would determine the median Final Grade for the class.

   Answer: To calculate the average, you add all the scores and then divide the total by the number of scores. To find the median, you place all final grades in value order and determine which score falls in the middle.
- **CUSTOMIZED INSTRUCTION: Special Needs Students:** Remind physically challenged students

that they can use the familiar Ctrl+C, Ctrl+X, and Ctrl+V shortcuts to copy, cut, and paste data. However, the Ctrl+V shortcut only pastes a picture of the data; it doesn't work when you need to link or embed data.

Editing Embedded Data

- **Try It! Editing Embedded Data, step 2:** Point out the thick gray border surrounding the selected Excel data in the figure.
- **DESIGN FORUM:** Most experts suggest that the font size for slide text should be 24 points or larger. While the exercises in this lesson are designed to illustrate the ease with which you can share and update Excel data in PowerPoint slides, you might note that data such as these test grades may be better suited to be embedded in a Word document.
- **QUICK QUIZ:** How do you edit embedded Excel data?

  Double-click the embedded data to activate the Excel Ribbon and then edit the data as you would in an Excel worksheet.

Editing Linked Data

- **Try It! Editing Linked Data, step 3:** For the linking procedure to work properly, make sure students do not change the location of either the source or destination files.
- **Step 4:** Students should arrange the PowerPoint and Excel windows side-by-side. They can do this by clicking the Restore Down button for each window and then resizing and repositioning the windows as necessary.
- **Try It! Updating Links Manually, step 4:** Make sure students right-click the linked object in order to display the shortcut menu.

Project 79—Inventory Projections

- **Step 5:** Make sure students are on the FORECAST worksheet.

Step 8: Make sure students click the Paste drop-down arrow on the bottom portion of the Paste button.

- If they inadvertently click the top portion of the Paste button, they can click the Paste Options button and then click Picture.
- Step 9: Instruct students on whether or not they are allowed to print their worksheets, and what they are to submit for grading.

Project 80—Inventory Projections

- Students embed and link Excel worksheet data in a Word document.
- Make sure to instruct students on where they are to save the files.
- Step 8: To edit embedded data, students should double-click it to activate the Excel Ribbon within the Word document.
- Step 9: To edit linked data, students should double-click it, thereby opening the workbook in Excel. When they return to the Word document, they may have to update the link manually by right-clicking the data and selecting Update Link on the shortcut menu.
- Step 12: Instruct students on whether or not they are allowed to print their worksheets, and what they are to submit for grading.
- **WORKPLACE SKILLS:** Instead of predicting inventory needs based on current or past usage, some companies utilize just-in-time strategies. This is a method of reducing costs while improving quality and efficiency by limiting the amount of inventory a company keeps in stock. The business orders new inventory just-in-time to produce an order, instead of keeping unused inventory sitting around in a warehouse or storage facility. Ask students how a just-in-time strategy might work for Whole Grains Bread. To be successful, the company would need to form partnerships with local suppliers of various ingredients who could guarantee supplying the product on short notice.

Data/Solution Files

Data files:
ETry36.xlsx
ETry36_Grades.pptx
EProj79.xlsx
EProj79_Projections.docx
EProj80.xlsx
EProj80_Projections.docx

Solution files:
ETry36_solution.xlsx
ETry36_Grades_solution.pptx
EProj79_solution.xlsx
EProj79_Projections_solution.docx
EProj80_solution.xlsx
EProj80_Projections_solution.docx

Lesson 37 Working with Workbooks

What You Will Learn
- ✓ Creating a Workbook from a Template
- ✓ Changing from Workbook to Workbook
- ✓ Comparing Workbooks

Words to Know
Template

Tips, Hints, and Pointers

- Discuss each of the skills listed in the What You Will Learn section, and ask students if they have used any of these skills before.
- Discuss the scenario covered in the Application Skills section, and preview the tasks students will perform for Whole Grains Bread.
- Key skills covered in this lesson include creating a workbook from a template or another workbook, switching between workbooks, and comparing workbooks.

Creating a Workbook from a Template

- Have students click the Sample templates link in the New Workbook dialog box and explore the available templates. Remind students how a template can save time in creating and formatting a worksheet.
- Discuss ways in which students might use the templates available in Excel; for example, they could use a budget template to set up a personal budget that helps them monitor how they spend and save money.
- **WORKPLACE SKILLS:** Explain to students the purpose of a billing statement. It is a business document that summarizes a customer's account with the issuing company. The statement is designed primarily for repeat customers who may purchase several goods and services from a business over a given period of time. It typically shows the charges the customer has made and any payments the customer has made toward the balance. Students may be familiar with billing statements from credit card companies.
- **CUSTOMIZED INSTRUCTION: Special Needs Students:** The worksheet templates provided with Excel can save formatting time and minimize the number of keystrokes a physically challenged person has to make.
- **CUSTOMIZED INSTRUCTION: More Advanced Students:** Have students open the Time Card template and modify it so they can track how they spend their time during a typical day. For example, they might change the categories (Regular Hours, Overtime, Sick, and Vacation) to School, Homework, Work, Leisure, etc.
- **Try It! Creating a New Workbook from an Office.com Template:** Students will need an active Internet connection in order to complete this Try It.
- **Try It! Searching Office.com for a Template:** Students will need an active Internet connection in order to complete this Try It.
- **Step 5:** You might note that some templates may contain paid advertisements that link you to the sponsor's Web site.
- **WORKPLACE SKILLS:** Help students understand the difference between an invoice and a billing statement. An invoice is a bill for goods or services provided whereas a billing statement summarizes the status of a customer's account at a particular point in time.

Changing from Workbook to Workbook

- The text discusses the Switch Windows method for change from workbook to workbook. This method is most useful when you have several workbooks open at a time.
- When fewer windows are open, you might find using taskbar buttons to be the easiest method for switching between windows.

Comparing Workbooks

- Demonstrate how to use the View Side by Side feature to view two workbooks simultaneously. Be

sure to point out how the Synchronous Scrolling option works and how to turn it off.
- Review how to arrange open documents on the desktop using options in the Arrange Windows dialog box.
- **QUICK QUIZ:** What is the difference between the Tiled window arrangement and the Cascade arrangement?

    Tiled windows are arranged in small, even rectangles within the window whereas cascaded windows are arranged in a stack with only the title bars in full view.

Project 81—Inventory Projections

- Step 9: Urge students to proofread the data when they are finished entering it.
- Step 10: Instruct students on whether or not they are allowed to print their worksheets, and what they are to submit for grading.

Project 82

- If students do not have an active Internet connection to download the invoice template from Office.com, they should use Windows Explorer or the Computer window to copy the **EProj82_Sales Invoice** template from the data files for this lesson.
- Step 4: If necessary, explain how to arrange windows side by side. On the View tab, click the View Side by Side button. Make sure students turn off Synchronous Scrolling.
- Step 13: Instruct students on whether or not they are allowed to print their worksheets, and what they are to submit for grading.

Data/Solution Files

Data files: ETry37.xlsx
EProj81.xlsx
EProj81_Schedule 7-20.xlsx
EProj82.xlsx
EProj82_Sales Invoice.xltx

Solution files: ETry37_solution.xlsx
EProj81_solution.xlsx
EProj82_solution.xlsx

- **WORKPLACE SKILLS:** An invoice is a business document prepared by a seller of goods or services listing all such items sold, and presented to the buyer for payment. Review the different parts of the invoice shown in Figure 37-2.
- **DESIGN FORUM:** Most templates available in Office 2010 programs are professionally designed. Have students evaluate the design of the Invoice template they used in this project. Ask students for ideas on how the design and appearance of the invoice could be improved or enhanced to more strongly communicate the Whole Grains Bread corporate image.
- **JOB FOCUS:** Many companies employ a billing manager or accounts receivable clerk to issue invoices and oversee billing practices. In addition to preparing, verifying, and processing invoices, this person may also be responsible for coordinating and resolving sales tax issues, tracking payments, developing payment plans, and collecting unpaid bills, and maintaining the company's general ledger.
- **CURRICULUM CONNECTION:** Have students calculate a sales tax of 6%, 6.5%, and 7% on the subtotal shown on the invoice in Figure 37-2.

    Answer: 6% sales tax = $116.13

    6.5% sales tax = $125.81

    7% sales tax = $135.49

    Have students research the sales tax rate in their state. How does it compare to neighboring states?

Lesson 38 Working with Comments and Modifying Page Setup

What You Will Learn

- ✓ Inserting Comments
- ✓ Printing Multiple Copies of a Workbook or Worksheet
- ✓ Modifying Page Setup
- ✓ Using Page Layout View
- ✓ Inserting Headers and Footers

Words to Know

Comment
Footer
Header
Page Setup
Print options
Scaling

Tips, Hints, and Pointers

- Discuss each of the skills listed in the What You Will Learn section, and ask students if they have used any of these skills before.
- Discuss the scenario covered in the Application Skills section, and preview the tasks students will perform for Voyager Travel Adventures.
- Key skills covered in this lesson include inserting comments, printing multiple copies of a workbook, modifying the page setup, and inserting headers and footers.

Inserting Comments

- Explain that you insert comments on a worksheet to annotate text, communicate with readers, or to attach reminders or questions to certain data.
- Demonstrate how to insert a comment in a worksheet cell.
- Identify the red triangle that appears in a cell containing a comment. Note how the comment pops open when you hover the pointer over it and how the author of the comment is identified.
- Review the options in the Comments group on the Review tab. Make sure students understand how to use each button.
- **Try It! Displaying and Editing Comments, step 1:** Point out that you can also right-click a cell containing a comment and click Show/Hide Comments to display or hide all comments in a worksheet.

- **Step 5:** Explain that you can also right-click a cell containing a comment and click Edit Comment on the shortcut menu.
- **CUSTOMIZED INSTRUCTION: Special Needs Students:** The Accessibility Checker is a new tool available in Microsoft Word, Excel, and PowerPoint 2010. It is designed to help you identify problems with your files that could potentially limit a person with a disability from accessing or understanding the content of the file. To use the Accessibility Checker, click File > Info. Under Prepare for Sharing, an alert will appear if any accessibility issues are detected. Click the Check for Issues button and then select Check Accessibility. You are returned to your file where the Accessibility Checker task pane displays, listing the issues it has detected.
- **CUSTOMIZED INSTRUCTION: Less Advanced Students:** Have students create a workbook that lists all the items they have purchased within the last week along with the cost for the item. This can include food, clothing, school supplies, and entertainment-related purchases. If they don't remember the price, have them estimate it. Have them insert at least three comments on the worksheet about whether or not they think their purchase was a wise one or a good deal. Encourage them to explain their opinions.

Printing Multiple Copies of a Workbook or Worksheet

- Demonstrate how to specify the number of copies to print in Backstage view.
- Have students click the drop-down arrows on the various printing and page setup options available in Backstage view.
- Explain the value of reviewing the preview of the worksheet before printing it. The preview enables you to identify awkward breaks in the data.
- Point out the Page Setup link in Backstage view that opens the Page Setup dialog box.
- **QUICK QUIZ:** What would happen if you chose to print multiple copies of a multipage worksheet as uncollated?

  Uncollated means you would print the specified number of copies of page 1, then page 2, then page 3, and so on. You would then have to manually collate the pages to assemble each copy of the file.

Modifying Page Setup

- Demonstrate the different methods for opening the Page Setup dialog box: 1.) Click File > Print. In Backstage view, click the Page Setup link at the bottom of the screen. 2.) Click the Page Layout tab and then click the Page Setup dialog box launcher.
- Explore the four tabs in the Page Setup dialog box and demonstrate how to change options to control how the worksheet will look when printed.
- Make sure students understand the various page setup options discussed in the text:
  - Orientation: This determines the way the content prints on the page. In landscape orientation, the file prints wider than it is long. In portrait orientation, the file prints longer than it is wide.
  - Scaling: This option enables you to control the height and width of the worksheet data so it fills a specified number of pages.
  - Paper size: This option enables you to print on various sizes of paper, labels, and envelopes.
  - Print quality: Through this option, you can control the print quality and set the file to print in color or black-and-white only.
  - Margins: Margins are the white space between the worksheet data and the edge of the paper. You can change these to better accommodate worksheet data.

Using Page Layout View

- Demonstrate how to switch to Page Layout view. Point out the differences between this view and Normal view; i.e., rulers are displayed as are headers and footers.
- Make sure students can identify the margin edge. The margin appears in a light shade of gray. The selected cell is in a darker shade of gray.
- Point out the margin identifiers on the ruler and distinguish between them and the highlights for the active cell, which is B6.
- **QUICK QUIZ:** How can changing print orientation save resources and time?

  Landscape orientation can often print a wide worksheet on one page rather than two, saving paper and printing time.
- **CUSTOMIZED INSTRUCTION: Special Needs Students:** Students with visual challenges may find it easier to work in Page Layout view when reviewing their documents and making adjustments because they can make most changes directly in the worksheet rather than within various dialog boxes.

Inserting Headers and Footers

- Remind students that headers print at the top of each page and footers at the bottom of each page.
- Demonstrate how to insert a header or footer in Page Layout view. Click in a header or footer placeholder to activate the Header & Footer Tools Design tab. On the tab, click the Header button or the Footer button, and then select from the list of supplied headers and footers and preview the result.
- Show students how to delete a header and footer (choose None from the Header or Footer drop-down lists).
- Demonstrate how to create a custom header in Page Layout view Click in a placeholder, and on the Header & Footer Tools Design tab, explore the options in the Header & Footer Elements group.
- Let students experiment with creating their own custom headers and footers in Page Layout view. Encourage students to create a custom header by typing or using the supplied buttons.
- Encourage students to change font, font style, and the font size of their custom header text and then preview the result.
- **Try It! Creating a Custom Header and Footer in Page Layout View, step 6:** Students may type text of their choice in the header, or select a predefined header element, such as the current date.

Chapter 5 | 99

- **Step 7:** Encourage students to experiment with the various options listed.
- **SKILLS EXTENSION:** Have students display the Header & Footer Tools Design tab in their ETry38 file. On a sheet of paper, have them write a header that has the sheet name in the left section, the file name in the center section, and the path name in the right section.
- **CUSTOMIZED INSTRUCTION: Less Advanced Students:** Have students open the Page Setup dialog box. On the Header/Footer tab, have them click Custom Header. Have them hover their mouse over each of the buttons to identify the elements that can be inserted in a custom header or footer.
- Discuss with students what text will appear in a header (or footer) when they click each of the buttons labeled. Explain that the buttons are the same in the Footer dialog box.
- Make sure students understand that in Normal view, they can change the format of header and footer text by using the Format Text button in the Header or Footer dialog boxes. In Page Layout view, they must select the header or footer text, and then switch to the Home tab to use the formatting options in the Font group.

Project 83—Printing a Cost Estimate

- Step 4: Students will need to click the Go to Footer button on the Header & Footer Tools Design tab in order to bring the footer sections into view.
- Step 5: Have students carefully review the preview of the worksheet before continuing to step 6. Ask them to comment on why the orientation and scaling of the worksheet should be changed.

Data/Solution Files

Data files: ETry38.xlsx
               EProj83.xlsx
               EProj84.xlsx
               EProj84_voyager_travel_logo.gif
Solution files: ETry38_solution.xlsx
               EProj83_solution.xlsx
               EProj84_solution.xlsx

- Step 8: Instruct students on whether or not they are allowed to print their worksheets, and what they are to submit for grading.
- **DESIGN FORUM:** Because a document such as this cost estimate is being prepared for a customer, it's important that it appear professional and easy to read and interpret. Changing the orientation and scaling the data so it fits on one sheet of paper provides the customer with a single, easy-to-read itemized list of the trip's costs. Ask students if there are other design and page setup formats that could be applied to make the estimate even more "customer-friendly."

Project 84—Printing a Cost Estimate

- Step 3: To insert a comment in a cell, click the Review tab and then click the New Comment button.
- Step 4: You can show all comments by clicking the Show All Comments button on the Review tab.
- Step 5: To delete a comment, right-click the cell containing it and click Delete Comment on the shortcut menu.
- Step 6: Students can create the header and footer in Page Layout view or through the Header/Footer tab in the Page Setup dialog box.
- Step 6c: To insert a picture, click the Picture button (on the Header & Footer Tools Design tab in Page Layout view or in the Footer dialog box accessed through the Page Setup dialog box) and navigate to the data files for this lesson.
- Step 10: Instruct students on whether or not they are allowed to print their worksheets, and what they are to submit for grading.

Lesson 39 Modifying the Print Options

What You Will Learn

- ✓ Inserting Page Breaks
- ✓ Using Page Break Preview
- ✓ Setting the Print Area
- ✓ Repeating Row and Column Labels
- ✓ Selecting Other Sheet Tab Options

Words to Know

Gridlines
Page break
Page Break Preview
Print area
Print titles

Tips, Hints, and Pointers

- Discuss each of the skills listed in the What You Will Learn section, and ask students if they have used any of these skills before.
- Discuss the scenario covered in the Application Skills section, and preview the tasks students will perform for HealthNow MedCenter.
- Key skills covered in this lesson include inserting page breaks, setting the print area, and repeating row and column labels.

Inserting Page Breaks

- Discuss with students how page breaks can be very important when working with long or wide worksheets. It is helpful to be able to specify where the worksheet can be divided for the best appearance.
- Have students enter data in a new workbook and use fill and copy and paste to create a large worksheet (at least 70 rows). Students should preview the worksheet and note the dashed line page breaks that display when they return to Normal or Page Break Preview view.
- Have students insert a manual page break at a logical point in their sample worksheets (such as between groups of data). Preview to see the result of the break.
- Encourage students to practice moving page breaks by dragging them with the pointer.
- **Try It! Setting Manual Page Breaks, step 5:** Ask students how they think the worksheet will print with the manual page break they just inserted. You might have them preview the worksheet at this point so they can see that the break will cause the worksheet to print on four pages.
- **DESIGN FORUM:** Managing the page breaks in a worksheet that contains many rows and columns of data can have a huge impact on the reader's ability to analyze and interpret the information. When designing your worksheets, pay special attention to where breaks occur in the data and how best to organize it for optimum readability.
- **QUICK QUIZ:** Why would you want to change the position of the automatic page breaks Excel inserts?

    To avoid breaking a section or to make sure a chart prints all on one page.

Using Page Break Preview

- Discuss Page Break Preview, a special view that displays automatic and manual page breaks and allows you to adjust their location.
- Differentiate between Print Preview and Page Break Preview. Have students display Page Break Preview and identify the page breaks (solid or dashed blue lines).
- Demonstrate the two methods for removing a page break: In Page Break Preview, you can drag the solid blue page break line of the worksheet page; or, click the cell below or to the right of the page break, and on the Page Layout tab, click the Breaks button and then click Remove Page Break.

Setting the Print Area

- Explain that you can set the print area using these different methods:

- In Normal view or Page Break Preview, highlight the print area, click the Page Layout tab, click the Print Area button, and then click Set Print Area.
- On the Page Layout tab, click the Page Setup dialog box launcher. On the Sheet tab, click the Collapse dialog button for the Print area. In the worksheet, select the range or ranges of cells to be included in the print area. Return to the Sheet tab, and click OK.

- **QUICK QUIZ:** When would you want to print only a selection of cells?

  When you want to keep the rest of a worksheet confidential, or to have a hard copy of a specific section of a large worksheet.

Repeating Row and Column Labels

- Make sure students understand the difference between titles and row and column headings. Titles are those labels entered on a sheet to identify the data below them or to the right. For example, in the figure on this page, the titles are the labels entered in row 8. The item numbers in column A could also be used as titles to print on each page of the worksheet printout. Row and column headings are the column letters and row numbers that identify cell addresses.
- **Try It! Repeating Row and Column Labels, step 5:** Students may choose to repeat columns if desired. Encourage them to repeat the first two columns of labels, which are the item numbers and product descriptions.

Selecting Other Sheet Tab Options

- Discuss the various printing options on the Sheet tab and when you might use each.
- Demonstrate the two methods for setting gridlines to print: 1.) Click the Page Layout tab and in the Sheet Options group, under Gridlines, click Print. 2.) Open the Page Setup dialog box, and on the Sheet tab, click the Gridlines box.
- **DESIGN FORUM:** When rows of data extend across many rows, it is a good idea to print gridlines so that the reader of a printout can more easily follow the data across the page. Another option is to apply alternating shades of color to rows or groups of rows.
- **QUICK QUIZ:** What is the difference between printing titles and printing row and column headings?

  Titles are those labels entered on a sheet to identify the data below them or to the right whereas row and column headings are the row numbers and column letters that identify cell addresses.

Project 85—Balance Sheet

- Step 4: Make sure students click through all the pages in the preview.
- Step 9: Students are referred to Figure 39-1. Make sure they drag the page break to include rows 36 and 37, which contain the Total Net Worth and Total Liabilities and Net Worth figures. This data is not visible on the figure.
- Step 12: Instruct students on whether or not they are allowed to print their worksheets, and what they are to submit for grading.

Project 86—Balance Sheet

- Step 5: To enter their name, students should click in the left header placeholder and type the name. Encourage them to format it similarly to the text on the rest of the worksheet.
- Step 6: To set non-contiguous print areas, select the first print area in the worksheet and then on the Page Layout tab, click the Print Area button, and then click Set Print Area. Select the second print area, click the Print Area button, and then click Add to Print Area.
- Step 9: Instruct students on whether or not they are allowed to print their worksheets, and what they are to submit for grading.
- Have students compare the worksheets shown in Figure 39-1 and 39-2. Ask them to comment on the differences and what caused them.
- **WORKPLACE SKILLS:** A balance sheet is an essential financial record for any type of business. It shows a business's financial situation at a particular time, such as the end of a quarter. A balance sheet shows the relationship between the business's assets, liabilities, and owner's equity.
  - Assets include cash on hand, checking or other money accounts, accounts receivable, real estate that the business owns, office equipment, and vehicles such as company cars or trucks.
  - Liabilities include all debts that the business must pay to creditors, suppliers, or banks. These are also called accounts payable.
  - Owner's equity (referred to as Net Worth in the worksheet shown in the figure) is the amount of money invested in the business by its owners or shareholders.

  In a financially healthy business, assets equal liabilities plus owner's equity; that is the liabilities and owner's equity must balance with the assets, which is why this financial document is called a balance sheet.

- **WORKLACE SKILLS:** Ask students to explain what the pie chart shown in Figure 39-3 is illustrating. Define the difference between fixed assets and current assets. A current asset is one that can be quickly converted into cash within one calendar year. It is said to have high liquidity. Point out that the largest share of the pie – long-term investments – often include bonds and shares in other publicly traded companies. Ask students who have taken accounting or business classes to share their thoughts on the medical center's asset distribution.

Data/Solution Files

Data files: ETry39.xlsx
                EProj85.xlsx
                EProj86.xlsx

Solution files: ETry39_solution.xlsx
                EProj85_solution.xlsx
                EProj86_solution.xlsx

Lesson 40 Using Copy and Paste Special

What You Will Learn

- ✓ Using Copy and Paste Options
- ✓ Transposing Data
- ✓ Combining Data with Copy and Paste Special

Words to Know

Copied cells
Destination cells
Paste Special
Transpose

Tips, Hints, and Pointers

- Discuss each of the skills listed in the What You Will Learn section, and ask students if they have used any of these skills before.
- Discuss the scenario covered in the Application Skills section and preview the tasks students will perform for Voyager Travel Adventures.
- Key skills covered in this lesson include using copy and paste special, and transposing data in a worksheet.

Using Copy and Paste Special

- Remind students that Paste Special options control how copied data is pasted from the Clipboard. They can use Paste Special, for example, to transpose data so that a copied column of cells can be pasted into a row of cells.
- Remind students of Word's Format Painter and point out that Excel's Format Painter works the same way. Encourage students to practice using it to copy formats.
- Have students open a new workbook and enter some labels and values and a formula or two. Ask them to copy some data and open the Paste Special dialog box. Encourage students to try each of the Paste options in their sample worksheet.
- **QUICK QUIZ:** When might you need to copy only the results of a formula to another location?

  Totals from one worksheet might be copied to a summary worksheet; because only the value is important in the summary, the formula would not need to be copied.

- **Try It! Using Paste Special Commands on the Paste Options Menu, step 4:** Make sure students click the top Paste portion of the button, and not the drop-down arrow.

- **Step 11:** Make sure students click the Values & Source Formatting button on the Paste drop-down menu after hovering over the various buttons in step 10.
- **Step 12:** Using the description of the various Paste options, quiz students on the name and function of each button shown in the figure of the Paste Options drop-down menu that follows this step.

Transposing Data

- In a sample worksheet, attempt to copy a column of data and paste it in a row of selected cells. You will not achieve the results expected. Repeat the operation using the Paste Special Transpose option. If the column you copied includes a formula, point out how the formula's cell references have adjusted.
- Point out that pasting data in a cell usually overwrites the cell's contents, but the user may sometimes want to combine the pasted data with the cell's existing contents to update them.
- Encourage students to think of situations when this feature might be useful, such as keeping a running total of sales or inventory amounts.

Combining Data with Copy and Paste Special

- Demonstrate how to combine data using the Paste Special dialog box's Operation options. Stress that this feature does not use formulas to change the data; there will be no record in the cell of the data's adjustment.
- **SKILLS EXTENSION:** Have students enter some single-digit values in a new worksheet, copy one value, and display the Paste Special dialog box. Have students practice using each of the Operation commands with their sample values.

- **QUICK QUIZ:** When would it be useful to combine copied data with existing data in worksheet cells?

  To keep track of a running sales total week by week, for example, or subtract sold items from an inventory.

Project 87—Project Analysis

- Step 12: Students can widen columns as needed to display all the data.
- Step 13: Instruct students on whether or not they are allowed to print their worksheets, and what they are to submit for grading.

Project 88—Project Analysis

- Step 3a: In the EProj88_Revenues file, select the first range, click Copy, and then in the second workbook, select the corresponding range, click the Paste drop-down arrow, and then click the Formatting button. Follow this procedure to copy the formatting from the second range.
- Step 4: To transpose value and number formats, click the range in EProj88_Revenues, and click Copy. In the second workbook, select the range B10:H10, click the Paste drop-down arrow, and click Paste Special. In the Paste Special dialog box, click the Values and number formats option and then click the Transpose box.
- Step 5: To combine the ranges using addition, select the range in the EProj88_Revenues file and click Copy. In the other workbook, click the range B10:H10, click the Paste drop-down arrow, and click Paste Special. In the Paste Special dialog box, in the Operation section, click Add, and then click OK. Repeat for the D10:D16 range in the EProj88_Revenues file.
- Step 6a: Enter the formula that subtracts the projected revenue for a project from the quarter 3 total.
- Step 7: Instruct students to switch to Page Layout view, click the center header placeholder, and enter their name.
- Step 8: Instruct students on whether or not they are allowed to print their worksheets, and what they are to submit for grading. To change orientation and scaling, students can open the Page Setup dialog box (either through the Page Layout tab or the Print tab on the File tab) and select the appropriate settings on the Page tab.
- **WORKPLACE SKILLS:** The revenue analysis sheet is a quick and easy way for a company to review its sales project by project. Ask students why a restoration project might not meet its projected revenue. Some reasons are the project was not completed on time so the company could not collect complete payment from the client; the markup on labor or supplies had to be modified due to changing market conditions; or expenses incurred were higher than anticipated, thus depleting revenue.

Data/Solution Files

Data files:	ETry40.xlsx
	EProj87.xlsx
	EProj88.xlsx
	EProj88_Revenues.xlsx
Solution files:	ETry40_solution.xlsx
	EProj87_solution.xlsx
	EProj88_solution.xlsx

Lesson 41 Moving and Linking Data Between Workbooks

What You Will Learn
- ✓ **Using Drag-and-Drop Between Windows**
- ✓ **Linking Workbooks**

Words to Know

Dependent
Drag-and-drop
External references

Link
Source

Tips, Hints, and Pointers

- Discuss each of the skills listed in the What You Will Learn section, and ask students if they have used any of these skills before.
- Discuss the scenario covered in the Application Skills section and preview the tasks students will perform for Whole Grains Bread.
- Key skills covered in this lesson include dragging and dropping data between workbooks and linking workbooks.

Using Drag-and-Drop Between Windows

- Explore situations in which it would be necessary to share data between workbooks. Remind students how to arrange open workbooks to display on the desktop at the same time, and show them how to drag data from one workbook to another.
- As students learned in Lesson 9 of Excel Chapter 1, the drag-and-drop feature enables you to use the mouse to copy or move a range of cells simply by dragging them.
- You drag and drop between workbooks the same way you do on the same worksheet. Select a range to copy or move, and then you use the border surrounding the range to drag the data to a different location. When you release the mouse button, the data is "dropped" in that location. An outline of the selection appears as you drag it to its new location on the worksheet.
- You can use drag-and-drop to move *or* copy data. To copy data using drag-and-drop, simply hold down the Ctrl key as you drag.
- Insert, delete, move, and copy operations may affect formulas, so you should check the formulas after you have used drag-and-drop to be sure that they are correct.
- **TROUBLESHOOTING:** If a drag-and-drop action does not move data correctly, use the Undo feature to undo it and try again. If you inadvertently move data instead of copying it, click the Undo button, and remember to hold down the Ctrl key as you drag.

Linking Workbooks

- Review the concepts related to linking. A link is a connection between a source file and a destination or dependent file.
- Demonstrate how to link a cell or range from the source workbook to a dependent workbook. Modify the data in the source workbook and then show students how the dependent workbook displays the update.
- Have students open two workbooks and arrange them side by side. Encourage students to practice moving and copying data between the workbooks using drag-and-drop. Then, have students designate one of the open workbooks as the source and the other as the dependent workbook. Ask them to enter a column of numbers in the source workbook and use AutoSum to sum the column.
- Have students copy the cell containing the sum and use Paste Link in the Paste Special dialog box to paste it in the dependent workbook. Ask students to view the external reference in the dependent workbook's Formula bar. They can change a number in the source workbook to see the sum update in both workbooks.

- Stress that saving [cut off]
  folder makes [cut off]
  locate the so[cut off]
  workbooks be[cut off]
  reestablish th[cut off]
- **QUICK QUIZ:**
  time and ensur[cut off]
  *Rather than ree[cut off]
  each time it cha[cut off]
  updated via the [cut off]
  automatic update[cut off]
  dependent workb[cut off]*

Project 89—Tax Re[cut off]

- The title of this proj[cut off] appear as "Inventor[cut off] should be Tax Retur[cut off]
- Steps 1 and 3: Stude[cut off] numbers in the works[cut off] These worksheets clo[cut off] from which they were [cut off] select the actual row n[cut off] line items.
- Step 9: Instruct students[cut off] submit for grading.
- **WORKPLACE SKILLS:** [cut off] concept of taxes. A tax is [cut off] government, which in turn [cut off] for public resources, such [cut off] schools, and libraries. Ther[cut off] …e basic categories of taxes:
  - Incomes taxes are based on wages and other earnings.
  - Consumption taxes are based on things we buy, such as computers or gasoline.
  - Asset taxes are based on things we already own, such as houses or cars.

  Many students may be familiar with paying income taxes. Income tax is a percentage of your income that you pay to the government. Each year, you must file income tax returns for the income you earned the previous year. Income tax returns are forms on which you calculate the amount of income tax you owe. You file federal tax returns to the Internal Revenue Services (IRS), the agency responsible for collecting federal taxes, and you file tax returns with your state's revenue …tment.

0—Tax Returns

e of this project in the student textbook may as "Inventory Analysis," but the correct title e Tax Returns.

and 2: Students will see two sets of row in the worksheets used in this project. rksheets closely replicate the IRS forms 1 they were derived. Make sure students actual row numbers instead of the tax

e that you are copying data from the book. In this case, it is the EProj90 file. _TaxWS workbook is the destination

's step, the source and destination reversed: The EProj90_TaxWS source and EProj90 is the

students on whether or not they int their worksheets, and what t for grading.

< filing forms can be complex and idenced by the extensive …n the form shown in Figure 41-2. … why many businesses employ a CPA (certified public accountant) to manage their financial documents and prepare their income tax returns. The duties and responsibilities of a CPA vary. According to the Bureau of Labor Statistics, some accountants focus on advising companies about the tax advantages and disadvantages of certain business decisions and preparing individual income tax returns. Others offer advice in areas such as compensation or employee healthcare benefits, the design of accounting and data processing systems, and the selection of controls to safeguard assets. Still others audit the company's financial statements and inform investors and authorities that the statements have been correctly prepared and reported. CPAs may work as employees of a company, but generally they have their own businesses or work for public accounting firms that are hired by businesses to perform these duties.

Data/Solution Files

Data files:	ETry41.xlsx	Solution files:	ETry41_solution.xlsx
	EProj89.xlsx		EProj89_solution.xlsx
	EProj89_TaxWS.xlsx		EProj89_TaxWS_solution.xlsx
	EProj90.xlsx		EProj90_solution.xlsx
	EProj90_TaxWS.xlsx		EProj90_TaxWS_solution.xlsx

Lesson 42   Working with 3-D Formulas

What You Will Learn
- ✓ Creating 3-D Formulas
- ✓ Duplicating a Workbook Window

Words to Know
3-D formula
3-D reference
Duplicate workbook window

Tips, Hints, and Pointers

- Discuss each of the skills listed in the What You Will Learn section, and ask students if they have used any of these skills before.
- Discuss the scenario covered in the Application Skills section and preview the tasks students will perform for Whole Grains Bread.
- Key skills covered in this lesson include using 3-D formulas and duplicating the workbook window.

Creating 3-D Formulas

- Remind students that they have worked with several workbooks containing data on multiple sheets. Point out that they can use 3-D formulas to summarize data from multiple sheets on a summary sheet. Stress that these formulas use the same cells or range of cells on each worksheet.
- Reinforce the guidelines discussed for creating 3-D references. Make sure students understand the syntax of referencing consecutive and nonconsecutive sheets and single cells or cell ranges.
- Show students a worksheet that contains 3-D formulas to sum or average data across several worksheets. Stress that these formulas require the user to select the same cell or range of cells on all sheets.
- Show students how to enter a 3-D formula by referencing cells on each worksheet rather than typing in the reference. Students may find it easier to build a 3-D formula in this manner; it also helps minimize keying errors.
- Have students open a new workbook, assign sheet names to at least three sheets, and practice creating 3-D formulas. They should try referencing consecutive and nonconsecutive sheets.

- **SKILLS EXTENSION:** After students have completed the steps in the Try It, have them build the Average formula by clicking cell references instead of typing them. The should follow these steps:
  - On the Grades sheet in cell E5, click the Formulas tab, click the Recently Used button, and click AVERAGE.
  - In the Function Arguments dialog box, click the Collapse dialog button on the Number 1 box. Click the Sem 1 sheet and then click cell H5. Click the Expand dialog button to return to the Function Arguments dialog box.
  - Click the Collapse dialog button on the Number 2 box. Click the Sem 2 sheet and click cell H5. Note how the 3-D formula is built in the formula bar as you click references. Click the Expand dialog button and then click OK in the Function Arguments dialog box. The average should be 98.

- **QUICK QUIZ:** How do sheet names speed the operation of creating 3-D formulas?

  Sheet names that relate to their data are easier to distinguish from each other than the default sheet names.

Duplicating a Workbook Window

- Creating 3-D formulas can be simplified by displaying multiple sheets from the same workbook. Demonstrate how to display duplicate workbook windows to display a workbook's worksheets.
- **QUICK QUIZ:** If you type a label or value in a duplicate window, do you have to copy it and paste it in other duplicate windows?

No. Whatever changes are made in one duplicate window appear in all other windows of the same workbook.

Project 91—Quarterly Sales

- The title of this project in the student textbook may appear as "Inventory Analysis," but the correct title should be Quarterly Sales.
- Before students proceed with building formulas, have them review the data on the July, August, and September worksheets.
- Step 3: Stress the importance of carefully checking the syntax of the 3-D formula before pressing Enter.
- Step 8: Instruct students on whether or not they are allowed to print their worksheets, and what they are to submit for grading.
- **WORKPLACE SKILLS:** The sales report shown in Figure 42-1 provides an overview of the net profit achieved by Whole Grains Bread in its various city markets. Explain that net profit is the profit left after all costs (coupons, ingredients, and labor) have been subtracted.

Project 92— Quarterly Sales

- The title of this project in the student textbook may appear as "Inventory Analysis," but the correct title should be Quarterly Sales.
- Step 3: To duplicate the window, click the View tab and then click the New Window button. Click the Arrange All button on the View tab and select Vertical.
- Step 5: Copy C27:G27 on the July worksheet. Switch to the Qtr 3 worksheet, select K12:O12, click the Paste drop-down arrow, and then click the Paste Link button.
- Steps 6-7: Follow the same procedure as in step 5 to link the August and September data.
- Step 8: Students can use the SUM function to total the data.
- Step 12: Instruct students on whether or not they are allowed to print their worksheets, and what they are to submit for grading.
- **WORKPLACE SKILLS:** Ask students why they think coupons represent such a large expense for Whole Grains Bread. Coupons are a popular marketing tool that companies spend hundreds of thousands and even millions of dollars on each year. The costs incurred for a coupon program include the following:
  - Designing and printing the coupons.
  - Distribution through vehicles, such as an insert in the local newspaper or through the mail.
  - Redemption value, which reduces the profit margins on the product.
  - Processing and/or destroying those coupons that customers have redeemed.

Data/Solution Files

Data files: ETry42.xlsx
                       EProj91.xlsx
                       EProj92.xlsx
Solution files: ETry42_solution.xlsx
                       EProj91_solution.xlsx
                       EProj92_solution.xlsx

Chapter Assessment and Application

Project 93   Finalize and Package Bakery P&L Statements

Tips, Hints, and Pointers

- In this project, students will use 3-D formulas and linking to develop a profit and loss statement for Whole Grains Bread.
- Step 3: On the View tab, click the Arrange All button and select Tiled.
- Steps 4-5: Copy the data specified, switch to the EProj93_P&L workbook, select the specified cells, click the Paste drop-down arrow, and then click the Paste Link button.
- Steps 9-10: Follow the same procedure as outlined above for steps 4 and 5 to link data within the same workbook.
- Step 11: Insert the Sum function and use the Function Arguments dialog box to reference the appropriate cells in the three worksheets.
- Step 13b: Click the Paste drop-down arrow and click Paste Special. Select the specified options in the Paste Special dialog box.
- Steps 16-17: Students can use the Page Setup dialog box or options on the Print tab in Backstage view.

- **WORKPLACE SKILLS:** A profit and loss statement is a financial document that summarizes a business's income and expenses over a given time period. Most are prepared once a month, quarterly, or once a year. A profit and loss statement has three parts:
  - Revenue. This is the money a company receives from selling its products, before taking into account how much money was spent on making and selling them.
  - Expenses. This is a list of everything a company pays to operate the business. It includes the cost of making, store, and selling its products, as well as rent for the company and wages for employees.
  - Net profit (or loss). Net profit is the amount of money a company actually makes, and net loss is the amount of money a company loses. Both are calculated by subtracting the expenses from the revenue.

  The health of a company is reflected by the numbers on the profit and loss statement.

Data/Solution Files

Data files: EProj93.xlsx
                  EProj93_P&L.xlsx
                  EProj93_Sales.xlsx
Solution files: Proj93_solution.xlsx
                  EProj93_P&L_solution.xlsx

Project 94 Publishing Bid Results

Tips, Hints, and Pointers

- In this project, students develop a bid summary and publish it to the Web for Michigan Avenue Athletic Club.
- Step 3: On the Data tab, click the From Web button to open the New Web Query dialog box.
- Enter the address for the data file. To copy the path, click Start > Computer and then navigate to your data files. Press Shift and right-click the EProj94_Samsung50InchTV file. Select Copy as path. Go back to the New Web query dialog box and select any text in the Address box, and press Ctrl + V.
- Steps 4-5: Follow the procedure as outlined above to create the other Web queries.
- Step 6: Click File > Save As and from the Save as type list, select Single File Web Page.
- Step 7a: Click File > New to access the Professional Memo template.
- Step 7f: Click the Paste drop-down arrow, and click Paste Special. Click the Paste link option and select Microsoft Excel Worksheet Object.
- Step 7h: Make sure students switch back to the EProj94 workbook to enter the formula.
- **WORKPLACE SKILLS:** Ask students to discuss the value of getting a number of bids for the television monitors. This is a smart business practice because it enables you to identify the lowest cost provider for the same products and equipment. Besides cost, there are other factors to consider. These include the scheduling requirements for the installation, customer service provided by the company, and any warranties on the equipment and installation.

Data/Solution Files

Data files: EProj94.xlsx
EProj94_Phillips50inchTV.mht
EProj94_Pioneer50inchTV.mht
EProj94_Samsung50inchTV.mht

Solution files: EProj94_solution.docx
EProj94_solution.xlsx
EProj94_solution.mht

Chapter 6: Managing Large Workbooks and Using Advanced Sorting and Filtering

Lesson 43 Customizing the Excel Interface and Converting Text

What You Will Learn

- ✓ Customizing the Quick Access Toolbar
- ✓ Customizing the Ribbon
- ✓ Customizing Excel Options
- ✓ Converting Text to Columns
- ✓

Words to Know
No Words to Know in this lesson.

Tips, Hints, and Pointers

- Discuss each of the skills listed in the What You Will Learn section, and ask students if they have used any of these skills before.
- Discuss the scenario covered in the Application Skills section, and preview the tasks students will perform for The Little Toy Shoppe.
- This lesson shows students how to customize the appearance of the Excel window and how to split text from a single column into multiple columns.

Customizing the Quick Access Toolbar

- Point out the Quick Access Toolbar and the drop-down arrow you click to display the customization options. Explain that only a few tools are included on this toolbar by default.
- Show students how to customize the toolbar. You can add buttons by clicking the Customize Quick Access Toolbar drop-down arrow and then selecting from the menu of options. Or, right-click a button and click Add to Quick Access Toolbar.
- Ask which additional buttons they think would be most useful to place on the toolbar. For example, many users display the Open button on this toolbar.
- **Try It! Customizing the Quick Access Toolbar:** Make sure students remove buttons they add to the QAT and reposition it in its default location above the Ribbon.

Customizing the Ribbon

- If necessary, review the parts of the Ribbon students. Students should be familiar with the tabs, the groups on each tab, and the buttons and commands in each group.
- Demonstrate how to minimize the Ribbon by clicking the Minimize the Ribbon button next to the Help button to the far right of the tab names. You can also right-click a tab name and select Minimize the Ribbon on the shortcut menu. Right-click again on a tab and deselect Minimize the Ribbon to redisplay it or click the Expand the Ribbon button.
- Reduce the Excel window size to show students how the Ribbon appearance changes to accommodate the reduced width.
- **Try It! Restoring the Ribbon:** Make sure students complete this exercise. Encourage them to apply customization options to the QAT and Ribbon on their own personal computers.
- **CUSTOMIZED INSTRUCTION: Less Advanced Students:** In a worksheet, have students enter the names of each tab on the Ribbon. Under each tab name, they should list the groups on the tab.

Customizing Excel Options

- Demonstrate how to open the Excel Options dialog box.
- **Try It! Customizing Excel Options:** This is the first exercise in which students access a data file. Make sure they know how to access the data files

for the lesson and where they are to save their work. Also, when students have completed this exercise, you should instruct them to return the options in the Excel Options dialog box to their default settings.

- **CUSTOMIZED INSTRUCTION: ESOL Students:** In the Excel Options dialog box, have students explore the options on the Language tab.

Converting Text to Columns

- Discuss situations where it might be useful to convert text to columns. For example, suppose you have a column called *Name* that holds the full names of each customer. You might want to change to having separate *First Name* and *Last Name* columns, but without having to retype everything.
- Demonstrate how to separate the data out when there are three pieces of data: City, State, and ZIP code, for example. The initial split will not be perfect; you will need to go back in and combine certain entries where the city name consists of more than one word, for example.
- Try a three-column split with the following data. Have students figure out how to do it, and how to clean up the data. First you would split it with a comma as the delimiter, and then you would split the state and ZIP with a space as a delimiter.
    - Dalton City, IL 64222
    - Indianapolis, IN 46240
    - Macon, IL 62544
    - Salt Lake City, UT 84101
- Have students close any sample workbooks without saving changes.
- **DESIGN FORUM:** Emphasize the importance of setting up worksheet data so that it is easy to read and interpret. While some cells will contain longer descriptive text, you should try to limit other cell contents to a single piece of data or information.

For example, a worksheet containing product information should have separate columns for the category of product, the name of the product, a product ID or inventory number, and a product description. Setting up your data in this way also makes it easier to integrate the data with other applications, such as a Word table or an Access database.

Project 95—Splitting Delimited Text

- Remind students to read and follow the instructions carefully, paying close attention to the cell addresses in which they are to enter data.
- Steps 13-14: Instruct students to remove the Quick Print and Spelling buttons from the Quick Access Toolbar before they log off their computers. To remove a button, right-click it and then click Remove from Quick Access Toolbar.

Project 96—Splitting Text into Multiple Columns

- Step 3c: If necessary, remind students that to delete a column, you right-click the column D column heading and then click Delete on the shortcut menu.
- Step 4: To insert a column, click in column F, click the Home tab, click the Insert button, and then click Insert Sheet Columns.
- Step 6b: To display the wizard, click the Data tab and then click the Text to Columns button.
- Step 9: To add a header, click the Insert tab and click the Header & Footer button. Students should enter their names in a header section of their choice.
- Step 11: Remind students that they can select the pages to print and change the orientation in Backstage view.

Data/Solution Files

Data files: ETry43.xlsx
                        EProj95.xlsx
                        EProj96.xlsx
Solution files: ETry43_solution.xlsx
                        EProj95_solution.xlsx
                        EProj96_solution.xlsx

Lesson 44 Formatting Cells

What You Will Learn
- ✓ Using Advanced Formatting of Dates and Times
- ✓ Creating Custom Number Formats
- ✓ Clearing Formatting from a Cell
- ✓

Words to Know
No Words to Know in this lesson.

Tips, Hints, and Pointers

- Discuss each of the skills listed in the What You Will Learn section, and ask students if they have used any of these skills before.
- Discuss the scenario covered in the Application Skills section, and preview the tasks students will perform for Giancarlo Franchetti's Go-Cart Speedrome.
- In this lesson, students apply various formatting options to cells to fine-tune a worksheet's appearance.

Using Advanced Formatting of Dates and Times

- Remind students of the dialog box launcher in the Home tab's Number group, which opens the Format Cells dialog box.
- Review how Excel displays numbers as dates and times, and show how to change the date/time number format via the Number tab in the Format Cells dialog box.
- **CURRICULUM CONNECTION:** The United States uses several different times zones. Using the Internet or other resources, have students investigate the different U.S. time zones. On a blank worksheet, have students list the time zones and then list each state that falls within that time zone.

Creating Custom Number Formats

- Discuss the purpose of a custom number format, and show several examples. Review the codes to use when creating a format.
- Ask students if they know where custom number formats are saved. They are saved with the worksheet. To copy a custom number format to another sheet, you can use Format Painter to copy the formatting from a cell in one worksheet to a cell in another.
- **SKILLS EXTENSION:** On a sample worksheet, have students click any cell. Then, have students open the Format Cells dialog box, click the Number tab, and then click Custom. They should select a custom format in the list box. On the worksheet, have them enter a random number in the selected cell to see how the custom format appears. Have them experiment with several other custom formats.

Clearing Formatting from a Cell

- Discuss why you would clear a cell's formats without clearing its content. Point out the Clear button on the Home tab, and discuss the options on its menu.

Project 97—Using Date and Time Formats

- Step 6: Make sure students click the Number Format drop-down arrow and not the button itself. Otherwise, they will apply the current number format to the selected cells.

Project 98—Using Custom Number Formats

- Step 3c: Remind students to carefully check what they enter in the Type box.
- Step 3d: Again, remind students to carefully proofread the data after they enter it.
- Step 4b: To clear formatting, click the Home tab, click the Clear button, and click Clear Formats.
- Step 6: To add a footer, click the Insert tab and click the Header & Footer button. On the Header & Footer Tools Design tab, click the Go to Footer button, if necessary.

Data/Solution Files

Data files: ETry44.xlsx
                  EProj97.xlsx
                  EProj98.xlsx

Solution files: ETry44_solution.xlsx
                  EProj97_solution.xlsx
                  EProj98_solution.xlsx

Lesson 45 Hiding and Formatting Workbook Elements

What You Will Learn

- ✓ Hiding Data Temporarily
- ✓ Hiding and Printing Worksheet Gridlines
- ✓ Hiding Row and Column Headings
- ✓ Using Custom Views

Words to Know

Gridlines
Headings
Hide
Unhide
View

Tips, Hints, and Pointers

- Discuss each of the skills listed in the What You Will Learn section, and ask students if they have used any of these skills before.
- Discuss the scenario covered in the Application Skills section, and preview the tasks students will perform for Intellidata Database Services.
- This lesson focuses on how to *hide* cells, rows, and columns, and even an entire worksheet in a workbook. Hiding data is a simple method for keeping sensitive information out of sight.
- **CUSTOMIZED INSTRUCTION: ESOL Students:** Have students make flash cards of the Words to Know listed on this page. They should print the word in English and their primary language on one side, and the definition in English only on the other side.

Hiding Data Temporarily

- This type of security is not very strong because anyone can *unhide* the hidden parts. It is more of a convenience to get unwanted parts of the worksheet out of the way.
- Point out that for greater security, when you hide a worksheet tab, you might want to rename the remaining tabs to make it less obvious that one is missing. For example, if you hide Sheet1 but leave Sheet2 and Sheet3, an alert viewer is going to understand that Sheet1 might be hidden.
- Point out that when a row or column is hidden, its letter or number is skipped in the numbering. For example, if you hide row 13, the numbering runs 11, 12, 14, and so on.

- One reason to hide a worksheet is to store macros on a sheet but not necessarily have them in view.
- One reason to hide a row or column is to print noncontiguous rows or columns as if they were contiguous.
- Point out that hidden data does not print, and if you copy or move it, it remains hidden, even if the destination location is not hidden.

Hiding and Printing Worksheet Gridlines

- Ask students why a user would want to hide worksheet *gridlines*. For example, in an on-screen form, the gridlines might make the form look less attractive or less like a paper form.
- Point out that gridlines display in gray when the cells are unbordered. Explain the difference between a border (a line around one or more sides of a cell) and a gridline (the boundary of the cell). Show how you can print gridlines or not, independently of whether you display gridlines onscreen or not.
- **QUICK QUIZ:** What is the difference between a cell border and cell gridlines?

  A border is the line around one or more sides of a cell and a gridline is the boundary of the cell.

Hiding Row and Column Headings

- Discuss why you might want to hide row and column *headings* onscreen on a worksheet. It makes the display look cleaner and fits more data onscreen at once.

- Demonstrate Full Screen view, and then contrast that to turning off row and column headings.

Using Custom Views

- Discuss custom *views*, and why you might use them. You can combine the skills learned previously for setting up the display (zooming, hiding rows/columns, and so on) with creating a custom view to save those settings.
- **CUSTOMIZED INSTRUCTION: Special Needs Students:** Visually challenged students may find it helpful to work at a zoom percentage greater than 100%. Help students find a zoom percentage comfortable for their needs.

Project 99—Creating a Custom View of a Worksheet

- Step 4: Remind students that they must hold down the Ctrl key to select noncontiguous row headings.
- Step 12: You might instruct students to delete the custom view before closing the file.

Project 100—Creating Multiple Views of a Worksheet

- Step 3: Instruct students to redisplay the row and column headings first. To do this, click the View tab and make sure the Headings box is checked. Then, they should select rows 6 through 26, right-click, and click Unhide.
- Step 9: You might instruct students to delete the custom views before closing the file.
- **JOB FOCUS:** Remind students that in Projects 5 and 6, they are working in the capacity of *bookkeeper* for Intellidata. Explain that a bookkeeper is responsible for keeping records of financial transactions for a business. Typical duties include verifying, allocating, and posting details of various business transactions to the appropriate accounts in journals or computer files from documents such as sales slips, invoices, receipts, check stubs, and computer printouts. Bookkeepers are also responsible for reconciling and balancing the business's accounts. Additional duties may include compiling reports to show cash receipts and expenditures, accounts payable and receivable, profit and loss, and other items pertinent to the operation of business. In some companies, the bookkeeper may also be charged with preparing payroll records.

Data/Solution Files

Data files: ETry45.xlsx
              EProj99.xlsx
              EProj100.xlsx
Solution files: ETry45_solution.xlsx
                EProj99_solution.xlsx
                EProj100_solution.xlsx

Lesson 46 Customizing Styles and Themes

What You Will Learn
✓ Customizing a Workbook Theme
✓ Creating a Custom Table Style

Words to Know
Excel table

Tips, Hints, and Pointers

- Discuss each of the skills listed in the What You Will Learn section, and ask students if they have used any of these skills before.
- Discuss the scenario covered in the Application Skills section, and preview the tasks students will perform for PhotoTown.
- In this lesson, students work with themes and table styles.

Customizing a Workbook Theme
- Review themes with students. Themes supply coordinated colors, fonts, and effects to give worksheets a distinctive look.
- All of the Office 2010 applications offer the same set of themes. Discuss how this kind of consistent formatting could make it easy to create coordinated communications across applications.
- Review what makes up a theme: fonts, colors, and graphic effects. The effects include line and fill settings such as borders and shadows.
- Point out the Themes gallery on the Page Layout tab. Have students open or create a sample worksheet that has several levels of headings, a block of data, and a total row. Have them practice previewing themes to see how the worksheet's appearance changes.
- In the sample worksheet, have students select a theme, and then make other changes to theme colors, fonts, or effects. When they are done, they should close the workbook without saving their changes.
- Demonstrate changing the theme, and then show how to create your own custom theme.
- Show the difference between creating themes (overall) and creating theme colors or theme fonts. Point out that you cannot create your own theme effects.

- **Try It! Modifying an Existing Set of Theme Colors:** You should have students remove the custom theme colors from their lab computers. To do this, click the Page Layout tab, click the Colors button, right-click the custom theme colors, and click Delete. Click Yes in the message box to confirm the deletion.
- **Try It! Modifying an Existing Set of Theme Fonts:** You should have students remove the custom theme fonts from their lab computers. To do this, click the Page Layout tab, click the Fonts button, right-click the custom theme fonts, and click Delete. Click Yes in the message box to confirm the deletion.
- **Try It! Saving a New Theme:** You should have students remove the new theme from their lab computers. To do this, click the Page Layout tab, click the Themes button, right-click the custom theme, and click Delete. Click Yes in the message box to confirm the deletion.
- **DESIGN FORUM:** The use of themes can give worksheets a professional look. Many businesses find that they can also create continuity among their internal and external documents by using the same themes, styles, and formatting on all of them. This applies to financial documents, brochures and other marketing materials, the corporate logo, letterhead, and even envelopes and mailing labels. The consistent use of formats on all documents can help a business enhance its image and strengthen corporate identity.

Creating a Custom Table Style
- Review the concept of Excel tables. An Excel table is a range of data with special features that enable you to reference a column of data in a formula more naturally and build formulas more easily.

- You can perform other functions with the special column headers in an Excel table, such as sorting and filtering data.
- Excel tables are best for data that's organized primarily by columns, because automatic totals and other functions can be inserted per column, but not by row.
- You select an overall table format and other formatting settings on the Table Tools Design tab.
- **Try It!: Creating a New Table Style:** You should have students remove the new table style from their lab computers. To do this, click the Table Tools Design tab. In the Table Styles gallery, right-click the table style and click Delete. Click Yes in the message box to confirm the deletion.
- **CUSTOMIZED INSTRUCTION: Special Needs Students:** Themes and table styles can save a great deal of formatting time and minimize the number of keystrokes a physically challenged person has to make. Create new styles to allow easier text formatting.

Data/Solution Files

Data files: ETry46.xlsx
              EProj101.xlsx
              EProj102.xlsx
Solution files: ETry46_solution.xlsx
                EProj101_solution.xlsx
                EProj102_solution.xlsx

Project 101—Creating a Custom Theme
- Instruct students to delete the custom colors, custom fonts, and custom theme before logging off their computers. On the Page Layout tab, select the respective button in the Themes group, right-click the custom design, and click Delete. Click Yes in the message box to confirm the deletion.

Project 102—Creating a Custom Table Style
- Step 5: Remind students to format the range as a table, click the Home tab and click the Format as Table button.
- Step 11: Before closing the file and exiting Excel, instruct students to delete the new table style they created in this project. To do this, click the Table Tools Design tab. In the Table Styles gallery, right-click the table style and click Delete. Click Yes in the message box to confirm the deletion.

Lesson 47 Using Advanced Sort

What You Will Learn
- ✓ Sorting Excel Items
- ✓ Understanding the Rules for Advanced Sorting
- ✓ Sorting on Multiple Columns
- ✓ Removing a Sort

Words to Know
Ascending order
Descending order
Key

Tips, Hints, and Pointers

- Discuss each of the skills listed in the What You Will Learn section, and ask students if they have used any of these skills before.
- Discuss the scenario covered in the Application Skills section, and preview the tasks students will perform for Wood Hills Animal Clinic.
- This lesson covers sorting. While these skills can refer to individual columns, a user is most likely to be sorting a data set contained in multiple rows and columns.

Sorting Excel Items
- Make sure students understand what is meant by *ascending* and *descending order*. Ask what happens when an entry begins with a number or symbol rather than a letter. If they don't know, have them experiment.
- Review the rules for sorting provided in this section. Point out that the symbols have their own arbitrary sort order. For example, ! comes before #.

Sorting on Multiple Columns
- Define *key*. A key is a sort level. For example, when you sort by City, City is the sort key.
- Point out that the Sort command can sort a list using a maximum of three keys in a single operation. Ask students how they would sort by more than three keys. For example, they could sort by three, and then sort the results by the others.
- Show and demonstrate the Sort buttons on the Data tab. Point out that they sort only by the leftmost column in the selected range.

- Show how you can use the Sort Options dialog box to sort left to right rather than top to bottom, or with case sensitivity or conditional formatting.

Removing a Sort
- Show how to undo a sort with the Undo button immediately after sorting. Caution students that other than Undo, there is no way to undo a sort. Ask students to identify some ways they could retain a memory of the original sort order if needed. For example, they could add a column in which records are consecutively numbered.
- **CUSTOMIZED INSTRUCTION: More Advanced Students:** Have students create a table of 12 to 15 items on the menu in your school cafeteria. For each item, they should include the price as well as any nutritional information, such as the number of calories. Have them apply different sorts to the data. Have them copy the data after each sort to another location on the worksheet and insert a title that summarizes the table.

Project 103—Sort a Patient List
- Step 5: If necessary, remind students how to insert a footer. Click the Insert tab and then click the Header & Footer button. On the Header & Footer Tools Design tab, click the Go to Footer button and enter the name in the desired section.

Project 104—Custom Sort a Patient List
- Step 3: Remind students to follow the instructions carefully in order to achieve the desired sorting results.

- Step 4: If necessary, remind students how to insert a header. Click the Insert tab and then click the Header & Footer button. Enter the name in the desired section.

Data/Solution Files

Data files: ETry47.xlsx
                 EProj103.xlsx
                 EProj104.xlsx
Solution files: ETry47_solution.xlsx
                 EProj103_solution.xlsx
                 EProj104_solution.xlsx

Lesson 48   Using Advanced Filtering

What You Will Learn

- ✓ Using AutoFilter to Filter Tables
- ✓ Using AutoFilter to Filter by Custom Criteria
- ✓ Filtering Items without Creating a Table
- ✓ Filtering by Using Advanced Criteria
- ✓ Removing an In-Place Advanced Filter
- ✓ Extracting Filtered Rows
- ✓ Using Sum, Average, and Count in a Filtered Table

Words to Know

Calculated column
Criteria range
Excel table
Extract
Extract range
Filter
List
Total row

Tips, Hints, and Pointers

- Discuss each of the skills listed in the What You Will Learn section, and ask students if they have used any of these skills before.
- Discuss the scenario covered in the Application Skills section, and preview the tasks students will perform for Wood Hills Animal Clinic.
- In this lesson, students learn how to filter items in a table.

Using AutoFilter to Filter Tables

- Remind students what an Excel table is. A table is a range of data with special features that enable you to reference a column of data in a formula more naturally and build formulas more easily.
- Define *filter*. A filter is a tool that enables you to filter out records in an Excel table that do not meet criteria you specify. Explain that one of the benefits of using a table is that you can more easily filter the data. However, using a table is not a requirement for filtering. This lesson shows how to filter with or without a table.
- Point out that filtering does not delete records; it just hides them.

Using AutoFilter to Filter by Custom Criteria

- Show how to set up a filter for both a text and a numeric column. For a text column, the submenu is Text Filters; for a numeric column, it is Number Filters.

- Show how to use multiple criteria with AND or OR.

Filtering Items without Creating a Table

- Show how to do a filter without creating a table, using the Filter button on the Data tab.
- When working with a table, you can use the down arrow at the top of a column to select a filter choice. Review the available options on one of these menus.
- Review the advantages of filtering with a table as discussed in this section. When using a table, the formulas can reference columns by name, and you can apply formatting more quickly. You can also add a total row and a calculated column.

Removing a Filter from a List

- Show how to remove all filters so that the full set of data reappears.

Filtering by Using Advanced Criteria

- Explain that the main advantage of an advanced filter is that it allows you to *extract* (copy) records to another location based on the filter criteria. Advanced filters also allow more complex criteria.
- Explain that you must set up your *criteria range* prior to using an advanced filter. Explain what a criteria range is, and show how to set one up. Mention that typically the criteria range is above

or to the right of the original list or table, separated by a few rows or columns.
- Show the Advanced Filter dialog box and explain the options there.
- Ask students why they think the Advanced Filter dialog box uses absolute references to the cells.
- Explain how to set up a criteria range and criteria, and explain the constraints on that.
- Review the difference between AND and OR operations and give some examples.
- Show how to use wildcards, and differentiate between the ? and the * wildcard characters.
- Show how to use operators in criteria, such as < and >=. Discuss how to use these for text entries as well as numeric ones.
- Demonstrate the use of a formula as a criterion. Remind students that formulas must be entered in cells that don't have a criteria label above them, because you need to select the blank cell(s) above the cells containing the formula when defining the criteria range.
- QUICK QUIZ: How do you distinguish between an AND condition and an OR condition when entering criteria for a filter?

  To enter an AND condition, where two or more criteria must be true for a record to match, type the criteria under their proper field names in the same row. To enter an OR condition, where any of two or more criteria will qualify a record as a match, type the criteria under their proper field names, but in separate rows.

Examples of Advanced Criteria
- Work through the examples of advanced criteria on page 362.

Data/Solution Files
Data files: ETry48.xlsx
                 EProj105.xlsx
                 EProj106.xlsx
Solution files: ETry48_solution.xlsx
                 EProj105_solution.xlsx
                 EProj106_solution.xlsx

Removing an In-Place Advanced Filter
- Show how to remove an advanced filter (Data tab, Clear button).

Extracting Filtered Rows
- Discuss reasons why you might want to extract records to another area of the worksheet, and show how to do that.
- Point out that editing extracted records does not affect the original data.

Using Sum, Average, and Count in a Filtered Table
- Demonstrate how to use the common functions with a filtered table: SUM, AVERAGE, MIN, and so on.
- Demonstrate how to create a calculated column. To do this, type a formula in a blank column in a table; it is filled automatically in the rest of the column.

Project 105—Filtering a Large Data Table
- Step 6b: Make sure students click in the Total cell for the Total Items2 column.
- Step 6c: Make sure students click in the Total cell for the Total Items column.
- Figure 48-2: Have students compare the data in their Total Items column against those shown in the figure.

Project 106—Using an Advanced Filter on a Large Data Table
- Step 2a: Remind students that to rename a worksheet, you right-click the worksheet tab, click Rename, and enter the new name.

Lesson 49 Customizing Data Entry

What You Will Learn
✓ Entering Labels on Multiple Lines
✓ Entering Fractions and Mixed Numbers

Vocabulary
Format
Line break

Tips, Hints, and Pointers

- Discuss each of the skills listed in the What You Will Learn section, and ask students if they have used any of these skills before.
- Discuss the scenario covered in the Application Skills section, and preview the tasks students will perform for the PhotoTown store.
- In this lesson, students learn how to create line breaks within a cell and enter fractions and mixed numbers.

Entering Labels on Multiple Lines
- To wrap text to multiple lines in a cell, you can either use the Wrap Text option on the Home tab or you can manually insert a line break where you want it (Alt+Enter). Show both methods, and discuss when one might be better than the other.

Entering Fractions and Mixed Numbers
- Ask students how to enter a fraction, and have them try out their methods. Entering a plain fraction such as 1/3 results in a date. Have them try it by entering a zero and space before each one, as in 0 1/3.
- Point out that the fraction appears in the cell, but the decimal equivalent appears in the formula bar.
- Any number can be substituted for the zero, such as 13 1/2.
- Point out that entering numbers as fractions this way automatically applies the Fraction number format to the cell. You can also apply the Fraction number format to a cell at any time, not just during data entry.
- **WORKPLACE SKILLS:** Discuss the importance of math not only at school and at work, but in situations you encounter every day. You calculate how much time you have to get to class. You count your change at lunch. You dole out portions of a pizza to friends. Then, take some time to review fractions and decimals with students. A fraction is a ratio—or comparison—of two whole numbers, or one whole number divided by another whole number. You write a fraction in a way similar to writing a division problem. A dividend, called the numerator, is written above a line, called the fraction bar. A divisor, called the denominator, is written below the fraction bar.

  For example, if you have three-quarters of an hour to travel to a meeting, you can write the fraction like this: ¾. The number 3 is the numerator, or dividend. It represents the number of quarter-hours you have. The number 4 is the denominator, or divisor. It represents the total number of quarter-hours in a whole hour.

  A mix of whole numbers and fractions is called a mixed fraction. For example, 1¼ is a mixed fraction.

  A decimal is a different way of writing a fraction. You write a decimal using a decimal point, or dot. Numbers to the left of the decimal point are whole numbers. Numbers to the right of the decimal point are less than one. Each place in a decimal represents a multiple of ten. The first place to the right of a decimal is tenths. The second place is hundredths. The third place is thousandths. For example, .25 means that there are two tenths and five hundredths. The number 2.25 means there are two wholes, two tenths, and five hundredths.

Project 107—Weekly Payroll Tracker
- Step 3: Remind students to hold the Alt key and press enter to insert a manual line break.

Project 108—Weekly Payroll Tracker
- Step 5: To set a specific column width, click the Home tab, click the Format button, and click Column Width. In the Column Width dialog box, enter the width as instructed.

- Step 6: Remind students to type a 0 and space before entering the fraction. Have them check the formula bar to be sure the decimal equivalent of 8/15 (0.533333333333333) appears in it.

- Step 7: For the first employee, remind students to enter a 0 and space before typing ¾.

Data/Solution Files

Data files: ETry49.xlsx
      EProj107.xlsx
      EProj108.xlsx
Solution files: ETry49_solution.xlsx
      EProj107_solution.xlsx
      EProj108_solution.xlsx

Lesson 50   Using Find and Replace

What You Will Learn
- ✓ Formatting Text with Formulas
- ✓ Replacing Text

Words to Know
No Words to Know in this lesson

Tips, Hints, and Pointers

- Discuss each of the skills listed in the What You Will Learn section, and ask students if they have used these skills before.
- Discuss the scenario covered in the Application Skills section, and preview the tasks students will perform for PhotoTown.
- In this lesson, students learn how to use text formatting functions, such as PROPER, UPPER, and LOWER, and text replacement functions, such as SUBSTITUTE and REPLACE.

Formatting Text with Formulas

- Review the syntax of the PROPER, UPPER, and LOWER functions. They are all the same; each takes only one required argument.
- Point out that these functions can be used not only on their own, but also as part of a nested set of functions to apply the formatting to the result of another function. For example, =UPPER(CONCATENATE(B1&" "B2)).

Replacing Text

- Contrast the SUBSTITUTE function with the REPLACE function. SUBSTITUTE replaces one text string with another; REPLACE changes characters based on their position in the cell.
- Show an example of SUBSTITUTE. For example, in cell A1, type Patrick Smith. Then in cell A2, type =SUBSTITUTE(A1,"Patrick","Jean"). Cell A2's result will be Jean Smith.
- Show an example of REPLACE. For example, in cell A1, type abcde. Then in cell A2, type =REPLACE(A1,3,2,"XY"). The result in cell A2 will be abXYe. Explain what each argument does. In this example, A1 contains the original, 3 is the position at which to start (3rd character), 2 is the number of characters to replace (c and d), and XY is the text with which to replace them.
- Note that the number of characters in the replacement need not be the same as the number of characters to be replaced.

Project 109—Updating the Employee Listing
- Step 4c and 5c: Remind students to click the drop-down arrow on the Paste button.

Project 110—Updating the Employee Listing
- Step 3d and 4f: Remind students to click the Paste drop-down arrow and click Values.
- **JOB FOCUS:** Remind students that in Projects 15 and 16, they were acting in the capacity of human resources manager for PhotoTown. Explain that a human resources manager must have broad knowledge and experience in employment law, compensation, organizational planning, employee relations, safety, and training and development.

  Human resource managers are typically responsible for managing the hiring/firing functions. They also oversee the administration of benefits and compensation programs and other employee training and development programs. Because the focus is on people, the human resource manager must have excellent interpersonal and coaching skills as well as strong oral and written communication skills.

Data/Solution Files

Data files:	ETry50.xlsx	Solution files:	ETry50_solution.xlsx
	EProj109.xlsx		EProj109_solution.xlsx
	EProj110.xlsx		EProj110_solution.xlsx

Lesson 51 Working with Hyperlinks

What You Will Learn

- ✓ Using a Hyperlink in Excel
- ✓ Creating a Hyperlink in a Cell
- ✓ Modifying Hyperlinks
- ✓ Modifying Hyperlinked Cell Attributes
- ✓ Removing a Hyperlink

Words to Know

Hyperlink
Internet
Intranet
URL
Web pages

Tips, Hints, and Pointers

- Discuss each of the skills listed in the What You Will Learn section, and ask students if they have used any of these skills before.
- Discuss the scenario covered in the Application Skills section, and preview the tasks students will perform for the Wood Hills Animal Clinic.
- Students work with hyperlinks in Excel worksheets in this lesson.

Using a Hyperlink in Excel

- Ask students if they have ever created a *hyperlink* in an Office application or a Web design application.
- Ask students to list some reasons to use hyperlinks in an Excel workbook, and some locations to which they might want to link. For example, they could link to Web sites, to other worksheets, to Word documents, and to e-mail addresses.
- Differentiate between *Internet* and *intranet*. Have students discuss the purpose of an intranet and the benefits of having one that is separate from the Internet.
- Demonstrate the shape the mouse pointer takes when it hovers over a hyperlink.
- Point out when a ScreenTip appears displaying the URL of a hyperlink and discuss how ScreenTips can be used to check a link when spoofing is suspected.
- Discuss why some text hyperlinks are blue and others are purple. (These are the default colors for visited and unvisited hyperlinks.)

- Talk about pages where the hyperlinks are not the default colors, and/or are not even underlined. This is done by HTML coding. Discuss the pros and cons of having a page like that.
- Discuss how to create a range name and then create a hyperlink to that range name to quickly jump to a certain section of a large worksheet.
- Show the setting in Excel Options that controls whether an URL becomes a live hyperlink automatically when typed. It's in Proofing, AutoCorrect Options, AutoFormat As You Type, Replace as you type.
- Point out that in some programs, such as Word and Outlook, you must hold down Ctrl as you click a hyperlink in order to follow it.
- **SKILLS EXTENSION:** In the ETry09 file, have students create a link from one of the cities listed to a Web page that shows a map for the city.

Modifying Hyperlinks

- Demonstrate the different methods for modifying a hyperlink.
- Show how to change the hyperlink's destination in the Edit Hyperlink dialog box. Also point out how to customize the ScreenTip that appears when you hover the mouse over a hyperlink.

Modifying Hyperlinked Cell Attributes

- Review how to use the Cell Styles gallery to apply a style to a hyperlink. Also explain that you can format a hyperlink using formatting that you apply to other cells on a worksheet.

Removing a Hyperlink
- Demonstrate the methods for removing a hyperlink. You can right-click the hyperlink and click Remove Hyperlink on the shortcut menu. Or, you can click Edit Hyperlink on the shortcut menu and click Remove Link in the Edit Hyperlink dialog box.

Project 111—Linking Patient Records
- Step 3d: Note that EProj111a is an Excel workbook file.
- Step 4: Remind students that they can use the Arrange All button on the View tab to display open workbooks on screen at the same time.

Project 112—Linking Patient Records
- Step 2d: Note that EProj112b is an Excel workbook file.
- Step 2e: To change the ScreenTip, click the ScreenTip button in the Insert Hyperlink dialog box.
- Step 18: If necessary, review with students how to insert a footer. Click the Insert tab and click the Header & Footer button. Click the Go to Footer button and enter the footer as instructed.

Data/Solution Files

Data files:
ETry51.xlsx
EProj111.xlsx
EProj111a.xlsx
EProj112.xlsx
EProj112b.xlsx

Solution files:
ETry51_solution.xlsx
ETry51b_solution.xlsx
EProj111_solution.xlsx
EProj112_solution.xlsx

Lesson 52   Saving Excel Data in a Different File Format

What You Will Learn

- ✓ Ensuring Backward-Compatibility in a Workbook
- ✓ Saving Excel Data in CSV File Format
- ✓ Saving a Workbook as a PDF or XPS File

Terms to Know
PDF Format

Tips, Hints, and Pointers

- Discuss each of the skills listed in the What You Will Learn section, and ask students if they have used any of these skills before.
- Discuss the scenario covered in the Application Skills section, and preview the tasks students will perform for Holy Habañero.
- This lesson covers how to save Excel data in different formats.

Ensuring Backward Compatibility in a Workbook

- Ask students to provide examples of situations in which you would want to save Excel files so that they can be opened in earlier versions of the program. For example, your lab computers at school are running Excel 2010 but your home computer has Excel 2003 installed.
- When you save in other formats, compatibility becomes an issue, and you might lose some of the Excel 2010 specific features.
- Demonstrate how to run the Compatibility Checker, and discuss how to evaluate the summary messages regarding loss of functionality. Show how the Help and Find hyperlinks there can help you investigate the details.
- **CUSTOMIZED INSTRUCTION: Special Needs Students:** The Check for Issues drop-down list also includes the Check Accessibility option that allows a user to check a file for content that would be difficult for people with disabilities to read or access. Have your special needs students investigate this feature and what types of problems it can find that might help everyone create more accessible files.

Saving Excel Data in CSV File Format

- Explain that CSV stands for comma-separated or character-separated values. CSV is a simple text format in which each value in a cell is separated by a comma.
- **SKILLS EXTENSION:** In the Save As dialog box, have students research the many file formats available on the Save as type drop-down menu. You might have students create a table that lists and defines each or some of the most commonly used types.

Saving a Workbook as a PDF or XPS File

- Discuss the difference between PDF and XPS. They are both page layout descriptions, but PDF is made by Adobe and read with Adobe Reader, whereas XPS is a Microsoft format and is read only by the XPS reader.
- Explain that you might want to create a PDF copy of a worksheet to distribute in situations where not everyone has Excel (but everyone does have or can get a PDF reader), or in situations where you want people to have an uneditable copy of worksheet data.

Project 113—Checking Compatibility

- Step 6: If necessary, discuss the summary in the Compatibility Checker dialog box with students.

Project 114—Saving a Worksheet in Different Formats

- Step 2: Note that after you click Create PDF/XPS Document under File Types in the middle pane of Backstage view, you will have to click the Create PDF/XPS button in the right pane.

- Step 5: Students should notice that the columns at the right side of the worksheet are cut off in the PDF.

Data/Solution Files

Data files:
ETry52.xlsx
EProj113.xlsx
EProj114.xlsx

Solution files:
ETry52_solution.xlsx
ETry52_solution.csv
ETry52a_solution.pdf
EProj113_solution.xlsx
EProj113a_solution.xls
EProj114_solution.xlsx
EProj114a_solution.pdf
EProj114b_solution.csv

Lesson 53 Working with Subtotals

What You Will Learn

- ✓ Using Go To and Go To Special
- ✓ Creating Subtotals
- ✓ Creating Nested Subtotals
- ✓ Hiding or Displaying Details
- ✓ Removing a Subtotal
- ✓ Manually Outlining and Adding Subtotals

Words to Know

Database function
Function

Tips, Hints, and Pointers

- Discuss each of the skills listed in the What You Will Learn section, and ask students if they have used any of these skills before.
- Discuss the scenario covered in the Application Skills section and preview the tasks students will perform for Intellidata.
- This lesson shows how to jump to a particular cell using the Go To and Go To Special features. It also shows students how to work with subtotals and levels of outlining detail.

Using Go To and Go To Special

- To access the Go To command, click the Find & Select button and then click Go To, or press F5. Once the box is open, type the cell reference and press Enter.
- To access the Go To Special dialog box, click the Find & Select button and then click Go To Special.
- **Try It! Using Go To and Go To Special, step 8:** Point out that Go To Special should highlight the formulas in the Value Sold column and in row 13.

Creating Subtotals

- Explain that the Subtotal feature provides an easy way of subtotaling, but is not the only way of doing it. You can manually create subtotals with database functions such as DSUM.
- Warn students that the Subtotals feature does not work on an Excel table; you have to convert it back to a list.
- Point out that the Subtotal feature provides access to not only DSUM but also DCOUNT, DAVERAGE, and other database-related functions.
- Warn students that the Subtotal feature works only when all records containing values that contribute to that subtotal are contiguous. Therefore, they need to sort the list beforehand so that all records to be calculated together are co-located. This is necessary because Excel inserts a subtotal line based on a change in the value of the chosen field.
- Click the Subtotal button on the Data tab and review the options in the dialog box for setting up a subtotal.
- Explain that when the Subtotal feature is used on a filtered list, the totals are based only on the displayed data, not on the original data set.

Creating Nested Subtotals

- Ask students for an example of a nested subtotal. Show how to create one based on one of their examples.

Hiding or Displaying Details

- Explain the Outline controls shown in both figures on page 396, and mention that they are available only when the Subtotal feature is used.
- Show how to use the Outline controls to display and hide details within the data set.

Removing a Subtotal

- Demonstrate how to remove a subtotal (by clicking Remove All in the Subtotal dialog box).

Outlining and Adding Subtotals Manually
- Show how to manually outline (group) a list, with the Group feature. Point out that this workaround enables you to add subtotals to an Excel table.

Project 115—Organizing Usage Statistics
- Step 12: Students may need to adjust the columns widths again so that all the data displays.
- Step 14: If necessary, review how to insert a footer. Click the Insert tab, click the Header & Footer button, click the Go to Footer button, and then enter the footer as instructed.

Project 116—Organizing Usage Statistics
- Step 3d: If necessary, students should clear any fields other than Avg. Bandwidth that are checked.
- **WORKPLACE SKILLS:** In Projects 21 and 22, students used subtotaling to help them interpret and analyze data for Intellidata. Explain that this type of data analysis, also referred to as statistics, is a type of math used to collect, organize, and analyze data. Statistics are bits of numerical information. They are used to make sense of things that have happened in the past, to help make decisions, and to predict—or forecast—what might happen in the future, based on what has happened before. The chance that something might happen is called probability.

Data/Solution Files
Data files: ETry53.xlsx
  EProj115.xlsx
  EProj116.xlsx
Solution files: ETry53_solution.xlsx
  EProj115_solution.xlsx
  EProj116_solution.xlsx

Data and statistics help to prove facts, illustrate goals, and forecast possibilities. Almost all careers use statistics and probability. Meteorologists collect statistics about weather and use the information for forecasting. Geologists collect statistics on mineral deposits and use the information to predict the probability of locating oil. Market researchers collect statistics about people's buying habits and use the information to predict the probability of a product's success.

- **CURRICULUM CONNECTION:** In a Word document or Excel worksheet, have students list and define some common statistics. These include:
  - Median: The middle value in a set
  - Average or mean: A typical value calculated by adding all values and dividing the total by the number of values
  - Mode: The number that occurs most often in a set
  - Range: The difference between the lowest and highest values in the set
  - Frequency: The number of times an event occurs

Chapter Assessment and Application
Project 117   Payroll Calculations

Tips, Hints, and Pointers

- Discuss the scenario, and preview the tasks students will perform for PhotoTown.
- In this activity, students convert text to columns, and insert and modify a hyperlink.
- Step 2: Remind students to press Alt and then Enter to insert a manual line break in a cell. Or, they can use the Wrap Text button on the Home tab.
- Step 3a: Right-click column D and click Insert on the shortcut menu.
- Step 4: If necessary, allow students extra time to type in the hours worked.
- Step 6: Click the Home tab, click the Number Format drop-down arrow, and click Short Date.
- Step 7b: Note that EProj117a is an Excel workbook file.
- Step 9a: Remind students that they can use the Custom Views button on the View tab to set up custom views.
- Step 9b: To hide columns, select the columns C-G column headings. Right-click and click Hide on the shortcut menu.
- Step 12: Instruct students to enter their name in the desired header or footer section.

Data/Solution Files

Data files: EProj117.xlsx
                 EProj117a.xlsx
Solution file: EProj117_solution.xlsx

Project 118 Women and Children First

Tips, Hints, and Pointers

- Discuss the scenario, and preview the tasks students will perform in this project.
- In this activity, students sort data on multiple columns, calculate subtotals, and filter data using advanced criteria.
- Step 3c: Remind students to click the Add Level button in the Sort dialog box to add each of the sort levels as instructed.
- Step 4a: Students should have a Yes count of 449 and a No count of 864.
- Step 4c: Students should find of those who survived the 1st class average age is 37, 2nd class average age is 24, and 3rd class average age is 21. Of those who didn't survive, the 1st class average age is 44, 2nd class average age is 32, and 3rd class average age is 26.
- Step 7: Refer students to Illustration A to help them determine where to set up their criteria ranges and the criteria they should enter.

Data/Solution Files

Data file: EProj118.xlsx
Solution file: EProj118_solution.xlsx

Chapter 7: Creating Charts, Shapes, and Templates
Lesson 54 Formatting Chart Elements

What You Will Learn
- ✓ Changing Chart Elements
- ✓ Setting Data Label Options
- ✓ Setting Data Table Options
- ✓ Formatting a Data Series

Words to Know
Categories
Data series
Data table
Legend key
Plot area

Tips, Hints, and Pointers

- Discuss each of the skills listed in the What You Will Learn section, and ask students if they have used any of these skills before.
- Discuss the scenario covered in the Application Skills section and preview the tasks students will perform for Special Events.
- This lesson teaches students how to improve a chart by changing label and table options, formatting a data series, and adding or removing data from the chart.
- **CUSTOMIZED INSTRUCTION: Less Advanced Students:** Have students look through newspapers or magazines for an article or regular column that uses a chart. They should cut out the article and chart and write a brief explanation of how the chart illustrates information in the article. You might also ask them to identify the type of chart used.

Changing Chart Elements
- Review the chart elements identified in Figure 54-1 on page 409. Most of these elements are defined in the Words to Know list on page 408. In addition, point out the horizontal (or X) axis and the vertical (or Y) axis. Review that Excel refers to the X-axis as the Category axis because it displays the categories for the chart and calls the Y-axis the Value axis because it shows the values being plotted. You might also point out the vertical axis title (Units), and the chart title (Q2 Home Construction).

- Review the options on the Chart Tools Design, Layout, and Format tabs. Allow students time to get familiar with the options on each, as this will help them work more quickly and efficiently with charts.
- Review how to select a chart. Make sure students know how to select the whole chart as well as the different parts of it. Point out the Chart Elements button in the Current Selection group on the Chart Tools Layout tab.
- **QUICK QUIZ:** What is the difference between the plot area in a chart and the chart area?

    The plot area contains the charted data only; it is contained within the chart area along with the chart title, legend, axes labels, and data table.

- **CUSTOMIZED INSTRUCTION: ESOL Students:** Have students write the name of each element of a chart labeled in Figure 54-1 on flashcards. They should write the element name in both English and their primary language on one side, and the definition of the element in English only on the other side.

Setting Data Label Options
- Discuss what data labels are, and show how to turn them on and off.
- Make sure students understand what the data label represents. As explained in the text, you can display the data series name, category name, the actual data value and/or percentage, and the

legend key, which is the color or pattern assigned to that particular data point in the legend.

Setting Data Table Options

- Define data table, and discuss why you might want to use one. A data table is especially helpful when the chart is on its own separate worksheet, for example, because the data is not visible at the same time as the chart unless you use a data table.

Formatting a Data Series

- Show some of the ways in which you can format a data series, including fills, borders, and shapes (for bar-type charts).
- Demonstrate how to adjust the amount of space between series in a group by changing the Series Options.
- **DESIGN FORUM:** To design an effective chart, you must select the appropriate chart type. For example, when you want to compare parts of a whole, such as sales by salesperson relative to total sales, you use a pie chart. When you want to show trends over time, such as how total sales change from month to month, you use a line chart. Here are some common chart types.
    - A column chart shows data changes over a period of time or illustrates comparisons among items.
    - A bar chart illustrates comparisons among individual items.
    - A line chart shows trends over time.
    - A circle—or pie—chart shows the relationship of parts to a whole.
    - A scatter chart compares pairs of values.
    - An area chart displays the magnitude of change over time.

Project 119—Formatting a Sales Column Chart

- Step 7: If necessary, remind students that the Chart Elements button is in the Current Selection group on the Chart Tools Format tab. They need to click the drop-down arrow on the button.
- Step 9: Students will need to refer to the legend to determine which columns are in the Private data series.

Project 120—Formatting a Sales Chart

- Step 4: To add a title, click the Chart Tools Layout tab, click the Chart Title button, and click the specified title style.
- Step 5a: Click the Chart Tools Layout tab, click the Data Table button, and click the specified style.
- Step 5b: Remind students to use the Chart Elements button on the Chart Tools Format tab to select the Plot Area.
- Step 6: Click the Chart Tools Layout tab, click the Data Labels button, and click the specified style.
- Step 7: Remind students to use the Chart Elements button to select any data series. Then, on the Chart Tools Format tab, click the Format Selection button to apply the series format as specified.

Data/Solution Files

Data files: ETry54.xlsx
              EProj119.xlsx
              EProj120.xlsx
Solution files: ETry54_solution.xlsx
                  EProj119_solution.xlsx
                  EProj120_solution.xlsx

Lesson 55   Formatting the Value Axis

What You Will Learn

✓ Creating a Stock Chart
✓ Modifying the Value Axis
✓ Formatting Data Markers
✓ Formatting a Legend
✓ Adding a Secondary Value Axis to a Chart

Words to Know

Data marker
Legend
Value axis

Tips, Hints, and Pointers

- Discuss each of the skills listed in the What You Will Learn section, and ask students if they have used any of these skills before.
- Discuss the scenario covered in the Application Skills section, and preview the tasks students will perform for Midwest Pharmaceutical.
- In this lesson, students learn how to create and interpret a stock chart.

Creating a Stock Chart

- Explain the purpose of a stock chart, and explore the differences between the four different types of stock charts (HLC, OHLC, VHLC, and VOHLC; see the student text for full names and definitions of stock information).
- **SKILLS EXTENSION:** Have students look up the Open, High, Low, and Close values for three different stocks for three consecutive days, and then create a chart for them. You can find this information online, on financial and business news radio and TV stations, and in major metropolitan newspapers.

Modifying the Value Axis

- Make sure students can distinguish between the horizontal (or X) axis and the vertical (or Y) axis. Excel refers to the X-axis as the Category axis because it displays the categories for the chart and calls the Y-axis the Value axis because it shows the values being plotted.
- **Try It! Modifying the Value Axis, Step 6:** Students can select the axis by clicking it in the chart (a rectangular box appears around the axis to indicate it is selected), or by clicking the Chart Elements drop-down arrow and selecting Vertical (Value) Axis.

Formatting Data Markers

- Show how to change the data marker format on a chart, in the Format Data Series dialog box. Include how to apply a special fill to a data marker, such as a gradient or texture.
- Point out that the Format Data Series dialog box contains a wide variety of options for customizing a chart's data series. You may want to allow students additional "playing" time to test how some of these options can be used to change chart appearance.

Formatting a Legend

- Demonstrate the different formats you can apply to a legend. Make sure students know how to change the position of the legend and how to apply different fill and outline colors to it.
- Show how to resize the legend without resizing the rest of the chart.

Adding a Secondary Value Axis to a Chart

- Discuss the reason for a secondary axis on a chart. For example, you might have two axes on a stock chart that include both the volume of the stock trading and the value of the stock. The chart students have been working on in this lesson has two value axes.

- **WORKPLACE SKILLS:** You might take some time to explain stocks to students. Stocks represent ownership in a company and entitle their owners to a share of a business's assets and profits. Your share—or return on investment—depends on the stock price. If the stock goes up, or increases in value, you gain. If it goes down, or decreases in value, you lose. Stock prices change by the minute, and their value often depends heavily on the perceived value of those assets and future profits. If profits begin to slip or a company starts losing money, the market value of its stock can decline or even be wiped out altogether in the case of a business that can't pay its bills and has to cease operating. Point out that you do not actually earn any money until you sell your stock.
- **JOB FOCUS:** Discuss with students the job of stock broker. A broker, also called a securities and commodities sales agent, buys and sells stocks, bonds, and other products for clients who want to invest in the stock market. They explain the advantages and disadvantages of investments and keep their clients up to date with price quotes and economic changes. Some agents help clients with insurance, tax planning, estate planning. Being a broker is a stressful and demanding job. Brokers generally work long hours and are always under pressure to make important financial decisions. The job can also be very rewarding: It's not unusual for brokers to make more than six figures per year. Most brokers have a bachelor's degree in business or finance.

Project 121—Formatting a Stock Chart
- Step 10: Students can select the axis by clicking it in the chart (a rectangular box appears around the axis to indicate it is selected), or by clicking the Chart Elements drop-down arrow and selecting Vertical (Value) Axis.
- Step 12: Make sure students type the value in the correct text box.
- Step 16: Remind students to click the Number option in the left pane of the dialog box. They should leave the Format Axis dialog box open for the next step.

Project 122—Formatting a Stock Chart
- Step 5: To change the position of the legend, click the Chart Tools Layout tab, click the Legend button, and then click the position as specified.
- Step 6: To open the Format Legend dialog box, click the Legend button and then click More Legend Options, or double-click the legend.

Data/Solution Files

Data files:　　　ETry55.xlsx
　　　　　　　　EProj121.xlsx
　　　　　　　　EProj122.xlsx
Solution files:　ETry55_solution.xlsx
　　　　　　　　EProj121_solution.xlsx
　　　　　　　　EProj122_solution.xlsx

Lesson 56 Creating Stacked Area Charts

What You Will Learn

✓ Creating a Stacked Area Chart
✓ Formatting the Chart Floor and Chart Walls
✓ Displaying Chart Gridlines
✓ Applying a Chart Layout and Chart Styles

Words to Know

Chart floor
Chart wall
Gridlines
Stacked area chart

Tips, Hints, and Pointers

- Discuss each of the skills listed in the What You Will Learn section, and ask students if they have used any of these skills before.
- Discuss the scenario covered in the Application Skills section, and preview the tasks students will perform for Premiere Formatting.
- This lesson explains how to create, format, and modify a stacked area chart.

Creating a Stacked Area Chart

- Define what is meant by a stacked chart, and show some examples of stacked charts. Show a stacked area chart, and then show a 100% stacked area chart. Discuss the difference, and talk about why you might use one over the other.
- **Try It! Creating a Stacked Area Chart, Step 6:** Have students look closely at their stacked charts and discuss what the chart illustrates. For example, veterinary salaries remain constant from month to month, but exam room supplies were much higher in January and April. Ask students to provide additional examples.

Formatting the Chart Floor and Chart Walls

- Make sure students can distinguish between the chart floor and the chart walls.
- Point out that you can control the appearance and format of these chart elements by using the Chart Wall and Chart Floor buttons on the Chart Tools Layout tab or the Chart Elements drop-down menu.
- **QUICK QUIZ:** What type of chart has a chart floor and chart walls?

  Only 3-D charts have a chart floor and chart walls. A 2-D chart does not have a chart floor.

- **Try It! Formatting the Chart Floor and Chart Walls, Step 4:** Make sure students select the chart area and not the plot area. To ensure that they pick the correct element, they can check the Chart Elements button on the Chart Tools Layout tab.

Displaying Chart Gridlines

- Ask students what the purpose of gridlines is. Show how to remove the gridlines for a chart, and ask students how they think it affects the chart's readability.
- Discuss the difference between major and minor gridlines, and show how to control their frequency.
- Allow students time to experiment with gridlines and modifying their color and other options.

Applying a Chart Layout and Chart Styles

- Explain that you can apply a different chart layout or style to any type of chart.
- The chart layout encompasses the placement of elements, such as the legend, data table, data labels, and gridlines. The chart style encompasses the color scheme of the chart area, plot area, and data series.
- **CUSTOMIZED INSTRUCTION: Special Needs Students:** Visually challenged students may find it necessary to change the colors of chart text or backgrounds so they can more easily read the text. Remind them how to change these chart settings as necessary.

Project 123—Formatting a Budget Chart

- Step 7: Remind students that the chart layouts are in numerical order. When they hover the mouse over a selection in the gallery, the layout number appears.
- Step 9: Make sure students click the Font Color drop-down arrow. If they click the button itself, they will apply the font color that was last used.

Project 124—Formatting a Budget Chart

- Step 9: After setting the solid line for the Border Color, students should click the Fill option in the left pane of the Format Data Table dialog box. Then, they should apply the Light Blue, Background, Darker 25% fill color.

- Step 10a: Remind students that they can either click on the horizontal axis or select Horizontal (Category) Axis from the Chart Elements drop-down menu to select it.
- **WORKPLACE SKILLS:** In Projects 29 and 30, students charted budget data. Explain that a budget is a plan for spending and saving money. It is designed to help an individual or a business balance income and expenses so that they can make sure they don't spend more than they have. When you make a budget, you keep a record of your income, which is the money that comes in, and your expenses, which is the money that goes out. The goal is to balance the budget, which means making sure that income is equal to or greater than expenses.

Data/Solution Files

Data files: ETry56.xlsx
              EProj123.xlsx
              EProj124.xlsx
Solution files: ETry56_solution.xlsx
              EProj123_solution.xlsx
              EProj124_solution.xlsx

Lesson 57   Working with Sparklines

What You Will Learn

- ✓ Inserting a Line, Column, or Win/Loss Sparkline
- ✓ Formatting a Sparkline
- ✓ Inserting a Trendline

Words to Know

Sparkline
Trendline

Tips, Hints, and Pointers

- Discuss each of the skills listed in the What You Will Learn section, and ask students if they have used any of these skills before.
- Discuss the scenario covered in the Application Skills section, and preview the tasks students will perform for PhotoTown.
- In this lesson, students learn how to use Sparklines and Trendlines to identify and illustrate trends in a series of data.

Inserting a Line, Column, or Win/Loss Sparkline

- Explain to students that a Sparkline is like inserting a miniature chart in a single cell to illustrate how selected data in a series changes over time.
- **Try It! Inserting a Line, Column, or Win/Loss Sparkline, Step 5:** Remind students that they can enter the range in the Data Range box or click the Collapse Dialog button, select the range directly on the worksheet, and then click the Expand Dialog button to redisplay the dialog box.
  Step 7: Take some time to discuss the Sparkline results for each series of data. Students should notice that beds and dresses both had a steady increase in sales over the three-month period whereas dining tables and china cabinets decreased.

Formatting a Sparkline

- Review the groups and buttons on the Sparkline Tools Design tab.
- Demonstrate how to apply different formats to Sparklines. Allow students time to experiment with the formatting options.

Inserting a Trendline

- A Trendline is placed within a chart to further illustrate changes in a series of data. Make sure students can distinguish between a Sparkline and a Trendline.
- **CUSTOMIZED INSTRUCTION: ESOL Students:** Ask students to write the words for Sparklines and Trendlines in their primary language. These terms are most likely not in any standard dictionaries, so they will have to form them from the individual parts of the words: "spark" and "line" and "trend" and "line."

Project 125—Inserting Trendlines

- Step 9c: Note that Intense Line – Accent 6 is the last style in the gallery.

Project 126—Adding Sparklines

- Step 4c: Remind students that they can enter the range in the Data Range box or click the Collapse Dialog button, select the range directly on the worksheet, and then click the Expand Dialog button to redisplay the dialog box.
- Step 4d: If necessary, show students how to select and drag the AutoFill handle.
- **JOB FOCUS:** In Projects 31 and 32, students conducted analyses of a company's sales force. Discuss the job of a company's sales force. The goal of a business is to sell its goods or services. Personal selling is a type of promotion, accomplished by using a sales force. A sales force is another term for salespeople, or sales representatives. It is the group of employees responsible for contacting customers and arranging the terms of a sale.

Personal selling has a few advantages over other types of promotion. It helps build personal relationships, because the salespeople meet face-to-face with customers. It allows for customized communication, which means the salespeople can customize their message to each potential customer.

A sales person represents the company to the customer. It is likely that a customer will form an opinion about an entire company based on the attitude and behavior of the sales person. It is very important for sales representatives to be professional, well dressed, knowledgeable, ethical, and polite.

Data/Solution Files

Data files:	ETry57.xlsx
	EProj125.xlsx
	EProj126.xlsx
Solution files:	ETry57_solution.xlsx
	EProj125_solution.xlsx
	EProj126_solution.xlsx

Lesson 58   Drawing and Positioning Shapes

What You Will Learn
✓ Drawing Shapes
✓ Resizing, Grouping, Aligning, and Arranging Shapes

Words to Know
Adjustment handle
Group
Order
Shape
Sizing handles
Stack

Tips, Hints, and Pointers

- Discuss each of the skills listed in the What You Will Learn section, and ask students if they have used any of these skills before.
- Discuss the scenario covered in the Application Skills section and preview the tasks students will perform for Sydney Crenshaw Realty.
- In this lesson, students work with the drawing tools in Excel. These are the same drawing tools as in other Office applications such as Word and PowerPoint. If students have already completed the Word section of this course, they should be familiar with shapes and how to work with them.

Drawing Shapes
- Point out that Excel 2010 uses the term *shapes* for the objects called AutoShapes in earlier versions.
- Review the Shapes button's palette of shapes, which is shown in Figure 58-1. Note that shapes are sorted by category.
- Review how to draw a shape by selecting it and then dragging.

Resizing, Grouping, Aligning, and Arranging Shapes
- Note that arranging, aligning, and grouping techniques apply to any floating objects in the worksheet, not just to drawn shapes.
- Point out the selection handles on the drawn shape, and show how to resize the shape by dragging them. Show how dragging a corner handle resizes in both dimensions, whereas a side handle resizes in only one dimension.
- Point out the green rotation handle at the top of the shape.
- Some shapes have a yellow diamond for reshaping the shape. Not all have this adjustment handle; draw a star or arrow so that you will have an example to work with.
- Review stacking order by placing some papers on your desk and then moving a sheet to the top or bottom of the stack. Then show how overlapping drawn shapes can be stacked.
- Demonstrate how to select multiple objects, and then how to group them and work with the group as if it were a single object.
- View the Selection Pane, and explain how to use it to select multiple objects, including ones that are obscured.
- Demonstrate the use of several of the line tools, including the straight line and the scribble.
- Allow students some free time to practice drawing lines and shapes.
- **TROUBLESHOOTING TIP:** When resizing a shape, remind students that dragging a corner handle will maintain the shape's aspect ratio. Dragging a side or top or bottom handle will distort the image.

Project 127—Drawing and Arranging Shapes
- Step 4: If necessary, point out that in the Themes gallery, under Built-In, the Office theme is listed first with the rest of the themes appearing after in alphabetical order.
- Step 10: Remind students to make sure the pointer is not resting on a sizing handle when they drag the shape. If they inadvertently move a sizing handle, they can click the Undo button to undo the sizing change.
- **SKILLS EXTENSION:** Have students use shapes to draw a more elaborate house graphic. They can add windows, doors, chimneys, and even shrubbery.

Chapter 7 | 145

Project 128—Drawing and Arranging Shapes

- Step 3: Remind students that a ScreenTip will display the name of the shape when they hover their mouse over it.
- Step 8: Note that the number of points displays in the middle of the stars with a greater number of points.
- Step 11: Remind students that to open the Selection Pane, click the Selection Pane button on the Drawing Tools Format tab.

- **CURRICULUM CONNECTION:** Formulas are used to save time when performing certain calculations. In geometry, formulas are used to calculate things like the area, perimeter, and volume of different shapes. Each shape requires a different formula. Have students create a worksheet that lists geometric formulas. Include columns for the shape name (square, circle, triangle, etc.), the actual drawn shape, the respective formulas required to find the area, perimeter, volume, etc., and an example of each formula.

Data/Solution Files

Data files:	ETry58.xlsx
	EProj127.xlsx
	Eproj128.xlsx

Solution files:	ETry58_solution.xlsx
	EProj127_solution.xlsx
	EProj128_solution.xlsx

Lesson 59 Formatting Shapes

What You Will Learn
- ✓ Formatting Shapes
- ✓ Adding Shape Effects

Words to Know
Effects

Tips, Hints, and Pointers

- Discuss each of the skills listed in the What You Will Learn section, and ask students if they have used any of these skills before.
- Discuss the scenario covered in the Application Skills section and preview the tasks students will perform for Sydney Crenshaw Realty.
- In this lesson, students learn how to format drawn lines and shapes and add special effects to them.

Formatting Shapes
- As students have already learned, the Format tab appears when a shape is selected, containing controls for applying formatting to it.
- Explain shape styles, and show some examples applied to a shape and to a line.
- Differentiate between shape fill, outline, and effects, and point out that a shape style can apply all three of these at once. Show how to apply each individually as well.
- Review the types of fills that can be applied to a shape: color, picture, gradient, or texture. Show examples of each.

Adding Shape Effects
- Review the shape effects and have students try out each effect. You can skip 3-D rotation for the moment if you like, as it is covered in Lesson 18.
- Show students how to create complex gradients and how to control where the colors break from one to the other.
- Demonstrate how to use one of your own photos as a custom texture fill, and then compare that to a picture fill. Have students identify the pros and cons of going one way vs. the other.

- Show how to change the color, thickness, and dash style of an outline around a shape.
- Demonstrate a shadow effect, and show how to format the shadow after applying it (different color, different angle, and so on).
- **QUICK QUIZ:** What happens when you create shapes with the Excel 2010 effects and then save in an earlier Excel format?

    The Compatibility Checker dialog box opens informing you that the effects are not supported in the earlier version and the features will be lost or degraded.

Project 129—Formatting Shapes
- Step 6: Note that the Moderate styles are in the next-to-last row in the Shape Styles gallery.

Project 130—Formatting Shapes
- Step 5: If necessary, remind students that Shape Styles are on the Drawing Tools Format tab.
- Step 6: Note that the Intense styles are in the last row in the Shape Styles gallery.
- Step 7: Note that the Subtle styles are in the first row in the Shape Styles gallery.
- Step 10: Note that the Offset Diagonal Top Left effect is the last one in the Outer group.
- **CUSTOMIZED INSTRUCTION: More Advanced Students:** In the EProj130 workbook, have students insert functions at the bottom of the Sales Price column that find the average sale price, the highest (MAX) sale price, and the lowest (MIN) sale price. Have them use shapes to highlight each value and format the shapes as desired.

Data/Solution Files

Data files:	ETry59.xlsx
	EProj129.xlsx
	EProj130.xlsx

Solution files:	ETry59_solution.xlsx
	EProj129_solution.xlsx
	EProj130_solution.xlsx

Lesson 60   Enhancing Shapes with Text and Effects

What You Will Learn

✓ Adding Text to a Text Box, Callout, or Other Shape
✓ Adding 3-D Effects
✓ Rotating Shapes
✓ Inserting a Screen Capture

Words to Know

Callout
Extension point
Rotation handle
Screenshot
Text box

Tips, Hints, and Pointers

- Discuss each of the skills listed in the What You Will Learn section, and ask students if they have used any of these skills before.
- Discuss the scenario covered in the Application Skills section, and preview the tasks students will perform for Sydney Crenshaw Realty.
- In this lesson, students learn how to add text to drawn shapes, how to add 3-D effects, and how to rotate them. They also work with screenshots.

Adding Text to a Text Box, Callout, or Other Shape

- Review what a text box is. A text box is a floating box, unconnected to any particular cell, that contains text. It is essentially a drawn shape (a rectangle) with text in it; you can create text boxes out of any shape by drawing the shape and then placing text inside it. Remind students that they have already worked with text boxes if they have completed the Word unit.
- Point out the Text Box tool on the Insert tab. Have students draw a text box and then type in it.
- Discuss the purpose of a text box on a worksheet. It could contain a note, for example, or be used as a callout to a chart or to a particular cell.
- Show how to change the shape of a text box to one of the other shapes such as a cartoon balloon callout.
- Show how to type text in an existing shape. You can double-click inside it to move the insertion point there, or you can right-click it and choose Add Text.

- Point out that formatting text in a text box is the same as formatting any other text. Use the controls on the Home tab, in the Font group.
- Demonstrate how to change the vertical and horizontal alignment of text in a text box.
- Explain text direction, and show how to set it. For example, show how to make text run uphill at a 45 degree angle within a text box.

Adding 3-D Effects

- Define 3-D effect—this refers to the amount of X, Y, and Z rotation. X rotation is side to side; Y is up and down; Z is pivoting on a center point.
- Show the rotation settings in the Format Shape dialog box, in the 3-D Rotation area. Point out that each of the three aspects, X, Y, and Z, can have a separate angle set for them (0 to 360 degrees).

Rotating Shapes

- Discuss how rotation can be done with the Z axis setting, or you can use the rotation handle. Show students how to drag this handle to rotate an object.
- Explain the difference between rotation and vertical or horizontal flipping. Flipping is like mirroring.

Inserting a Screen Capture

- Discuss instances when you might want to take a screenshot of another open file. For example, if you're tracking stock prices of a company, you might want to capture the company's logo from

- one of its Web pages or other documentation saved in electronic format.
- Explain that screenshots inserted on a worksheet can be formatted using the Picture Tools Format tab. This tab contains many of the same tools students worked with on the Drawing Tools Format tab.

Project 131—Adding Text Effects
- Step 3c: To select the text, hover the pointer over it until it changes to the insertion point. Click and drag to select it.
- Step 5: Mention to students that they will add text to the callout in Project 132.

Project 132—Enhancing Shapes
- Step 3: On the Drawing Tools Format tab, click the Shape Effects button, click Preset, and then click Preset 4.
- Step 4: Click the callout and begin typing.
- Step 5: Remind students that they can apply all the formats listed by using buttons on the Drawing Tools Format tab.
- Step 6: Refer students to Figure 18-2 to see how to position the extension point.
- Step 10: You might note to students that the worksheet shown in the figure still displays gridlines. In the Preview screen in Backstage view, they should not see gridlines on their worksheets.

Data/Solution Files

Data files:	ETry60.xlsx
	ETry60a.jpg
	EProj131.xlsx
	EProj132.xlsx
Solution files:	ETry60_solution.xlsx
	EProj131_solution.xlsx
	EProj132_solution.xlsx

Lesson 61 Working with Templates

What You Will Learn

✓ Changing Cell Borders
✓ Filling Cells with a Color or Pattern
✓ Adding a Watermark or Other Graphics
✓ Creating a Workbook Template

Words to Know

Border
Pattern
Reverse type

Template
Watermark

Tips, Hints, and Pointers

- Discuss each of the skills listed in the What You Will Learn section, and ask students if they have used any of these skills before.
- Discuss the scenario covered in the Application Skills section, and preview the tasks students will perform for Pete's Pets.
- In this lesson, students learn how to customize a worksheet with cell borders, fills, and watermarks. They also work with templates.

Changing Cell Borders

- Review the difference between a border and a gridline. The gridlines are always there no matter what (and can be displayed and printed or not); a border is added formatting for the cell(s).
- Show the various methods of applying a cell border. You can use the Border tab in the Format Cells dialog box or the Borders button in the font group on the Home tab.
- Ask students to evaluate each of those methods and identify the unique benefits of each, and when each one might be most appropriate.

Filling Cells with a Color or a Pattern

- Define *pattern* (as used in Excel fills) and discuss the benefits and drawbacks of using pattern fills. One of the most significant drawbacks to using a pattern in the background of a cell is that it can make the text harder to read.
- When is a pattern not exactly a pattern? Several of the patterns are named with numbers, such as 25% Gray. These blend together the colors you choose for the pattern background color and pattern color. Show examples of these, and then compare the effect to a solid custom color.
- Show how to create a gradient fill, and allow students time to experiment with gradients.
- Define *reverse type*, and discuss its uses. Demonstrate that on a dark background, white text is more readable than black.
- **DESIGN FORUM:** Point out to students that while borders, fills, and patterns add visual interest to worksheets, you should limit their use in worksheets with many rows and columns of numeric data. They can be distracting and may also make the data difficult to read.

Adding a Watermark or Other Graphics

- Define *watermark*, and show examples. Point out that a watermark is actually part of the header or footer.
- Explain that a watermark appears only on the worksheet on which it was added, and show how you can copy a watermark from one worksheet to another.

Formatting the Worksheet Background

- Discuss the pros and cons of using worksheet backgrounds. They liven up the look of the worksheet, but may make it more difficult to read.
- Point out that worksheet backgrounds do not print (unlike watermarks). They are for on-screen viewing only.
- Point out that fill colors for cells are at a higher stacking level than worksheet backgrounds, so any background you use can be partially

obscured by background formatting applied to individual cells.

Creating a Workbook Template
- Discuss the benefits of creating templates versus starting from scratch each time, and versus opening a workbook and saving it under a different name each time.
- Point out the .xltx extension on templates and demonstrate how to create a template and where to store it.
- **CUSTOMIZED INSTRUCTION: Special Needs Students:** The workbook templates provided with Excel can save formatting time and minimize the number of keystrokes a physically challenged person has to make.

Project 133—Formatting the Worksheet
- Step 3d: Instruct students to navigate to the data files for this lesson to select the EProj133a.jpg file.
- Step 10: Point out to students that the watermark is visible in Page Layout view but not in Normal view.

Project 134—Creating a Workbook Template
- Step 4: Remind students to click the Page Layout tab and click the Background button. Navigate to the data files for this lesson and insert the EProj133a.jpg file.
- Step 6: To hide the gridlines, click the View tab and deselect the Gridlines check box.
- Step 10: To save as a template, click the File tab and click Save As. From the Save as type list box, select Excel Template.

Data/Solution Files

Data files: ETry61.xlsx
                    ETry61a.jpg
                    EProj133.xlsx
                    EProj133a.jpg
                    EProj134.xlsx

Solution files: ETry61_solution.xlsx
                    EProj133_solution.xlsx
                    EProj134_solution.xlsx
                    EProj134a_solution.xltx

Lesson 62 Protecting Data

What You Will Learn
- ✓ Locking and Unlocking Cells in a Worksheet
- ✓ Protecting a Range
- ✓ Protecting a Worksheet
- ✓ Protecting a Workbook

Words to Know
Lock
Protect
Unlock
Unprotect

Tips, Hints, and Pointers

- Discuss each of the skills listed in the What You Will Learn section, and ask students if they have used any of these skills before.
- Discuss the scenario covered in the Application Skills section, and preview the tasks students will perform for Marcus Furniture.
- In this lesson, students learn various ways of protecting cells, ranges, worksheets, and workbooks.

Locking and Unlocking Cells in a Worksheet

- Ask students why they would want to protect various parts of a worksheet. Examples include to protect cells against accidental changes you would make yourself, and to protect them against others who might make unwanted changes.
- Discuss the pros and cons of using a password when protecting. Review how to construct a strong (difficult to guess) password.
- Explain that all cells are locked by default, but because the sheet is unprotected by default, that lock is not enabled. Protecting the sheet turns on the lock for all cells except those that have been specifically unlocked.
- Demonstrate what happens when you unlock a cell that contains a formula. An Error Options button appears, which you can ignore if you intended to unlock the cell.
- Show how to protect and unprotect a sheet.
- Demonstrate how to move between unlocked cells by pressing Tab when a sheet is protected.
- Point out that data in a locked cell can be copied, but not moved, changed, or deleted.

Protecting a Range
- Demonstrate how to protect a cell or a range of cells against changes made by selected individuals.

Protecting a Worksheet
- Show the Protect Sheet dialog box and discuss the check boxes there for protecting various aspects of the worksheet.

Protecting a Workbook
- Discuss the difference between protecting a sheet and protecting the entire workbook. Demonstrate how to protect the entire workbook.
- Explain the difference between protecting the workbook's structure and protecting the data.

Project 135—Protecting a Worksheet
- Step 3: Make sure students are on the Feb Earnings worksheet.
- Step 4b and 4d: Remind students to carefully type in the password exactly as it is shown in the text.

Project 136—Protecting Data
- Step 6: Remind students to carefully check they are entering the data in the correct cells.
- Step 7: To copy a worksheet, right-click the worksheet tab, click Move or Copy on the shortcut menu, select Comm-Bonus in the Before sheet box, click the Create a copy box, and click OK. Rename the sheet tab as instructed.
- Step 9: Students should find that they cannot select any cells other than those in the Sales column.

- **JOB FOCUS:** Remind students that in Projects 135 and 136, they were acting in the capacity of Payroll Manager. Payroll is simply the total sum of money that a company pays to employees at a given time. Companies employ a payroll manager to ensure that the payroll department operates as efficiently as possible.

    The payroll department may be responsible for two main functions: timekeeping (tracking employee time cards, hours worked, salary, and overtime) and payroll processing. The payroll manager oversees employee benefits processing and payroll tax reporting. These responsibilities require the manager to work closely with the company's accounting and finance department as well as human resources.

    In addition, the payroll manager must ensure the payroll system functions appropriately. This requires him or her to work closely with the company's information technology department.

Data/Solution Files

Data files: ETry62.xlsx
               EProj135.xlsx
               EProj136.xlsx
Solution files: ETry62_solution.xlsx
               EProj135_solution.xlsx
               EProj136_solution.xlsx

Chapter Assessment and Application
Project 137 Cash Flow Projection

Tips, Hints, and Pointers

- Discuss the scenario, and preview the tasks students will perform for Jones PR.
- In this activity, students use Excel tools to forecast cash flow and track the data in different charts.
- Step 3: Allow students sufficient time to adjust the formatting on the worksheet. Encourage them to use the features they've learned about in this chapter, including fills, patterns, borders, watermarks, and page backgrounds.
- Step 5c: Remind students to select the plot area in the chart and then click the Paste button to add the new data series.
- Step 5f: One way to do this is to right-click a data series and click Select Data on the shortcut menu. In the Select Data Source dialog box, click the Hidden and Empty Cells button. Click Connect data points with line and click OK. Click OK again.
- Step 5g: Click the Chart Tools Design tab and click the Select Data button. In the Select Data Source dialog box, in the Horizontal (Category) Axis Labels, click Edit. In the Axis Labels dialog box, click the Collapse Dialog button, and select the range on the Comparison sheet as instructed. Click the Expand Dialog button to redisplay the Select Data Source dialog box and then click OK.
- Step 6f: Click the Chart Tools Layout tab, click the Trendline button, and click Linear Trendline.
- Refer students to the charts shown in Illustration A and Illustration B.

Data/Solution Files

Data file: EProj137.xlsx
Solution file: EProj137_solution.xlsx

Project 138 Daily Sales Report

Tips, Hints, and Pointers

- Discuss the scenario, and preview the tasks students will perform for Country Crazy Antiques.
- In this activity, students create a format a worksheet, create a template from a worksheet, and create a logo using shapes.
- Step 3: Remind students that the worksheet will serve as a template and that it currently contains only column labels and a sales summary formula.
- Step 5: Remind students to select the Excel Template option from the Save as type drop-down menu in the Save As dialog box. Make sure they include the letter "a" in the file name to distinguish the template from the original workbook.
- Step 6: Note that students should open the EProj138a supplied with the data files, and *not* the EProj138a template file they just saved.
- Step 8: Allow students sufficient time to create their logos. Encourage them to be creative in their designs.
- Step 11: Refer students to Illustration B for an example of a logo and its positioning on the worksheet.

Data/Solution Files

Data files: EProj138.xlsx
                EProj138a.xlsx
Solution files: EProj138_solution.xlsx
                EProj138a_solution.xltx

Chapter 8: Using the Data Analysis, Scenario, and Worksheet Auditing Features

Lesson 63 Inserting Functions and Using Logical Functions

What You Will Learn

- ✓ Using Insert Function
- ✓ Creating an IF Function
- ✓ Creating SUMIF and AVERAGEIF Functions
- ✓ Creating SUMIFs and AVERAGEIFS Functions

Words to Know

AVERAGEIF function
AVERAGEIFS function
IF function
Insert Function
Logical function
SUMIF function
SUMIFS function

Tips, Hints, and Pointers

- Discuss each of the skills listed in the What You Will Learn section, and ask students if they have used any of these skills before.
- Discuss the scenario covered in the Application Skills section, and preview the tasks students will perform for Wood Hills Animal Clinic.
- This lesson teaches students how to use the Insert Function dialog box and how to build IF functions.

Using Insert Function

- Review functions, explaining that they are predefined formulas that perform specific types of calculations based on values the user specifies. Excel offers hundreds of functions that perform financial, statistical, mathematical, and logical calculations.
- Discuss the function categories and other commands in the Function Library on the Formulas tab.
- Remind students that the Insert Function dialog box can be accessed by clicking the Insert Function button on the formula bar or in the Function Library group on the Formulas tab.
- After you select a function in the Function Arguments dialog box, the Function Arguments dialog box appears to prompt you to enter the arguments needed for the function.
- In the Function Arguments dialog box, you can select cells instead of typing them by using the Collapse Dialog button.
- Remind students that required arguments appear in bold. As you enter the arguments, the value of that argument is displayed to the right of the text box.
- **CUSTOMIZED INSTRUCTION: Special Needs Students:** Remind physically challenged students how to use Key Tips to access specific functions from the Formulas tab. They can press Alt+M, F to quickly open the Insert Function dialog box.

Creating an IF Function

- Explain that IF functions enable you to test for particular conditions and then perform specific actions on whether those conditions exist or not.
- For example, with an IF function, you could calculate the bonuses for a group of salespeople on the premise that bonuses are only paid if a sale is over $1,000.
- Explain that the IF function requires three arguments: the condition to be tested, the answer

to return if the test is true, and the answer to return if the test is false.

Creating SUMIF and AVERAGEIF Functions

- The SUMIF and AVERAGEIF functions use a condition to add or average certain data.
- If the condition is true, then data in a corresponding cell is added to the total or averaged in with the other values. If it is false, then the corresponding data is skipped.
- **Try It! Inserting a SUMIF Function:** Take a minute to review with students the results of the SUMIF function. The function evaluated the data in D4:D13 to find those cells in which "Yes" is entered. It then summed the values in the range C4:C13 that correspond to the cells with the "Yes" value. In other words, it totaled all the items that have been paid for.

Creating SUMIFS and AVERAGEIFS Functions

- The SUMIFS and AVERAGEIFS functions are similar to SUMIF and AVERAGEIF except that they allow you to enter multiple qualifying conditions.
- **Try It! Inserting an AVERAGEIFS Function:** Again, take some time to review the results of the AVERAGEIFS function. The function will find the average of values entered in the range C4:C13 where the corresponding cells in the range D4:D13 are equal to "No" and the corresponding cells in the range E4:E13 are equal to "Dog." In other words, it finds the average amount due for dog items that have not yet been paid for, which is $541.

Project 139—Pet Drug Sales

- Step 5: Students should have the following formula entered in cell D100: =SUMIF(C8:C94,"Dog",K8:K94).
- Step 6: Students should have the following formula entered in cell D101: =SUMIF(C8:C94,"Cat",K8:K94).
- Step 7: Students should have the following formula entered in cell D103: =SUMIF(B8:B94,"Flea",K8:K94).
- Step 8: Students should have the following formula entered in cell D104: =SUMIF(B8:B94,"Flea and Tick",K8:K94). Students should have the following formula entered in cell D105: =SUMIF(B8:B94,"Heartworm",K8:K94).
- Step 9: Students should have the following formulas entered:
  D108: =AVERAGE(K8:K94)
  D109: =AVERAGEIF(C8:C94,"Dog",K8:K94)
  D110: =AVERAGEIF(C8:C94,"Cat",K8:K94)
  D112: =AVERAGEIF(B8:B94,"Flea",K8:K94)
  D113: =AVERAGEIF(B8:B94,"Flea and Tick",K8:K94)
  D114: =AVERAGEIF(B8:B94,"Flea and Tick",K8:K94)
- Step 11: Students should have the following formula entered in cell D115: =AVERAGEIFS(K8:K94,B8:B94,"<>Flea",B8:B94,"<>Flea and Tick",B8:B94,"<>Heartworm").

Project 140—Pet Store Sales

- Step 4: Students should have the following formula entered in cell D62: =SUMIF(E10:E49,"Alice Harper",F10:F49).
- Step 5: Students should have the following formula entered in cell D63: =SUMIF(E10:E49,"Bob Cook",F10:F49).
- Step 6: Students should have the following formula entered in cell E62: =AVERAGEIF(E10:E49,"Alice Harper",F10:F49).
- Step 7: Students should have the following formula entered in cell E63: =AVERAGEIF(E10:E49,"Bob Cook",F10:F49).
- Step 8: Students should have the following formula entered in cell D66: =SUMIFS(F10:F49,D10:D49,"Fish",E10:E49,"Alice Harper").
- Step 9: Students should have the following formula entered in cell D67: =SUMIFS(F10:F49,D10:D49,"Fish",E10:E49,"Bob Cook").
- Step 10: Students should have the following formula entered in cell E66: =SUMIFS(F10:F49,D10:D49,"Accessory",E10:E49,"Alice Harper").
- Step 11: Students should have the following formula entered in cell E67: =SUMIFS(F10:F49,D10:D49,"Accessory",E10:E49,"Bob Cook").
- Step 12: Students should have the following formula entered in cell D70: =AVERAGEIFS(F10:F49,D10:D49,"Fish",E10:E49,"Alice Harper").
- Step 13: Students should have the following formula entered in cell D71: =AVERAGEIFS(F10:F49,D10:D49,"Fish",E10:E49,"Bob Cook").

Data/Solution Files

Data files: ETry63.xlsx
EProj139.xlsx
EProj140.xlsx

Solution files: ETry63_solution.xlsx
EProj139_solution.xlsx
EProj140_solution.xlsx

Lesson 64 Working with Absolute References and Using Financial Functions

What You Will Learn

- ✓ Using Absolute, Relative, and Mixed References
- ✓ Using Financial Functions

Words to Know

Absolute reference   PMT
FV   PV
Mixed reference   Relative reference
NPER

Tips, Hints, and Pointers

- Discuss each of the skills listed in the What You Will Learn section, and ask students if they have used any of these skills before.
- Discuss the scenario covered in the Application Skills section, and preview the tasks students will perform for Sally's Shoes.
- In this lesson, students work with financial functions and learn more about applying relative, absolute, and mixed cell references.

Using Absolute, Relative, and Mixed References

- Review cell references with students. Cell references that adjust automatically are called relative cell references because they change relative to the formula's position. For example, the formula =B4+B5 entered in column B becomes =C4+C5 when copied to column C, =D4+D5 when copied to column D, and so on.
- Relative references make it easy to copy formulas across a row to total values above, for example.
- Relative references also work best when you want to fill formulas across a row or down a column.
- Show students how to create absolute cell references to lock the cell's reference when a formula is copied to a new location.
- For example, the formula =$B$4+$B$5 contained in a cell in column B remains the same when copied to column C. The cell addresses do not adjust based on the new formula location.
- You can also create mixed cell references, where the column letter part of a cell address is absolute, and the row number if relative, or vice-versa.

- For example, the formula =B$4+B$5 contained in a cell in column B changes to =C$4+C$5 when copied to any cell in column C. The cell addresses partially adjust based on the new formula location.
- Press the F4 key as you type a cell reference in a formula to change to an absolute reference. Pressing F4 additional times cycles through the mixed references and then returns to a relative reference.
- **QUICK QUIZ:** How can you designate an absolute reference in a formula?
  You can designate a reference as absolute by typing the $ sign before the column letter and the row number or you can press the F4 key as you type a cell reference.

Using Financial Functions

- Students of an age to be considering a car purchase should be able to relate to uses for the PMT and PV functions. Older students who own or hope to own a home will also find these functions, as well as the FV function, particularly useful.
- Review the financial functions listed in the table and provide examples of situations in which you would use them.
- Stress that the rate and the number of payment periods must be expressed in the same time intervals, either monthly or yearly. If the interest rate is annual, for example, it must be divided by 12 to match monthly payment periods.

- **CUSTOMIZED INSTRUCTION: More Advanced Students:** Have students use the PMT function to determine the monthly payment for a car where the loan length is 60 months, the loan rate is 4.75%, and the loan amount is $12,000. The answer is $225.08.

Project 141—Shoe Sales Evaluation

- Step 4: Remind students to click cell C5 and position the pointer on the fill handle in the lower right corner. When the pointer changes to a solid + sign, drag down to cell C9. Students should continue to fill in the rest of the chart using the fill handle. Refer them to Figure 64-3 to ensure they have the correct values in the cells.
- **WORKPLACE SKILLS:** A worksheet that shows estimated sales like the one in Figure 64-3 can be a valuable tool to a company like Sally's Shoes. By estimating sales, a business can determine if its pricing structure will allow it to make a profit on the product or service. Profit can be defined simply as the money left over after all the bills are paid.

Project 142—Loan and Investment Analysis

- Step 3: Refer students to Figure 64-4 to see how to set up the Payment Calculation grid. In cell B7, they should enter the formula: =PMT(B5/12,B6,-B4).
- Step 4: Again, refer students to Figure 64-4 to see how to set up the Present Value Calculation grid. In cell B11, they should enter the formula: =PV(B12/12,B13,-B14).
- Step 5: Refer students to the Compound Interest Calculation grid in Figure 64-4. In cell B22, make sure students enter the formula: =B19/B20. In cell B23, they should enter the formula: =FV(B19/12,B21*B20,0,-B18).
- **WORKPLACE SKILLS:** Explain that many business owners rely on loans to help start up and run their company. When you borrow money, you increase the company's debt, which is called debt financing.

Banks and credit unions are sources of debt financing. They issue business loans for a set amount of time—called the term—at a specific interest rate. The bank may ask for collateral against the loan. Collateral is property or other assets that you pledge to the bank. If you fail to repay the loan, the bank takes ownership of the collateral. For example, if you own a truck, you might use it as collateral. The bank may also ask for a co-signer for the loan. A co-signer is an individual who agrees to make the loan payments if you cannot.

Data/Solution Files

Data files:	ETry64.xlsx
	EProj141.xlsx
	EProj142.xlsx
Solution files:	ETry64_solution.xlsx
	EProj141_solution.xlsx
	EProj142_solution.xlsx

Lesson 65 Creating and Interpreting Financial Statements

What You Will Learn

- ✓ Loading the Analysis Toolpak Add-On
- ✓ Calculating a Moving Average
- ✓ Calculating Growth Based on a Moving Average
- ✓ Using Trendlines
- ✓ Charting the Break-Even Point with a Line Chart

Words to Know

Break-even point
Moving average
Trendline

Tips, Hints, and Pointers

- Discuss each of the skills listed in the What You Will Learn section, and ask students if they have used any of these skills before.
- Discuss the scenario covered in the Application Skills section and preview the tasks students will perform for the small business owner.
- This lesson explains how to use moving averages, growth calculations and projections to create and analyze financial statements and scenarios.

Loading the Analysis Toolpak Add-On

- You may want to check student computers before class to determine if they will need to load the analysis Toolpak Add-On. If it is already loaded, skip to the next section.

Calculating a Moving Average

- **Try It! Calculating a Moving Average, Step 5:** Remind students that they can click the Collapse Dialog button on the Input Range box and select the range directly on the worksheet.
- **SKILLS EXTENSION:** Have students click the Help button in the Data Analysis dialog box and select a few of the other analysis tools listed to learn more about them. If time permits, have them discuss the different tools and how they might use them.

Calculating Growth Based on a Moving Average

- **Try It! Calculating Growth Based on a Moving Average, Step 6:** With cell B19 selected, you might instruct students to click the Insert Function button on the formula bar to open the Function Arguments dialog box. Make sure students understand the arguments in the dialog box and how they are used to calculate the growth.
- **CURRICULUM CONNECTION:** In a worksheet, have students enter their expenses for the last six weeks. If they do not keep a record of expenses, have them estimate them. Expenses can include things such as clothing, food, entertainment, gas, school supplies, etc. Have them use the Growth function to estimate expenses for the next six weeks.

Using Trendlines

- Students worked with Trendlines in Lesson 15 of Chapter 2. Remind them that Trendlines can be used to show trends in recorded data, or to suggest a forecast of future data.
- Display the Trendlines drop-down menu on the Chart Tools Layout tab. Review the types of Trendlines listed.
- **QUICK QUIZ:** When would it be useful to use functions that attempt to predict future trends?
  Analyzing marketing results, the stock market, the economy, or scientific data.

Charting the Break-Even Point with a Line Chart

- **WORKPLACE SKILLS:** Explain that the break-even point is the point at which a business sells enough units at a specified price to cover all of its costs. That includes the cost of goods sold (which includes the cost of materials and labor to produce each unit). It also includes the business's fixed costs, such as the money paid for the building it occupies and any administrative expenses that pretty much stay the same regardless of how many units the business produces.

- **DESIGN FORUM:** Ask students to consider the expression, "A picture is worth a thousand words," and discuss in class what it means.

  Pictures and other graphical representations are a way of conveying information without words. They can be a great way of communicating ideas without saying them directly or writing them down. And there are times when this is the best way to communicate. For instance, visual aids can sometimes make us see ideas, designs, and trends that would be difficult to explain otherwise. Graphs and charts like the ones you can create in Excel are excellent examples of this.

  Businesses often find that using visual aids is the most effective way to communicate. This includes making a chart instead of describing a trend in your data set, putting a picture or graph in your presentation, or drawing a picture to explain what you are talking about. Visual aids are often helpful in communicating ideas that you have so far been unsuccessful at communicating with words.

Project 143—Best Movie Theater

- Steps 5 and 7: Remind students that they can click the Collapse Dialog button at the end of the Input Range box and Output Range box and select the ranges directly on the worksheet.

Data/Solution Files

Data files: ETry65.xlsx
                     EProj143.xlsx
                     EProj144.xlsx
Solution files: ETry65_solution.xlsx
                     EProj143_solution.xlsx
                     EProj144_solution.xlsx

Project 144—Formatting a Budget Chart

- Step 3: Students should click the Data tab and then the Data Analysis button. If necessary, they should reselect the Input Range and Output Range. Make sure they change the Interval from 7 to 5 and that the Chart Output box is selected.

- Step 4: Students should click cell B19 and use either the Insert Function button on the formula bar or directly enter the GROWTH function. The function is: =GROWTH(B2:B16,A2:A16,A19:A33). Make sure students copy the function to B20:B33.

- Step 5: Remind students that to apply the Linear Trendlines, they should click the Chart Tools Layout tab, click the Trendline button, and then click Linear Trendline. In the Add Trendline dialog box, click Income. Repeat for the Expenses.

- Step 6: In cell B6, students should enter the formula: =$B$1+(A6*$B$2). In cell C6, they should enter the formula: =$B$3*A6. In cell D6, they should enter the formula: =C6-B6. Make sure the copy the formulas down their respective columns.

- **JOB FOCUS:** Many entrepreneurs create worksheets like those that students worked on in Projects 49 and 50 to help them evaluate their company's financial status. An entrepreneur is a person who organizes and runs his or her own business. Entrepreneurs are often both owners and employees. An entrepreneur is responsible for the success or failure of his or her business. A successful business sells products or services that customers need, at prices they are willing to pay. Ask students to comment on their own entrepreneurial interests and pursuits. Discuss entrepreneurs in the community and those who have started businesses from which you buy products or services.

Lesson 66   Creating Scenarios and Naming Ranges

What You Will Learn

- ✓ Creating a Scenario Using the Scenario Manager
- ✓ Naming a Range
- ✓ Creating a Scenario Summary

Words to Know

Scenario
Scenario Manager
Variable

Tips, Hints, and Pointers

- Discuss each of the skills listed in the What You Will Learn section, and ask students if they have used any of these skills before.
- Discuss the scenario covered in the Application Skills section, and preview the tasks students will perform for Breakaway Bike Shop.
- In this lesson, students create and save versions of worksheet data based on "what-if" data, and then use Scenario Manager to work with the various versions.

Creating a Scenario Using the Scenario Manager

- Explain what a scenario is. It's like a situation; you can plug variables into it and save it for later reuse.
- Create a few scenarios for use in demonstration. Show the Scenario Manager dialog box, and explain that you can use it to switch between scenarios and create, summarize, delete, and manage them.
- Try It! Creating a Scenario Using the Scenario Manager, Step 3: If necessary, point out that the formulas in B9:D9 calculate the cost to produce by multiplying the hours in cell B7 by the Hourly labor cost ($45) and the units in cell B8 by the Material and supplies cost ($57).
- Step 14: Students should use Most Likely case and Best case as the names for the scenarios. They can add to the Comment box if desired.

Naming a Range

- Discuss the uses of cell ranges and explain that ranges can be named to make it easier for a user to identify a specific area of a worksheet.

- Show students how to name a range and then use the named range in a formula or to print a portion of a worksheet.
- Discuss rules for naming ranges, with special emphasis on avoiding row or column labels, which can cause confusion for users of the worksheet.
- Have students practice naming several ranges in a sample worksheet using both the Define Name command and the Name Box. Remind them to use Go To (F5) to move quickly to a named range.
- Show students how the range name displays on the Name Box drop-down menu.
- Demonstrate how to open the Name Manager dialog box where you can edit and delete named ranges.

Creating a Scenario Summary

- Explain to students that they can set which scenario's values display in the worksheet through the Scenario Manager dialog box. The scenario they choose will appear in the Current Values column on the Scenario Summary worksheet.

Project 145—Theater Profits

- Steps 5 and 7: You might have students click the Name Box drop-down arrow to view the range names assigned to the cells.
- Step 17: Students will need to scroll the list of changing values in the Scenario Values dialog box in order to see the Ticket-price cell.

- Step 18: Point out that the profit decreases by more than $600 when the ticket price is lowered by 50 cents.

Project 146—Repair Scenarios
- Step 3: Click the Data tab, click the What If Analysis button, and click Scenario Manager. Click Add. Type the name as instructed in the Scenario Name box. In the Changing cells text box, type the ranges as instructed, separating each with a comma.
- Step 4: In the Scenario Values dialog box, students can press Tab to move down the list of changing cells and enter the new values.
- Step 5: Make sure students follow the recommended procedure as instructed in the note following this step.

Data/Solution Files

Data files:	ETry66.xlsx
	EProj145.xlsx
	EProj146.xlsx
Solution files:	ETry66_solution.xlsx
	EProj145_solution.xlsx
	EProj146_solution.xlsx

Lesson 67 Finding and Fixing Errors in Formulas

What You Will Learn

- ✓ Using Formula Error Checking
- ✓ Understanding Error Messages
- ✓ Showing Formulas
- ✓ Evaluating Individual Formulas
- ✓ Using the Watch Window
- ✓ Tracing Precedents and Dependents

Words to Know

Circular reference
Dependents
Evaluate
Error Checking
Precedent
Watch Window

Tips, Hints, and Pointers

- Discuss each of the skills listed in the What You Will Learn section, and ask students if they have used any of these skills before.
- Discuss the scenario covered in the Application Skills section, and preview the tasks students will perform for Wood Hills Animal Clinic and Old Southern Furniture.
- This lesson explains how to correct common errors in formulas and functions.
- CUSTOMIZED INSTRUCTION: ESOL Students: Have students make flash cards of the terms in the Words to Know list. They should write the term in both English and their primary language on one side and the definition in English only on the other side.

Using Formula Error Checking

- Intentionally create a formula with an error, to show the Error Checking icon that appears next to the cell. Open its menu and review the options there.
- Review the types of errors on page 496 of the textbook.

Understanding Error Messages

- If time permits, have students try to reproduce all the errors in the Error Messages section (pages 496-497) of the textbook by intentionally creating the errors.
- Explain circular references, and how to correct one.

- **Try It! Correcting Formula Errors, Step 6:** Make sure students click the Error Checking button and not its drop-down arrow. Instruct students to click the Resume button.
- **Step 9:** Remind students that the Format Painter button is on the Home tab.
- **Steps 14-15:** Make sure students read the notes following each of these steps for helpful tips.

Showing Formulas

- Demonstrate how to show formulas in a worksheet and then redisplay the results.

Evaluating an Individual Formula

- Demonstrate the Evaluate Formula feature, which shows each intermediate step involved in the formula. Discuss the benefits of using this to troubleshoot a complex formula. To show this, use a formula that has three levels of nested functions.
- **Try It! Evaluating a Formula:** You might point out how each evaluation is carried out as students work through the exercise. If you think it would be helpful, have them use a calculator to carry out the evaluations in steps 6 and 9.

Using the Watch Window

- Display the Watch Window, and show how the results in it change as you make changes to the worksheet. Show that the Watch Window can be docked as a task pane.

Tracing Precedents and Dependents

- Define precedent and dependent and show examples. Set up a worksheet that references a formula in several jumps from one reference to another, and then turn on Trace Precedents to show how they connect.
- **CUSTOMIZED INSTRUCTION: Less Advanced Students:** Provide several worksheets containing formulas where students can trace precedents and dependents. Take extra time to point out precedents and dependents.

Project 147—Wood Hills Animal Clinic

- Step 9: The value in cell E64 should be $1.84.
- **WORKPLACE SKILLS:** A profit and loss statement is a financial document that summarizes a business's income and expenses over a given time period. Most are prepared once a month, quarterly, or once a year like the one students worked on in this project. A profit and loss statement has three parts:
    - **Revenue.** This is the money a company receives from selling its products, before taking into account how much money was spent on making and selling them.
    - **Expenses.** This is a list of everything a company pays to operate the business. It includes the cost of making, store, and selling its products, as well as rent for the company and wages for employees.
    - **Net profit (or loss).** Net profit is the amount of money a company actually makes, and net loss is the amount of money a company loses. Both are calculated by subtracting the expenses from the revenue.
- The health of a company is reflected by the numbers on the profit and loss statement.

Project 148—Earnings

- Step 4a: Note that students will enter values in cells B9 and B10 later in this exercise. In cell C13, they should enter the formula: =B13*$B$9.
- Step 4c: In cell D13, students should enter the formula: =IF(B13>40000,$B$10,0).
- Step 6: Remind students that the Trace Precedents button is on the Formulas tab. The arrows should point to cells B9 and B16.
- Step 7: The arrows should point to cells B10 and B14.
- Step 8: The arrows should point to cells B16, C16, and D16.
- Step 10: The arrows should point to cells C13 through C24.
- Step 11: The arrows should point to cells D13 through D24.
- Step 12: The arrows should point to cells C13, D13, and E13.
- Step 13: Remind students that the Evaluate Formula button is on the Formulas tab.
- Step 14: Remind students that the Show Formulas button is on the Formulas tab.

Data/Solution Files

Data files: ETry67.xlsx
 EProj147.xlsx
 Eproj148.xlsx
Solution files: ETry67_solution.xlsx
 EProj147_solution.xlsx
 EProj148_solution.xlsx

Lesson 68 Ensuring Data Integrity

What You Will Learn

- ✓ Turning Off AutoComplete
- ✓ Controlling Data Entry with Data Validation
- ✓ Circling Invalid Data
- ✓ Copying Validation Rules
- ✓ Removing Duplicate Data

Words to Know

Input message
Paste Special
Validation

Tips, Hints, and Pointers

- Discuss each of the skills listed in the What You Will Learn section, and ask students if they have used any of these skills before.
- Discuss the scenario covered in the Application Skills section, and preview the tasks students will perform for PhotoTown.
- In this lesson, students learn how to create data validation rules and identify invalid and duplicate data.

Turning Off AutoComplete

- You will probably want to have students turn the AutoComplete feature back on before shutting down their lab computers.

Controlling Data Entry with Data Validation

- Ask students to identify the most common data entry mistakes in worksheets. For example, people might enter states as full words or as two-letter codes, and might make typos in typing city names.
- Summarize the various ways of preventing user errors, including drop-down list lookups and validation.
- Explain what validation is, and show some examples, such as preventing states from being entered as anything other than a two-character code.
- Show the Data Validation dialog box and discuss the options there. For example, to restrict entry to a predefined list, you could put the list in a separate part of the worksheet (such as a hidden column) and then refer to it in the Source box.

- Point out that the entry list can be a range of cells with one item per cell or a single cell with a list of items separated by commas.
- To use a named range as the list, type the name preceded by an equals sign.
- Warn students that data validation doesn't work if the data is placed into the cell using the fill handle, or moved/copied from another location, or appears there as the result of a formula.
- **Try It! Setting Up a Simple Data Validation Rule, Step 4:** Make sure students click the Data Validation button and not its drop-down arrow.
- Show how to set up a custom error message on the Error Alert tab of the Data Validation dialog box.
- Mention that there are different alert styles you can choose, and they affect whether the user can proceed or not. A Stop alert refuses the entry. A Warning alert asks whether the user wants to proceed. An Information alert presents the error message only.

Circling Invalid Data

- Show how to use the Circle Invalid Data command to find errors in validation that have already been entered in the sheet.
- **Try It! Circling Invalid Data, Step 1:** Make sure students click the Data Validation drop-down arrow.

Copying Validation Rules
- Show how to copy and paste validation rules between cells with the Paste Special command.

Removing Duplicate Data
- Discuss why you would want to remove duplicate data from a list, and show how to use the Remove Duplicates command to do so.

Project 149—PhotoTown Order Form
- Step 5b: Remind students to click the Data Validation button and not its drop-down arrow.
- **DESIGN FORUM:** Most businesses require employees to do some degree of data entry, and many have departments of employees devoted to data entry. It is an important and tedious function and one in which errors can lead to misleading or just plain wrong results.

  Because of this danger, it is critical that data entry forms (such as the PhotoTown order form) be designed to eliminate or minimize the possibility of incorrect or inaccurate data being entered. Explain to students the importance of taking measures to limit the amount of new data that must be entered on a form. This can be achieved through the use of lookup functions. You can also use data validation to ensure the accuracy of data that users enter.

Project 150—PhotoTown Order Form
- Step 4: In the Data Validation dialog box, on the Settings tab, click the Allow drop-down arrow and click Whole number; click the Data drop-down arrow and click greater than; and in the Minimum box, type 0. On the Error Alert tab, select the Stop style if necessary. In the Error Message box, type a message such as, "Enter Positive Whole Numbers."
- Step 6: In the Data Validation dialog box, on the Settings tab, click the Allow drop-down arrow and click Text length; click the Data drop-down arrow and click less than or equal to; and in the Minimum box, type 180. On the Input Message tab, in the Input message box, type Enter up to 180 characters. On the Error Alert tab, select the Stop style; type Too Long for the Title; and in the Error message box, type Please enter a message of no more than 180 characters.
- Step 10: Remind students that the Remove Duplicates button is on the Data tab.

Data/Solution Files

Data files: ETry68.xlsx
               EProj149.xlsx
               EProj150.xlsx

Solution files: ETry68_solution.xlsx
                EProj149_solution.xlsx
                EProj150_solution.xlsx

Chapter Assessment and Application
Project 151 Analyzing a Business Opportunity

Tips, Hints, and Pointers

- Discuss the scenario, and preview the tasks students will perform as they evaluate the business purchase.
- In this activity, students use financial functions to evaluate business loans.
- Step 2: Remind students that they can group the sheets and add the header to all the sheets at once. To group sheets, click the first sheet and hold down Shift as you select the other sheets.
- Step 3: Students should enter the following formula in G5: =SUMIF($C$5:$C$124,"Facility Rental",$D$5:$D$124).
- Step 4: Students should enter the following formulas in the specified cells:

    G6: =SUMIF($C$5:$C$124,"Loan Payment",$D$5:$D$124)

    G7: =SUMIF($C$5:$C$124,"Materials",$D$5:$D$124)

    G8: =SUMIF($C$5:$C$124,"Payroll",$D$5:$D$124)

    G9: =SUMIF($C$5:$C$124,"Utilities",$D$5:$D$124)

    G12: =SUMIF($C$5:$C$64,"Facility Rental",$D$5:$D$64)

    G13: =SUMIF($C$5:$C$64,"Loan Payment",$D$5:$D$64)

    G14: =SUMIF($C$5:$C$64,"Materials",$D$5:$D$64)

    G15: =SUMIF($C$5:$C$64,"Payroll",$D$5:$D$64)

    G16: =SUMIF($C$5:$C$64,"Utilities",$D$5:$D$64)

    G19: =SUMIF($C$65:$C$128,"Facility Rental",$D$65:$D$124)

    G20: =SUMIF($C$65:$C$128,"Loan Payment",$D$65:$D$124)

    G21: =SUMIF($C$65:$C$128,"Materials",$D$65:$D$124)

    G22: =SUMIF($C$65:$C$128,"Payroll",$D$65:$D$124)

    G23: =SUMIF($C$65:$C$128,"Utilities",$D$65:$D$124)

    I5: =SUMIF($B$5:$B$128,"Fixed",$D$5:$D$128)

    I6: =SUMIF($B$5:$B$128,"Variable",$D$5:$D$128)

    I9: =SUMIF($B$5:$B$64,"Fixed",$D$5:$D$64)

    I10: =SUMIF($B$65:$B$128,"Variable",$D$5:$D$64)

    I13: =SUMIF($B$65:$B$124,"Fixed",$D$65:$D$124)

    I14: =SUMIF($B$65:$B$128,"Variable",$D$65:$D$124)

- Step 6: Make sure students read the notes following the step for helpful tips on completing the task.
- Step 8: Select A5:A28, hold down the Ctrl key, and select E5:E28. Then, click the Insert tab, click the Line button, and click Line.
- Step 9: On the Chart Tools Layout tab, click the Trendline button, and click Exponential Trendline.
- Step 11: Students should enter the following formula in B9: =PMT(B7/12,B8,-$B$4). They should enter the following formula in C9: =PMT(C7/12,C8,-$B$4).
- Step 12: Students should enter the following formula in B10: =IF(C9<MIN(Summary!$E$5:$E$28),"OK","No").
- Steps 13-14: Remind students to set up the scenarios using the Scenario Manager. Click the Data tab, click the What-If Analysis button, and click Scenario Manager.

Data/Solution Files

Data file: EProj151.xlsx
Solution file: EProj151_solution.xlsx

Project 152 Projecting Business Scenarios

Tips, Hints, and Pointers

- Discuss the scenario, and preview the tasks students will perform as they evaluate the business purchase.
- In this activity, students use scenarios and a moving average to help them evaluate the business.
- Step 3: Remind students to click the Data Analysis button on the Data tab. Then, click Moving Average in the Data Analysis dialog box and click OK. The Input Range should be the data in column E and the Output Range should be the cells in column F. Make sure they click the Chart Output box in the Moving Average dialog box.
- Step 4: Students should enter the formula, =GROWTH(B17:B28,A17:A28,A29:A40), in cell B29.
- Step 10: Make sure students enter =$I$29 in cell C29.
- Steps 13-15: Remind students to use the Scenario Manager to create the scenarios. Click the Data tab, click the What-If Analysis button, and click Scenario Manager.
- Step 16: Make sure students have displayed the Most Likely scenario before printing.

Data/Solution Files

Data file: EProj152.xlsx
Solution file: EProj152_solution.xlsx

Chapter 9: Importing and Analyzing Database Data
Lesson 69 Recording a Macro

What You Will Learn

- Adding the Developer Tab to the Ribbon
- Setting the Macro Security Level
- Setting Trusted Locations
- Saving a Workbook That Contains Macros
- Recording a Macro
- Running a Macro

Words to Know

Absolute recording
Developer tab
Macro
Macro security
Relative recording
Trusted location
VBA
.xlsm

Tips, Hints, and Pointers

- Discuss each of the skills listed in the What You Will Learn section, and ask students if they have used any of these skills before.
- Discuss the scenario covered in the Application Skills section, and preview the tasks students will perform for the Small business Professional Organization.
- This lesson teaches students how to record, run, and edit a macro.

Adding the Developer Tab to the Ribbon

- You might want to check student computers before class to see if the Developer tab has already been added. If it has been added, skip ahead to the next section.
- If desired, you might want to have students remove the Developer tab before they log off of their computers.

Setting the Macro Security Level

- Explain to students that "malware" is short for malicious software and is a type of program designed to infiltrate a computer without the user's permission or informed consent.

Setting Trusted Locations

- **SKILLS EXTENSION:** Have students open the Excel Options dialog box, click Trust Center, and click Trust Center Settings. If there are other User Locations listed as trusted locations, have students write down the list on a sheet of paper.
- **Try It! Setting Trusted Locations:** Once students have successfully completed this exercise, you might want to have them remove the trusted location from the Trust Center. To do this, click the File tab and then click Options. In the Excel Options dialog box, click Trust Center. Click Trust Center Settings. In the Trusted Locations list box, click the desired location and then click the Remove button.

Saving a Workbook That Contains Macros

- Make sure students understand that they cannot save a workbook containing macros in the default workbook format (.xlsx). Instead, it must be saved in macro-enabled format, which has the file extension of .xlsm.
- Saving in this format increases the security level to help prevent potential risks to your computer.

Recording a Macro

- Explain that you record a macro to automate tasks or actions that you perform frequently.
- A single macro can store an unlimited number of keystrokes or mouse actions.

- Macros can save time and help eliminate data entry and formatting errors.
- Show students where the Record Macros is on the Developer tab and on the status bar. Point out that the button changes to Stop Recording when you are recording the macro.
- Record a sample macro and demonstrate how to complete the Record Macro dialog box. Make sure students understand that macro names cannot contain spaces.
- As soon as you start recording, everything you input into your computer is stored in the macro.
- If a macro doesn't work the way you want, you can delete it and record it again.
- **CUSTOMIZED INSTRUCTION: Special Needs Students:** Macros are an effective way for physically challenged students to reduce the number of keystrokes and mouse clicks they make. Ask students to comment on the tasks they perform routinely in Excel that they could create macros to complete for them.
- **QUICK QUIZ:** Distinguish between absolute recording and relative recording.

  With absolute recording, the macro begins recording your actions based on the cell that is active. When you run the macro, it begins on that cell, regardless of which cell is currently active. With relative recording, the macro begins on whatever cell or range is currently selected.
- **Try It! Recording a Macro, Steps 7-12:** Point out to students that if they make a mistake, they can click the Stop Recording button and start over again on the macro.

Running a Macro

- Review the various ways you can run a macro and demonstrate each one.
- Students will add a button for the macro to the Quick Access Toolbar. They will remove the button in a later exercise.

Editing a Macro

- This section of the text provides a very brief introduction to Visual Basic for Applications (VBA), which is the programming language used to create macros.
- **Try It! Editing a Macro, Step 4:** Make sure students type the code exactly as it is shown in the text.

Project 153—Business Meeting Attendance

- Step 5: Make sure students select the .xlsm format options from the Save as type drop-down list.
- Step 23: Before closing the workbook, you might want to have students remove the macro. To do this, click the Developer tab and then click the Macros button. In the Macro dialog box, select the macro and then click Delete. Click yes to confirm the deletion.

Project 154—Revenue Chart

- Step 1: Make sure students save the workbook in .xlsm format as well.
- Step 2: Remind students that they can also group the two worksheets and enter the header information on both at the same time.
- Step 3: Click the Developer tab and click the Record Macro button. Enter the macro information as instructed.
- Step 6: To delete the chart, click it and press Delete. To run the macro, press Ctrl + s.
- Step 7: Click the Developer tab, click the Macros button, select the macro, and click Edit. In the VBA window, go to the ActiveChart.ChartStyle = 3 line and change the 3 to a 4. Click File and then click Close and Return to Microsoft Excel.
- Step 9: Before closing the workbook, you might want to have students remove the macro. To do this, click the Developer tab and then click the Macros button. In the Macro dialog box, select the macro and then click Delete. Click yes to confirm the deletion.

Data/Solution Files

Data files: ETry69.xlsx
                   EProj153.xlsx
                   EProj154.xlsm
Solution files: ETry69_solution.xlsm
                   EProj153_solution.xlsm
                   EProj154_solution.xlsm

Lesson 70 Importing Data into Excel

What You Will Learn

- ✓ Importing Data from an Access Database
- ✓ Importing Data from a Web Page
- ✓ Importing Data from a Text File
- ✓ Importing Data from an XML File

Words to Know

Data source
Database
Datasheet
Delimited
Delimiter character

Field
Markup language
Table
Record
XML

Tips, Hints, and Pointers

- Discuss each of the skills listed in the What You Will Learn section, and ask students if they have used any of these skills before.
- Discuss the scenario covered in the Application Skills section, and preview the tasks students will perform for World Services Real Estate.
- In this lesson, students work with data imported to Excel from other sources.

Importing Data from an Access Database

- Explain to students that because you can set up Excel ranges as tables, you can perform many of the same database tasks on worksheet data as you would on table data in a database.
- **Try It! Importing Data from an Access Database, Step 1:** Point out to students that the workbook does not contain data yet, but they will import data from various sources to the designated worksheets.
- **Step 4:** If necessary, remind students where the data files for this lesson are stored. Point out the extension .accdb on Access database files.

Importing Data from a Web Page

- Discuss situations in which a user might want to copy data from a Web page into Excel. "Data" may consist of tabular data, text, hyperlinks, or even graphics.
- Caution students that Web page copyrights must be respected; no user should ever copy data from a Web page and pass it off as his or her own data. When data is copied for a report or other publication, proper permission should be secured and the source of the data should be indicated.
- If students have Internet access, have them log in to the browser's start page and practice copying information from this page and pasting it in an Excel worksheet. Or, you might have students visit your school's home page from which they can copy information.
- **Try It! Importing Data from a Web Page:** Note that students will need Internet access in order to complete this exercise.
- **CURRICULUM CONNECTION:** When traveling abroad or conducting business internationally, it is important to know the exchange rate for converting American dollars to other currency. In some countries, the dollar will be worth more, and in others it will be less. Exchange rates change daily, but usually not by much.

  Have students look up the exchange rate of American dollars to Australian dollars. They should create a worksheet that lists the price of at least five items that they use on a regular basis and then use the conversion formula to list the equivalent cost of the same item in Australian dollars. Encourage them to expand the worksheet to include other foreign currency, such as the euro, or the Japanese yen.
- **CUSTOMIZED INSTRUCTION: ESOL Students:** Have students determine the currency exchange rate between the U.S. dollar and the currency from their country of origin. They can use an online currency conversion calculator, look up the

176 | Learning Microsoft Excel 2010 | Teacher's Manual

information in the business section of a daily newspaper, or contact a local bank.

Importing Data from a Text File
- **Try It! Importing Data from a Text File, Step 3:** If necessary, remind students where the data files for this lesson are stored.
- **Step 6:** Students can click anywhere in the second column in order to select it.

Importing Data from an XML File
- Explain that XML stands for Extensible Markup Language. It is a set of rules for encoding documents electronically, typically to be viewed and read online.
- **Try It! Importing Data from an XML File, Step 4:** If necessary, remind students where the data files for this lesson are stored.

Project 155—Consumer Price Index
- Note that students will need Internet access in order to download the specified information.
- **Step 11:** Allow time for students to format the data attractively.
- **WORKPLACE SKILLS:** Review with students the topic of plagiarism and how it applies to obtaining data from the Internet. Plagiarism is when you copy someone else's work and pass it off as your own. The Internet, unfortunately, makes plagiarism easy, because you can copy and paste data and information from a Web page into another file by simply copying and pasting. In some cases, you do not need permission to copy data from a Web site, such as the Bureau of Labor Statistics site from which you copied data for Project 61. But, generally, you should expect that content on a Web site has been copyrighted and subject to restrictions on its use. You should not submit content that you get from a Web site as your own work as it may result in failing grades, job loss, and even legal penalties.

Project 156—Real Estate Listings
- Step 4: To import Access data, click the Data tab and click the From Access button. Make sure students have cell A3 entered as the location where the data will be inserted.
- Step 5: Click the List Price filter arrow and click Sort Largest to Smallest.
- Step 6: Once the data is pasted to the Bedrooms sheet, click the Bedrooms filter arrow and click Sort Largest to Smallest.
- Step 7: To print the first page only, click the File tab and click Print. Under Print Settings, specify that you only want to print page 1 to page 1.

Data/Solution Files

Data files:
ETry70.xlsx
ETry70.accdb
ETry70.txt
axml.xml
EProj155.xlsx
EProj156.xlsx
EProj156.accdb

Solution files:
ETry70_solution.xlsx
EProj155_solution.xlsx
EProj156_solution.xlsx

Lesson 71 Working with Excel Tables

What You Will Learn

- ✓ Converting Ranges to Tables
- ✓ Showing a Totals Row in a Table
- ✓ Viewing Two Tables Side-by-Side
- ✓ Applying Icon Sets

Words to Know

Banded columns
Banded rows
Filter
Icon Sets
Table

Tips, Hints, and Pointers

- Discuss each of the skills listed in What You Will Learn section, and ask students if they have used any of these skills before.
- Discuss the scenario covered in the Application Skills section, and preview the tasks students will perform for Rural Estates Real Estate.
- This lesson explains how to use tables to filter, sort, and visually illustrate worksheet data.

Converting Ranges to Tables

- An Excel table is a range of data with special features that enable you to reference a column of data in a formula more naturally and build formulas more easily.
- Excel tables are best for data that's organized primarily by columns, because automatic totals and other functions can be inserted per column, but not by row.
- Formatting a range as an Excel table enables you to apply formatting and create calculations with more ease.
- You also can sort and filter the data in the table to organize it for analysis.
- You create a table by clicking in a range of data that includes headings for every column, and then using the Table button in the Tables group of the Insert tab.
- Explain that banding is applied automatically when you create a table out of a range that does not already have fill colors applied. You can add or removing banding as desired.
- Point out that Excel will automatically identify the proper range for a table if there are no blank columns or rows within the data and the column headers are contiguous to the range of data.
- Point out the drop-down arrows that appear on the column headings in a table. Explain that clicking the arrow displays a drop-down menu with options for sorting and filtering the data in the table according to criteria set for that column.

Showing a Totals Row in a Table

- Explain that a Totals row is a quick, easy way to summarize data in a table.
- Demonstrate how to add a Totals row. You can right-click a cell in the last row of the table, click Table on the shortcut menu, and then click Totals Row. Or, you can click the Table Tools Design tab and click the Total Row check box.

Viewing Two Tables Side-by-Side

- **Try It! Viewing Two Tables Side-by-Side by Moving a Table, Steps 2 and 10:** After you have selected the table, make sure the pointer is in the shape of a four-headed arrow and *not* a plus sign.
- **Try It! Viewing Two Tables Side-by-Side by Opening an Additional Window:** Make sure students click the window they want to be active before they attempt to scroll or perform another action. The window must be active before any actions can be performed on it.

Applying Icon Sets

- Explain that Icon Sets are a form of conditional formatting.
- Conditional formatting is a volatile type of formatting that changes depending on what the values or calculated results in the cells are.

- This type of formatting enables you to visually identify key data, and it updates automatically if you update worksheet values and formulas.
- **Try It! Editing the Icon Definitions, Steps 3-4:** Take time to explain to students how they are changing the rules, or conditions, the data must meet in order to be assigned the green arrow and the yellow arrow.
- **DESIGN FORUM:** Point out to students that while conditional formatting highlights important information and can add visual interest to a worksheet, you should be careful in the specific formats you select. In the financial world, red usually indicates a negative number whereas green indicates positive. The red, green, and yellow colors used on icon sets have the same meanings as the red, green, and yellow traffic light colors. In addition, dark fill colors and data bars that are sometimes used for conditional formatting can make the values in cells hard to read.
- **CUSTOMIZED INSTRUCTION: More Advanced Students:** Have students create a table of 10 to 15 items on their cafeteria menu along with prices. Have them create four copies of the table and place them at different locations on the worksheet. Have them apply each of the five different types of conditional formats that are available. These are:
  - Highlight cells rule, which applies specified formatting to cells whose contents meet a certain rule.
  - Top/bottom rule, which applies specified formatting to cells with the top or bottom values.
  - Data bars, which applies a horizontal bar that varies in length depending on the value in the cell.
  - Color scales, which applies different cell fill colors based on the values in the cells.
  - Icon sets, which applies a graphic to cells based on their values.

Project 157—Real Estate Recommendations
- Step 8: Remind students that to select a column, then can click on the column letter.

Data/Solution Files
Data files: ETry71.xlsx
                     EProj157.xlsx
                     EProj158.xlsx
Solution files: ETry71_solution.xlsx
                     EProj157_solution.xlsx
                     EProj158_solution.xlsx

- **SKILLS EXTENSION:** Have students study the Icon Set conditional formatting applied to the SqFt column. Ask them to explain what the green, yellow, and red flags indicate. You can determine this by opening the Edit Formatting Rule dialog box. The green flag indicates that the square footage is in the top 33% of square footage for all properties listed; the yellow flag indicates that the square footage is in the middle range of square footage for all properties listed; and the red flag indicates that the square footage is in the lower 33% of square footage for all properties listed.

Project 158—Real Estate Recommendations
- Step 4: Click the SqFt filter arrow, and click Sort Largest to Smallest; click the Area filter arrow, and check only the Coastal option; click the Type filter arrow, and check only Single Family; click the Pool filter arrow, and check True; and click the HOA Fees filter arrow and check False.
- Step 5: Select the column, click the Home tab, click the Conditional Formatting button, and click Icon Sets. Select the specified set. (These are referred to as the 3 Traffic Lights.)
- Step 6: Click the Conditional Formatting button, and click Manage Rules. Click the rule and click Edit Rule. Click the Reverse Icon Order button and click OK twice.
- Step 13: To clear filters, click the Data tab and then click the Clear button. Click the Area filter arrow and check only the Coastal option; and click the Type filter arrow and check Condo and Duplex.
- Step 15: Click the Home tab, click the Conditional Formatting button, click Clear Rules, and then click Clear Rules from This Table.
- Steps 17-18: Click the Conditional Formatting button and click Manage Rules. Click the rule and click Edit Rule. Make the modifications to the rule as instructed.
- Step 19: Click the List Price filter area, point to Filter by Color, and then click the green flag icon.

Lesson 72 Using Advanced Filters and Database Functions

What You Will Learn
✓ Using Advanced Filters
✓ Using Database Functions

Words to Know
Argument
Criteria range
Database range
Extract

Tips, Hints, and Pointers

- Discuss each of the skills listed in the What You Will Learn section, and ask students if they have used any of these skills before.
- Discuss the scenario covered in the Application Skills section, and preview the tasks students will perform for Pete's Pets and Katt's Catering.
- This lesson reviews advanced filtering and shows students how to use database functions on filtered data.

Using Advanced Filters

- Advanced filters were introduced in Lesson 6 of Chapter 1.
- Explain that the main advantage of an advanced filter is that it allows you to *extract* (copy) records to another location based on the filter criteria. Advanced filters also allow more complex criteria.
- Instead of selecting criteria from a drop-down list as students did in exercises in the previous lessons, you enter it in a criteria range.
- Explain that you must set up your *criteria range* prior to using an advanced filter. Explain what a criteria range is, and show how to set one up. Mention that typically the criteria range is above or to the right of the original list or table, separated by a few rows or columns.
- Show the Advanced Filter dialog box and explain the options there.
- Show how to remove an advanced filter (Data tab, Clear button).
- **Try It! Using an Advanced Filter to Extract Records, Step 3h:** Students can either enter the cell reference as shown in the figure below in the Copy to box, or they can click the Collapse Dialog button and select J8 directly on the July Race worksheet.
- **Step 3k:** Point out to students the data in the Qualifying Heat column of the Copy to range. The values should be 1, 2, or 3.
- **Try It! Using an Advanced Filter to Filter In-Place, Step 3g:** Point out that the filter is applied to the original table on the June Race worksheet because you did not specify a Copy to range in the Advanced Filter dialog box.
- **Try It! Using an Advanced Filter with a Comparison Operator, Step 5:** Note that $A$6:$K$93 should appear in the List range box.
- **Step 7:** Point out that the values in column H should be less than three times the corresponding values in column E.

Using Database Functions

- Make sure students understand the term *database*, and that they know about records and fields.
- As a simple introduction to database functions, show how to use DCOUNT to count the number of records that have a particular value in a particular field.
- Review the three arguments common to all database functions as discussed in the text. These are *database range*, *field*, and *criteria range*.
- Show the database function syntax that uses these arguments, and show some examples.
- Point out that you can use named ranges in functions, and remind students how to name a range.

- Review the table of database functions listed in the text, and have students come up with examples of situations where some of these might be useful.
- **Try It! Using Database Functions, Step 3:** Make sure students click the Define Name button and not its drop-down arrow.
- **Steps 14, 16, and 19:** Reminds students to enter the database functions exactly as they appear in the text.

Project 159—Pete's Pets
- Step 2: Remind students that they can group the worksheets to enter the information on both at the same time.
- Step 3d: Remind students that they can either enter the Criteria range as shown or click the Collapse Dialog button and select it directly on the worksheet.
- Step 3g: Point out that the values in the Current Inventory column should be less than or equal to the corresponding values in the Reorder When column.
- Step 12: Remind students that the Format Painter is on the Home tab.
- Step 14: Remind students that they can type lowercase characters for the function name and cell references.

Project 160—Katt's Catering
- Step 2: Remind students that they can group the worksheets to enter the information on both at the same time.
- Step 3: Make sure students type the database function exactly as shown in the text. Include a comma after each argument.
- Step 5: Students should enter the following function in cell B7: =DAVERAGE(Order,"Cost per Case",B4:B5).
- Step 6: Students should enter the following function in cell B8: =DSUM(Order,"Total Weight",B4:B5).
- Step 7: Students should enter the following function in cell B9: =DSUM(Order,"Total Cost",B4:B5).
- Step 8: Students should enter the following function in cell B10: =(B8/50)*20.
- Step 9: Students should enter the following function in cell B11: =B9+B10.
- **JOB FOCUS:** Many companies, such as Pete's Pets and Katt's Catering, employ an inventory manager to order, track, and manage the business's inventory of products. The responsibilities of an inventory manager vary depending on the type of business, but in general, they include the following:
  - Manages the storage and distribution of a company's products as well as materials it uses in the production of products.
  - Oversees the bookkeeping of accounts and financial control of the department's budget.
  - Maintains all inventory records.
  - Establishes and maintains good communication between the department and other departments in the company, such as Production, Quality Control, Purchasing, and Sales.
  - Logs the receipt of stock and notifies all interested departments of the arrival of stock.
  - Inspects and checks all deliveries and the return to the supplier of rejected stock.
  - Manages the distribution of products as well as production materials.

Data/Solution Files

Data files:
ETry72a.xlsx
ETry72b.xlsx
ETry72c.xlsx
EProj159.xlsx
EProj160.xlsx

Solution files:
ETry72a_solution.xlsx
ETry72b_solution.xlsx
ETry72c_solution.xlsx
EProj159_solution.xlsx
EProj160_solution.xlsx

Lesson 73 Using Data Consolidation

What You Will Learn
- ✓ Consolidating Data
- ✓ Working with Consolidated Data

Words to Know
Consolidation by category
Consolidation by position

Tips, Hints, and Pointers

- Discuss each of the skills listed in the What You Will Learn section, and ask students if they have used any of these skills before.
- Discuss the scenario covered in the Application Skills section, and preview the tasks students will perform for Holy Habanero.
- In this lesson, students learn about data consolidation. This feature consolidates data from separate ranges into a single worksheet. Contrast this process with 3-D formulas, if students are familiar with this feature.

Consolidating Data
- Discuss that you can consolidate by category or by position, and show examples of each.
- Point out that consolidating by position requires the data to be in the exact same cells on each sheet. In contrast, consolidation by category relies on column and row labels, rather than cell references.
- **Try It! Consolidate Data:** Students will consolidate the data from three different data files into a new workbook they create.

Working with Consolidated Data
- **Try It! Working with Consolidated Data, Steps 2 and 4:** Point out that when you click the plus sign to expand the listing, the records associated display above the value.
- **Step 7:** Make sure students click the Insert button and not its drop-down arrow.

Project 161—Sales Breakdown
- **Step 3d:** Make sure students do not skip over this important step.
- **Step 8:** Have students note the value in cell J27 on the Totals worksheet before they edit the value on the January worksheet.

Project 162—Daily Sales
- **Step 3:** Instruct students to click the Data tab, and click the Consolidate button. In the Consolidate dialog box, make sure they select the Sum function. For the Reference, click the Collapse Dialog button and select the B9:H13 on the August Week 2 worksheet. Click Add in the Consolidate dialog box. Repeat for the rest of the days. When they are done, there should be seven references in the All references box. Make sure they copy the Total Sales and Commission formulas from the August Week 2 worksheet.
- **Step 4:** In the Consolidate dialog box, make sure students select the Average function.

Data/Solution Files

Data files:
- ETry73a.xlsx
- ETry73b.xlsx
- ETry73c.xlsx
- EProj161.xlsx
- Eproj162.xlsx

Solution files:
- ETry73_solution.xlsx
- EProj161_solution.xlsx
- EProj162_solution.xlsx

Chapter Assessment and Application
Project 163 Chamber of Commerce Presentation

Tips, Hints, and Pointers

- Discuss the scenario, and preview the tasks students will perform for the Center City Chamber of Commerce.
- In this activity, students consolidate real estate information, filter data, and create macros.
- Step 3: Point out to students that the EProj163a.xlsx workbook they use in this step is a data file. They will be copying data from this file to the workbook they saved in step 1. Make sure students follow the instructions in the note below this step for copying the worksheet data.
- Step 4: Click the sheet tab of the worksheet that follows the Real Estate worksheet. Click the Home tab, click the Insert drop-down arrow, and then click Insert Sheet. Rename the sheet as instructed.
- Step 5: In the Consolidate dialog box, make sure students select the Average function.
- Step 6: Click the Bedrooms filter arrow and remove the check from 1. Remind students that they can add icon sets by clicking the Home tab, the Conditional Formatting button, and then Icon Sets.

- Step 7: To import the XML file, click the Data tab, click the From Other Sources button, and click From XML Data Import. Have them navigate to the specified data file.
- Step 10: Students should filter the avgsat column using the Number Filters Top 10 option.
- Step 12: Make sure students save the file in macro-enabled format (.xlsm).
- Step 13: Students can use data consolidation to total the data from the three months.
- Step 15: To convert to a table, click the Insert tab and then click Table. To add a Totals row, click the Table Tools Design tab and click the Total check box.
- Step 16: Remind students that to start recording a macro, they click the Developer tab and then click the Record Macro button. Remind them to carefully execute each step and then to click the Stop Recording button to end the macro.
- Step 18: The easiest way to do this is to copy and paste the data from one workbook to the other.

Data/Solution Files

Data files:	EProj163a.xlsx
	axm.xml
	EProj163b_xlsx
Solution files:	EProj163a_solution.xlsx
	EProj163b_solution.xlsm

Project 164 Basketball Team Data

Tips, Hints, and Pointers

- Discuss the scenario, and preview the tasks students will perform for the Indiana Visitors Bureau.
- In this activity, students collect data about professional basketball teams, convert the data to tables, and summarize and chart the data.
- Step 3: Note that students will need Internet access in order to complete this project. Make sure they gather the team data as specified.
- Step 4: In their Win/Loss column, students should insert a formula similar to the following: =IF(D4>E4,"WIN","LOSS"), where D4 is the Indiana team's points and E4 is the opponent's points.
- Step 5: Click the Insert tab and click the Table button.
- Step 7: Some statistics students might provide include the total games, total wins, total losses, total home games, total away games, and average point difference.
- Step 8: Students will need to have a cell with the team's wins and one with the team's losses in order to apply the conditional formatting.
- Step 9: Students should add this column to the individual team tables on their respective worksheets.
- Step 10: Students should use named ranges to determine the average point difference for each team.
- Step 11: Remind students how to determine a moving average. Click the Data tab, click the Data Analysis button, and in the Data Analysis dialog box, click Moving Average. In the Moving Average dialog box, they will need to specify the Input Range, Interval, and Output Range.

Data/Solution Files

Data file: None
Solution file: EProj164_solution.xlsx

Chapter 10: Collaborating with Others and Preparing a Final Workbook for Distribution

Lesson 74 Tracking Changes

What You Will Learn
- ✓ Creating and Modifying a Shared Workbook
- ✓ Tracking Changes in a Shared Workbook
- ✓ Merging Changes
- ✓ Removing Workbook Sharing

Words to Know
Track Changes
Shared workbook
Change history

Tips, Hints, and Pointers

- Discuss each of the skills listed in the What You Will Learn section, and ask students if they have used any of these skills before.
- Discuss the scenario covered in the Application Skills section, and preview the tasks students will perform for Grounds for Thought.
- In this lesson, students learn how share workbooks and how to track and merge changes.

Creating and Modifying a Shared Workbook
- Briefly talk about the concept of file locking, in which normally only one user can have a given workbook file open at once.
- With a *shared workbook*, several people can make changes at the same time.
- Ask students what the pros and cons are of shared workbooks. What problems might occur?

Tracking Changes in a Shared Workbook
- Introduce the *Track Changes* feature, and show how it enables you to see who has made what changes.
- Review the options in the Highlight Changes dialog box and demonstrate how changes are highlighted on screen and listed on a history worksheet.

- As an experiment, have students share their workbooks with a classmate. Have the classmate make tracked changes and give it back to them. Then have them accept or reject the changes.
- Warn students that changes are only tracked within a workbook for 30 days by default, and show them how to change this interval as you are turning tracked changes on.
- Note that some changes are not tracked. These include formatting changes, hiding or unhiding of rows and columns, and additional or changed comments.
- **QUICK QUIZ:** How would you use the history worksheet to re-insert data that was deleted?

  Because the history worksheet includes a record of all deleted data, you can copy that data back to the original cells in the shared workbook.
- **CUSTOMIZED INSTRUCTION: Special Needs Students:** Having tracked changes highlighted on-screen can help special needs students identify the specific changes made, who made them, and when they were made.

Merging Changes
- Demonstrate how to merge the changes between two workbooks by using Compare and Merge Workbooks.

- **Try It! Merging Workbook Data, Step 8:** You may want to have students remove the Compare and Merge Workbooks button on the Quick Access Toolbar. To do this, right-click the button and then click Remove from Quick Access Toolbar.

Removing Workbook Sharing
- Show how to unshare an unprotected workbook, and how to unprotect a shared workbook.

Project 165—Expense Report
- Step 3: Note that the Allow changes check box is on the Editing tab of the Share Workbook dialog box.
- Step 11: Make sure students save their files; otherwise, they will not be able to view changes on the history worksheet.

Project 166—Inventory Analysis
- Step 3: To set up the workbook for sharing, click the Review tab, click the Share Workbook button, and then click the Allow changes check box on the Editing tab.
- Step 4: To turn on change history, click the Review tab, click Track Changes, and click Highlight Changes. Click List changes on a new sheet.

- Step 13: If necessary, have students add the Compare and Merge Workbooks button to the Quick Access Toolbar. Click the File tab and then click Options. In the left pane, click Quick Access Toolbar. In the Choose commands from list, click All Commands. Click Compare and Merge Workbooks, and click Add.
- Step 17: To turn off sharing, click the Review tab and click Share Workbook. In the Share Workbook dialog box, click the Allow changes check box to clear the check mark. Click Yes in the message box.
- **DESIGN FORUM:** Remind students that in these projects, they were working on files for the coffee shop that would eventually be presented to the bank. Explain that business owners often need to provide historical financial data, as well as projected figures such as estimated expenses and sales, to banks in order to convince them to provide financing for startup and ongoing operations. "Financing" simply means raising money to start or run a business. While a lender will focus on the data, presenting accurate data in an attractive, professional format shows that you are conscientious about your effort and attentive to details.

Data/Solution Files

Data files:
ETry74.xlsx
ETry74b.xlsx
ETry74b_merge.xlsx
EProj165.xlsx
EProj166.xlsx
EProj166b.xlsx

Solution files:
ETry74_solution.xlsx
ETry74b_solution.xlsx
EProj165_solution.xlsx
EProj166_solution.xlsx

Lesson 75 Securing Workbooks

What You Will Learn

- ✓ Using Document Inspector
- ✓ Encrypting a Workbook
- ✓ Protecting the Current Sheet
- ✓ Protecting Workbook Structure
- ✓ Identifying Workbooks Using Keywords

Words to Know

Document Inspector
Worksheet structure

Tips, Hints, and Pointers

- Discuss each of the skills listed in the What You Will Learn section, and ask students if they have used any of these skills before.
- Discuss the scenario covered in the Application Skills section and preview the tasks students will perform for the environmental organization.
- In this lesson, students learn how to use the Document Inspector to remove private information. They also learn various ways of protecting cells, ranges, worksheets, and workbooks.

Using Document Inspector

- Discuss the security risks in distributing a document that contains hidden properties or personal data.
- Explain that workbook properties, or metadata, are bits of unique information that you save as part of a file.
- A workbook's properties display on the Info tab in Backstage view.
- Some properties are updated automatically when you create or modify a file, such as the file name and type, the author, and the file size.
- You can enter more specific properties to help differentiate the file from other similar files.
- Open the Document Inspector and review the list of items that the Document Inspector will search for.
- Show how to use the Document Inspector to remove some or all of these types of information.
- **TROUBLESHOOTING TIP:** Warn students that they might want to save a copy of the workbook first, before using Document Inspector, in case any of the metadata needs to be retrieved later.

Encrypting a Workbook

- Emphasize the importance of keeping a password in a safe place. If you forget the password, you will not be able to open the workbook.
- **CURRICULUM CONNECTION:** Have students create a worksheet that lists U.S. states, their capitals, and their current population. Have them set a password for the workbook that is the name of their home state's capital city.

Protecting the Current Sheet

- Ask students why they would want to protect various parts of a worksheet. Examples include to protect cells against accidental changes you would make yourself, and to protect them against others who might make unwanted changes.
- Discuss the pros and cons of using a password when protecting. Review how to construct a strong (difficult to guess) password.
- Show how to protect and unprotect worksheet elements in the Protect Sheet dialog box. Discuss the check boxes there for protecting various aspects of the worksheet.

Protecting Workbook Structure

- Explain the difference between protecting the workbook's structure and protecting the data.
- **Try It! Protecting Workbook Structure, Step 3:** Have students try to insert a new sheet in the workbook by clicking the Home tab and then the Insert button. The Insert Sheet option is grayed

out, indicating it is unavailable because the workbook structure has been protected.

Identifying Workbooks Using Keywords

- Explain that keywords are properties you can assign to a file to help you locate it more easily in a search.
- You assign keywords to a file in the Properties section of the Info tab in Backstage view.
- Open the Info tab in Backstage view and demonstrate how to add keywords in the Tags box.
- **Try It! Add Keywords to the Workbook, Step 1:** If necessary, point out the Tags text box in the right pane of the Info tab, under Properties.
- **CUSTOMIZED INSTRUCTION: Less Advanced Students:** Have students open a few of the workbooks they have completed in previous projects and insert keywords in their Tags property. Make sure the keywords are reflective of the workbook's content.

Project 167—Inventory Report

- Step 5: After removing all sensitive information and clicking Reinspect, the Document Inspector should not display any new results.
- Steps 8-9: Make sure students enter the password exactly as it appears in the text.
- Step 17: Have students compare their Info tab for the workbook to that shown in Figure 75-1.

Project 168—Marketing Budget Plan

- Step 3: To run the Document Inspector, click the File tab and click Info. Click Check for Issues, click Inspect Document, and then click Inspect. Click Remove All, and click Reinspect to make sure all sensitive data has been removed.

- Step 4: Click the File tab and click Info. Click Protect Workbook, and then click Encrypt with Password. Enter the password exactly as it appears in the text.
- Step 5: Click the File tab, and click Info. Click Protect Workbook, and then click Protect Current Sheet. In the Protect Sheet dialog box, select Format cells, and Insert hyperlinks.
- Step 6: Click the Review tab and click Protect Workbook. Click Structure and Windows in the Protect Structure and Windows dialog box.
- Step 7: Click the File tab and click Info. In the right pane under Properties, click the Tags text box and type the tags as specified. Have students compare their Info tab for the workbook to that shown in Figure 75-2.
- **WORKPLACE SKILLS:** The budget worksheets students worked on in Projects 73 and 74 are part of a grant proposal prepared by an environmental group. Explain that a grant proposal is a formal request submitted to a government agency, private foundation, or public corporation for the purpose of obtaining funding for a specific project. The funding, called a grant, does not have to be paid back as long as it is used to fund the project for which it was allocated. Grants can be awarded to individuals, non-profit or not-for-profit companies, charitable organizations, or educational facilities.

   In order to receive the funding, the grant proposal must be well-written with strong documentation on how the funding will be used and why the project qualifies to receive the funding. In fact, some organizations have employees whose sole responsibility is to write grant proposals and secure funding for various projects.

Data/Solution Files

Data files: ETry75.xlsx
                 EProj167.xlsx
                 EProj168.xlsx
Solution files: ETry75_solution.xlsx
                 EProj167_solution.xlsx
                 EProj168_solution.xlsx

Lesson 76 Finalizing a Workbook

What You Will Learn
✓ Adding a Digital Signature
✓ Marking a Workbook as Final

Words to Know
Encryption
Digital Signature

Tips, Hints, and Pointers

- Discuss each of the skills listed in What You Will Learn section, and ask students if they have used any of these skills before.
- Discuss the scenario covered in the Application Skills section and preview the tasks students will perform for the bookstores.
- In this lesson, students learn about digital signatures and how to mark a workbook as final.

Adding a Digital Signature

- Note that digital signatures were also covered in Word Chapter 4. If you have already covered Word, review the purpose of a digital signature. If this concept is new to students, define the term and show an example of a digitally signed workbook.
- A digital signature can be used like a written signature to verify the authenticity of information.
- A digital signature indicates the following: The signer is who he or she claims to be. The content has not changed since the digital signature was applied. The signer read and approved the document.
- A personal digital certificate is authorized only on the computer on which it is created.
- Once a digital signature is added, the document is marked as final, and the Signatures icon displays in the status bar.
- **Try It! Creating a Digital Signature for Your Workbook, Step 9:** Point out the Marked as Final bar below the Ribbon tabs and the Signatures icon in the lower left corner of the status bar.
- **CUSTOMIZED INSTRUCTION: More Advanced Students:** Have students investigate a signing certificate and how you would obtain one from a certificate authority. If their computers have Internet access, they can click the Signature Services from the Office Marketplace button in the Microsoft Excel dialog box that displays when you click the option to Add a Digital Signature.

Marking a Workbook as Final

- Show how to mark a workbook as final, and discuss why you would do this.
- Show how to un-finalize a workbook if you later decide you need to make further changes. To do this, simply click File, click Info, and then click Protect Workbook. Click Mark as Final again.
- **Try It! Marking a Workbook as Final, Step 6:** Have students return to the workbook, and point out the Marked as Final bar under the Ribbon tabs and the Marked as Final icon in the status bar.

Project 169—Monthly Time Sheet

- Step 10: Have students point out the Marked as Final bar, and the Marked as Final and Signatures icons on the status bar.

Project 170—Real Estate Recommendations

- Step 3: To add a digital signature, click the File tab, click Info, click Protect Workbook, and then click Add a Digital Signature. Click OK in the Microsoft Excel dialog box.

Data/Solution Files

Data files: ETry76.xlsx
                 ETry76b.xlsx
                 EProj169.xlsx
                 EProj170.xlsx

Solution files: ETry76_solution.xlsx
                 ETry76b_solution.xlsx
                 EProj169_solution.xlsx
                 EProj170_solution.xlsx

Lesson 77   Sending and Sharing a Workbook

What You Will Learn

✓ Sending a Workbook as an E-mail Attachment
✓ Setting Precise Margins for Printing
✓ Uploading a Workbook to a Windows Live SkyDrive

Words to Know

Windows Live SkyDrive
Excel Web App

Tips, Hints, and Pointers

- Discuss each of the skills listed in the What You Will Learn section, and ask students if they have used any of these skills before.
- Discuss the scenario covered in the Application Skills section, and preview the tasks students will perform with their colleagues on the research project.
- In this lesson, students will learn how to e-mail a file, how to set print margins, and how to access Windows Live SkyDrive.

Sending a Workbook as an E-mail Attachment

- Discuss reasons why e-mail distribution of a worksheet may be more convenient than paper or disk distribution.
- There are two ways of e-mailing a worksheet—you can send the workbook as an attachment, or you can embed it. However, embedding is available only using a legacy feature that must be manually added to the Quick Access Toolbar. Also when embedding, only one worksheet can be sent at a time, not the entire workbook.
- If necessary, review the difference between PDF and XPS. They are both page layout descriptions, but PDF is made by Adobe and read with Adobe Reader, whereas XPS is a Microsoft format and is read only by the XPS reader.
- Explain that you might want to create a PDF copy of a worksheet to distribute in situations where not everyone has Excel (but everyone does have or can get a PDF reader), or in situations where you want people to have an uneditable copy of worksheet data.

Setting Precise Margins for Printing

- Demonstrate how to set a print area. Explain that once you set the print area, this is the only portion of the worksheet that shows in the Preview window in Backstage view.
- Show how you can change the margins of a printout to fit more or less on the page. This can be useful in making data fit on a certain number of pages, for example. Show the Margins tab in the Page Setup dialog box, from which you can enter precise values.

Uploading a Workbook to Windows Live SkyDrive

- **Try It! Adding a Workbook to Windows Live SkyDrive:** In order to complete this Try It, students will need a Windows Live ID. To obtain the ID, they must have an active Internet connection and supply their e-mail address.

Project 171—Monthly Time Sheet

- Step 5: Instruct students on what e-mail address, if any, to enter in the To box. Encourage them to write a short message in the body of the e-mail that explains the file they have attached.
- Step 8: If necessary, students can click the Page Setup link at the bottom of the Print tab to open the Page Setup dialog box.
- Step 10: Students will need a Windows Live ID and an active Internet connection in order to complete the rest of this project.

Project 172—Research Results

- Step 3: Instruct students on whether or not they can send the file as an attachment and who they should send it to. To send as an attachment, click the File tab and then click Save & Send. Click Send Using E-mail, and then click Send as Attachment. Have students write a short note in the body of the e-mail that explains the content of the file they have attached.
- Step 4: To set the print margins, click the File tab and then click Print. Click the Page Setup link. On the Margins tab of the Page Setup dialog box, enter the margins as instructed and click the Horizontally and Vertically boxes.
- Step 5: Students will need a Windows Live ID and an active Internet connection in order to complete the rest of the project. Click the File tab, click Save & Send, and click Save to Web. Have students sign in to their Windows Live ID account, click the SkyDrive folder in which they are instructed to save the file, and click Save As.

Data/Solution Files

Data files: ETry77.xlsx
              EProj171.xlsx
              EProj172.xlsx

Solution files: ETry77_solution.xlsx
                  EProj171_solution.xlsx
                  EProj172_solution.xlsx

- **JOB FOCUS:** In Projects 77 and 78, students worked with files that contained research and survey data. Gathering and analyzing data is often the responsibility of a market research analyst. A market research analyst examines information and data gathered from various sources to help an organization understand the types of products and services people want and how much they are willing to pay. Market research analysts also work to build customer profiles and identify target markets, gather data about competitors, and analyze sales data to predict future sales.

Market research analysts generally work in offices on a regular schedule. They may work alone, or as part of a market research team. They benefit from strong communication skills, because they must be able to explain the data to others. They must be able to pay attention to detail and should have solid problem-solving skills.

Chapter Assessment and Application
Project 173 Assessing Educational Outcomes

Tips, Hints, and Pointers

- Discuss the scenario, and preview the tasks students will perform for the educational assessment project.
- In this activity, students track changes, add a digital signature, and share workbook data with others.
- Step 3: Remind students to click the Share Workbook button, and then select the Allow changes by more than one user at the same time check box.
- Step 4: To set Track Changes, click the Review tab, click Track Changes, and then click Highlight Changes. Click the Track changes while editing check box and click the Highlight changes on screen check box.
- Step 6: Click the Review tab, click Track Changes, and then click Highlight Changes to open the Highlight Changes dialog box.
- Step 8: To remove sharing, click the Review tab and click Share Workbook.
- Step 9: Instruct students on whether or not they can send the file as an attachment and who they should send it to. To send as an attachment, click the File tab and then click Save & Send. Click Send Using E-mail, and then click Send as Attachment. Have students write a short note in the body of the e-mail that explains the content of the file they have attached.
- Step 10: Click the File tab and then click Info. Click Protect Workbook, click Add a Digital Signature, and enter the text in the Sign dialog box as instructed.
- Step 12: To remove a signature, in the Signatures task pane, click the signature drop-down arrow, and click Remove Signature.
- Step 13: Students will need a Windows Live ID and an active Internet connection in order to complete the rest of the project. Click the File tab, click Save & Send, and click Save to Web. Have students sign in to their Windows Live ID account, click the SkyDrive folder in which they are instructed to save the file, and click Save As.

Data/Solution Files

Data file: EProj173.xlsx
Solution file: EProj173_solution.xlsx

Project 174 Budgeting a Movie

Tips, Hints, and Pointers

- Discuss the scenario, and preview the tasks students will perform for the video producer.
- In this activity, students set up a workbook for sharing.
- Step 3: To set up the workbook for sharing, click the Review tab, click the Share Workbook button, and then select the Allow changes by more than one user at the same time check box.
- Step 4: To set Track Changes, click the Review tab, click Track Changes, and then click Highlight Changes. Click the Track changes while editing check box and click the Highlight changes on screen check box.
- Step 5: Students may enter the same dollar values as shown in Illustration A.
- Step 6: Click the Review tab, click Track Changes, and then click Highlight Changes to open the Highlight Changes dialog box. In the Highlight Changes dialog box, click the List changes on a new sheet check box.
- Step 7: To open the Page Setup dialog box, click the File tab, click Print, and then click the Page Setup link. On the Margins tab, students can set the margins and centering options.
- Step 8: To remove sharing, click the Review tab, and click Share Workbook.
- Step 9: To protect the workbook structure, click the Review tab, and click Protect Workbook. In the Protect Structure and Windows dialog box, click Structure and Windows.
- Step 10: To mark the file as final, click the File tab, click Info, click Protect Workbook, and then click Mark as Final.
- Step 11: Instruct students on whether or not they can send the file as an attachment and who they should send it to. To send as an attachment, click the File tab and then click Save & Send. Click Send Using E-mail, and then click Send as Attachment. Have students write a short note in the body of the e-mail that explains the content of the file they have attached.
- Step 12: Students will need a Windows Live ID and an active Internet connection in order to complete the rest of the project. Click the File tab, click Save & Send, and click Save to Web. Have students sign in to their Windows Live ID account, click the SkyDrive folder in which they are instructed to save the file, and click Save As.

Data/Solution Files

Data file: EProj174.xlsx
Solution file: EProj174_solution.xlsx